John Keats and Benjamin Robert Haydon

The Pursuit of Beauty and Truth

Colin Silver

Text copyright © 2012 Colin Silver
All Rights Reserved

First published as an ebook in 2012
This paperback edition first published in 2014

Iamus Press
Oxford
Y
Email: iamuspress@gmail.com

Contents

Author Acknowledgements	Page 4
Chapter 1	Page 7
Chapter 2	Page 27
Chapter 3	Page 49
Chapter 4	Page 89
Chapter 5	Page 116
Chapter 6	Page 147
Chapter 7	Page 174
Chapter 8	Page 199
Chapter 9	Page 222
Chapter 10	Page 247
Chapter 11	Page 279
Chapter 12	Page 305
Chapter 13	Page 332
Epilogue	Page 364
Notes	Page 374
Select Bibliography	Page 394

Author's Acknowledgements

My special thanks go to my copy editor Alison Chapman for her excellent work in copy-editing the book, and for the many suggestions she made for its improvement. Her help and advice were invaluable. I would like to thank the staff at the British Library in London where I did a good deal of my research, and the staff of the Oxfordshire Library Service who were always helpful. I owe thanks to Bridget Howlett, Senior Archivist at the London Metropolitan Archives for help with my research into Messrs Harman & Co., and Dr Robin Darwall-Smith of Magdalen College, Oxford, for help with my research into the painting in the college chapel. I am very grateful to the staff at the Special Collections Dept., University of Iowa Libraries, Iowa City, Iowa, for permission to quote from the Leigh Hunt / Haydon correspondence of December 1817 and January 1818. My thanks go to the National Portrait Gallery in London for permission to use the cover drawings of Haydon and Keats. As does every student of Haydon's life and work, I owe a great debt to Professor Willard Bissell Pope's masterly edition of his diaries.

I am grateful to Ryan Ashcroft (www.fireclawfilms.com) for creating a book cover which I think captures the spirit of the book perfectly, and to Jo Harrison (www.ebook-formatting.co.uk) for her excellent work in preparing the book for publication. I wish to thank the literary agent Andrew Lownie (www.andrewlownie.co.uk) who took an interest in the book during its early stages and offered me valuable advice and encouragement. When I wanted a sustained period of writing without too many distractions, my good friend Michael Richards invited me to stay at his house in the South of France. I am grateful for his generous hospitality.

When I expressed a desire for a paperback edition of the book, my friend and neighbour Alistair Williamson offered to do the 'technical' work involved. I am grateful to him for making such an excellent job of it.

Cover images:
(Detail of) Benjamin Robert Haydon
By Mary Dawson Turner (née Palgrave), after Sir David Wilkie
Etching (1815)
© National Portrait Gallery, London

(Detail of) John Keats
By Benjamin Robert Haydon
Pen and ink, 1816
© National Portrait Gallery, London

Chapter 1

Thoughts tending to ambition, they do plot unlikely wonders.
Shakespeare: *Richard II*

In the early nineteenth century the Post Office mail coaches were the fastest and safest method of travelling in England, and the coaching inns where they changed their horses and fed their passengers were the equivalent of our modern-day railway stations. The White Horse Cellar, near the site of what is now the Ritz Hotel in Piccadilly, was one of London's finest, a colourful, noisy place with a steady stream of porters and passengers transporting luggage to and from a seemingly endless array of coaches, carts and wagons. Announcing its arrival in the early hours of Wednesday, 16 May 1804, was a mail coach from Devon and on board were two men who had boarded at Plymouth and a woman who had joined them at Exeter. The elder of the male passengers fancied himself something of a sophisticate because he knew where to find the most comfortable inns, the finest port and the best oyster shops in the capital. The younger man was just 19 years old, but he had a high forehead, blue-grey eyes and a mass of black curly hair which made him look imposing and intellectual. Earlier in the morning, when the dome of St Paul's had come into view, the bon viveur had cautioned the young man to be careful in London, and to make his point clear he had 'winked and glanced sideways at the dozing lady'.[1]

The young man was called Benjamin Robert Haydon and his family owned a bookshop and printing business in Plymouth, a major shipping port on the south west coast of England. Always clever and curious, Haydon had been the head boy of the Grammar School at nearby Plympton, among whose distant alumni was the celebrated portrait painter Sir Joshua Reynolds, one of the most successful artists of the eighteenth century. Reynolds had counted amongst his personal friends the great writer, lexicographer and conversationalist Samuel Johnson (James Boswell dedicated his *Life of Samuel Johnson* to Joshua Reynolds), David Garrick, who was one of London's leading actors and playwrights of the day, and Oliver Goldsmith, the author of *The Vicar of Wakefield*. In 1768, Reynolds had been elected the first President of the newly founded Royal Academy of Art.

As the head boy of the school, Haydon would have been very aware of the achievements of Sir Joshua Reynolds, as would, of course, all the masters in the school. Haydon's schoolmaster was the Reverend Dr Bidlake, a cultured man who wrote poems, played the organ and dabbled in painting. When Haydon developed a taste for drawing landscapes, Dr Bidlake allowed him and another boy to become his assistants as he mixed his paints and prepared his palettes in his painting room. Haydon absorbed all the details carefully before returning to the family bookshop where the head man in the binding department, an Italian called Fenzi, encouraged him to pursue his love of drawing. On one memorable occasion, the Neapolitan bared his muscular arm and advised Haydon not to draw landscapes, but to draw the figure.[2]

When Haydon completed his studies at the Grammar School he was sent to Exeter to study merchant accounting. His loathing of these studies – of cash books and ledgers – was almost pathological. He was around 17 years old when he first read Sir Joshua Reynolds' treatise on art, the *Seven Discourses Delivered in the Royal Academy by the President*, which became more simply known as *The Seven Discourses of Joshua Reynolds*. This had a profound effect upon him:

> [the book] placed so much reliance on honest industry, it expressed so strong a conviction that all men were equal and that application made the difference, that I fired up at once... The thing was done. I felt my destiny fixed. The spark which had for years lain struggling to blaze, now burst out for ever.[3]

Haydon sallied down to breakfast one morning to inform the family of his intention to follow in Sir Joshua's footsteps. Many years later, his own son would have the story related to him and recorded it in a memoir:

> In the midst of breakfast he appeared, his toilet showing evident marks of haste, 'Reynolds' Discourses' under his arm, his eyes wild with want of rest and excitement. He opened the campaign by briefly stating his wish to go to London and enter the Royal Academy... If he had dropped a shell on the breakfast table he could not have

astounded the family more. His uncle...stopped cracking his egg, gazed dubiously at the boy's face to see if any intellects were there, raised his eyebrows, and being a very powdered and precise man, wiped his mouth twice with his napkin...[4]

Haydon himself continued the story:

My mother, regarding my looks, which probably were more like those of a maniac than of a rational being, burst into tears.[5]

Haydon's parents knew their son's mind was made up, so they reluctantly agreed to support him for three years until he could establish himself and make his own way in the world. So, on this bright Wednesday morning in mid-May 1804, as the mail coach from Devon arrived in Piccadilly, Haydon must have felt a certain degree of self-satisfaction. He had arrived in Sir Joshua's London with 20 pounds in his pocket and lodgings already arranged.

After bidding goodbye to the other passengers – the bon viveur and the now wide awake lady passenger – Haydon opted to stay aboard the coach since his lodgings were on the Strand, a mile or two further into the city, and the coach would pass them on its way to the main post office. He was in a hurry because it was approaching breakfast time and he had much to do. First, he had to unpack his possessions, wash and have some breakfast, then he planned to visit Somerset House, the home of the Royal Academy and the place he had so often dreamed about whilst poring over Sir Joshua Reynolds' *Discourses* back in Plymouth.

The guard advised him to disembark at Clement's coffee house, one of the many coffee houses situated on the Strand and Fleet

Street. The coach headed along Pall Mall, past the Kings Mews in Charing Cross (then a stable block, now the site of the National Gallery in Trafalgar Square), and when it drew abreast of a splendid, ornamented, Italianate building, Haydon shouted up to the guard to enquire what it was. 'Somerset House' replied the guard. The home of the Royal Academy.

Having found his lodgings, Haydon quickly washed, changed and sallied out for breakfast. After breakfast, he hurried along to the Italianate building, bounded up the stairs and offered the man on the door (who was bedecked in a 'cocked hat and lace cloak') the money he thought would be required to get in. The fellow laughed. He was the beadle, the uniformed doorman of St Mary le Strand, a relatively new church built in 1717. Haydon was incredulous as he peered past the beadle – this was like no church he had ever seen. It was an early taste of just how much more splendid was London than anything he could have imagined. The beadle pointed to Somerset House – across the road and on the north bank of the Thames.

We have a picture of Somerset House as it appeared in 1805, painted by William Daniell from a high vantage point on the south side of the river. It is a realistic, atmospheric depiction of the building that Haydon visited on the morning of Wednesday, 16 May 1804. It dominates the Thameside view, and just to its right can be seen the spire of St Mary le Strand. One notable aspect of the picture is the greyness of the air caused by the trails of smoke from the myriad chimneys that were so prominent a feature of the London skyline. (Though to the modern ear it sounds somewhat perverse, Haydon loved the effect of the London smoke: 'Often have I studied its peculiarities from the hills near London, whence in the midst of its drifted clouds you catch a glimpse of the great dome of St Paul's, announcing at once civilisation and power.')[6] Even today, 200 years later, to walk through the vestibule of Somerset House is to enter one of the most impressive public buildings in London. It can readily be imagined how the young Haydon felt when the building was pristine and its pale stones glowed as the sunlight broke through the 'drifted clouds' and lit up the imposing statue of George III that dominated the courtyard.

The Royal Academy's exhibition room was on the top floor and accessed by a spiral staircase. Haydon prowled around the main gallery, scouring the paintings for historical subjects. He found at least two, both of which he studied carefully. Then he walked away. 'I don't fear you,' he said to himself.

***

Haydon's lodgings would have amounted to little more than a room or two. At the time, the Strand in London was in the middle of the world's greatest commercial district, and if the young man had been surprised by the splendour of the area in the morning, he would have been transfixed by its glitter at night. Throughout the length of Cornhill, Cheapside, Fleet Street, the Strand, Covent Garden and Charing Cross, jewellers, watchmakers, booksellers, perfumers and drapers competed with each other to show off their wares in brightly-lit window displays. The shopkeepers themselves were paradigms of finesse and courtesy as customers were welcomed at the door and gracefully shown into the premises. Interspersed with these arresting displays of fine goods and even finer manners were the taverns and coffee houses for which Fleet Street, in particular, was famous. It is little wonder that London's major shopping streets were widely considered the most splendid in Europe. In 1786 a German visitor described them in a letter:

> The spirit booths are particularly tempting... Here crystal flasks of every shape and form are exhibited, which makes all the different coloured spirits sparkle. Just as alluring are the confectioners and fruiterers, where, behind the handsome glass windows, pyramids of pineapples, figs, grapes, oranges and all manner of fruit are on show. Most of all we admired a stall with Argand and other lamps, situated in a corner house, and forming a really dazzling spectacle... right through the excellently illuminated shop one can see many a charming family scene enacted.[7]

Above all this colourful activity, Haydon spent his first three months in London alone, diligently drawing from plaster casts and reading books about Italian art. His enthusiasm was impressive; he would climb out of bed the moment he woke, be it three, four or five o'clock in the morning, and study until eight. After breakfast he drew from his casts until one o'clock in the afternoon. He would then take a short break before settling down to more drawing from half-past one until five, at which time he would saunter along the Strand to dine at one of the many 'ordinaries' or 'chop-houses' in the area. Upon returning to his rooms he would rearrange his casts and draw again from eight until ten or eleven o'clock in the evening. He kept up this demanding routine throughout the summer and autumn of 1804, week after week, month after month. 'I was once so long without speaking to a human creature,' he later wrote, 'that my gums became painfully sore from the clenched tightness of my teeth.'[8]

The reasons why Haydon was driven to such extremes of hard work are not difficult to discern. Many years earlier his father, also called Benjamin, had been very badly treated by a man whom he had assisted in some commercial way, and Haydon believed that his father had been so hurt by the betrayal that he had sunk into drunkenness and depression, a state that eventually led to his ruin and bankruptcy. Old Benjamin had been rescued by his brother-in-law, Mr Cobley, who subsequently became a financial partner in the family bookselling business, but in Haydon's eyes uncle Cobley was far from perfect. Although he was 'fond of reading, and accustomed to the best society', having spent some of his youth in Italy where he acquired a taste for art, he was, Haydon later reported, 'so habitually indolent that when he came to see my mother on a six weeks' visit he never had the energy to remove, got embedded in the family, stayed thirty years and died.'[9]

All of his life, Haydon tried to avoid drinking alcohol to excess, and despised idleness. He saw idleness as a sign of weakness, even effeminacy. 'The agonies of disappointment,' he once wrote, 'the agonies of sickness, the agonies of any agony on Earth, are nothing in comparison with the agonies of idleness...' But apart from his grim determination to work as hard as he possibly could, there was another factor which drove him inexorably towards his ambition to succeed as an artist. Although a relatively pious young man, he was powerfully attracted to the grandeur – the rituals and pageantry – that he saw in the lives of the rich. Sir Joshua Reynolds had been born into a working class family in Plymouth but through his vocation as an artist had reached the very pinnacle of the English social strata, painting the portraits and becoming the friend of a large number of aristocrats and royals. To Haydon, Sir Joshua was proof that art was valued by the English aristocracy as a worthy and respectable occupation, and that a great painter, from however humble a background, would always be welcome in its ranks.

The elements of naivety and affectation revealed by this rather starry eyed view of aristocratic society did not detract from the high degree of self-knowledge, or at least well-considered appraisal of his own talent, that underpinned Haydon's artistic ambition. Back in 1776, in his first *Discourse to the Academy*, Joshua Reynolds had specifically stated his hope that the works of the English painters during the reign of the then king, George III, might compare favourably with those of the Italian painters under the reign of Pope Leo X, in other words the High Renaissance of early sixteenth-century Rome.[10] Haydon had read of Sir Joshua's wish when he was living in Plymouth and, acutely aware of his own discerning intelligence and creative gifts, had come to believe that he had been chosen by providence to fulfil it. As was the young William Turner, he was determined to rescue the art of England from what he perceived to be its fashionableness and foppery, its languidness and dissipation, its taste for petty portraiture and lacklustre landscapes.

Turner, of course, turned to landscapes with a new vision – a bright and golden vision – but Haydon wanted to teach his fellow Englishmen the intellectual and moral benefits of having great historical art all around them. It was almost as if Sir Joshua Reynolds had been speaking to *him*, to Benjamin Robert Haydon, when he wrote:

> The value and rank of every art is in proportion to the mental labour employed in it... [The subject] ought to be either some eminent instance of heroic action or heroic suffering... Such are the great events of Greek and Roman fable and history... Such, too, are the capital subjects of Scripture history.[11]

One day in the spring or early summer of 1804, Haydon sat down in his rooms near the corner of the Strand and Catherine Street (perhaps glancing at the splendour of Somerset House from a window) and added some notable events from history, the Bible and Shakespeare's plays to Sir Joshua's list. Perusing this new list, he began writing a catalogue of the subjects he wanted to paint. This is a representative selection:

1. The assassination of Dentatus
2. The Judgement of Solomon
3. The Crucifixion
4. The raising of Lazarus
5. Milton playing on his organ – blind
6. The spirit of Caesar appearing to Brutus
7. Lear bidding defiance to the storm

8. Duncan's murder. The door open, and Lady Macbeth seen listening.

With his mind made up, his path was now clear to him. 'To apply night and day,' he wrote, 'to seclude myself from society, to keep the Greeks and the great Italians in view, and to unite form, colour, light, shadow, and expression was my constant determination.'[12]

***

For all his self-belief, Haydon was realistic; he knew that he would have to perfect his technique as a draughtsman before he could create paintings that would be pre-eminent at a Royal Academy exhibition. The first part of his plan was to gain membership of the Royal Academy itself, as a student. But his most important aim was to follow the path of study which he believed the greatest artists of the Renaissance had themselves pursued – the study of surgical anatomy. Above all else, he believed that an historical painter had to be an expert in the construction of the human body. Very soon after moving into his new lodgings he visited a plaster shop in Drury Lane and bought a cast of the head from the famous *Laocoon and his Sons* (it is said that Michelangelo himself was present when this magnificent sculpture was uncovered at a vineyard in Rome in 1506)[13] as well as casts of parts of the human body – 'some arms, hands and feet'.

Haydon was certainly correct in his assessment. He may or may not have known that Leonardo da Vinci, as early as the late fifteenth or early sixteenth centuries, wrote that an artist needed to understand the structure of bones, muscles and tendons in order to understand how they interact and move. With this knowledge, the painter could portray only those muscles that are actually being employed in any physical movement, and avoid joining the ranks of those who

> ...to seem great draughtsmen, draw their nude figures looking like wood, devoid of grace, so that you would think you were looking at a sack of walnuts rather than the human form, or a bundle of radishes rather than the muscles of figures'.[14]

Leonardo, of course, was one of the greatest anatomists in history and the drawings of bones, nerves and muscles he produced while dissecting dead criminals in Renaissance Milan have never been surpassed. Giorgio Vasari tells us that Michelangelo, Leonardo's great rival, also

> ...did anatomical studies on countless occasions, dissecting human beings in order to observe the principles and the ligatures of the bones, the muscles, nerves, veins and their various movements... And he not only studied the parts of the human body but those of animals, and most particularly, of horses, which he took great delight in keeping...[15]

The Renaissance artists were by no means the first anatomists. The practice had been pursued for generations, but it had been undertaken for the purposes of science and medicine, not as a means to an artistic end. By Haydon's time, even though Leonardo's beautiful anatomical studies were relatively unknown (his manuscripts were still scattered around the various private and royal collections of Europe), it was considered at least justifiable for a painter to be practised in anatomy.

The Pursuit of Beauty and Truth

During those early months in the Strand, Haydon studied anatomy in books. He had brought from Devon a copy of the *Tabulae sceleti et musculorum corporis humani*, a treatise on the skeleton and muscles of the human body by Bernhard Siegfried Albinus, the eighteenth century Professor of Anatomy and Surgery at the University of Leiden, which contains (to modern eyes) some gruesome pictures by an artist called Jan Wandelaar. A human body is shown, in successive pictures, peeled and pared, with layer after layer of its skin, flesh and muscle removed. Somewhat bizarrely, the bodies are shown against backdrops of classical carvings, flowers and foliage. The book was a serious attempt to depict the human skeleton and musculature in as accurate a manner as possible and Haydon pored over it. Indeed, before he had even set off for London, he had studied the book with the help of his sister, Harriet:

> She and I used to walk about the house with our arms round each other's necks – she saying, 'How many heads to the deltoid? Where does it rise? Where is it inserted?'... By these means, in the course of a fortnight, I got by heart all the muscles of the body.[16]

Not long after his arrival in London, during one of his daily sojourns along the Strand, Haydon went into Cawthorn's bookshop and bought a copy of *The Anatomy of the Human Body, Vol. 1, containing the Bones, Muscles and Joints*. It was written and illustrated by a brilliant and celebrated Scottish surgeon called John Bell. When it came to accuracy Bell was pertinacious; his drawings of human corpses make those of Albinus look prosaic. Bell's corpses hang from their necks by ropes, with the skin from their skulls flapping over their faces and from their arms hanging in shreds. Haydon was joyful at his serendipitous find. 'I took the book home, hugging it,' he said.

***

In Georgian England, the letter of introduction was a valuable commodity for a young gentleman starting out, for it was the primary means by which he could negotiate the labyrinth of contacts needed for the pursuance of a chosen career. If he wanted to become, say, a soldier or a doctor or a lawyer, he would seek out a friend or a relative, perhaps even a very distant one, who had the requisite connections and who might be willing to help. The letter of introduction was in fact a system of gate-keeping, of authorising access to persons of consequence in a society which had strictly imposed limits upon social mobility. Haydon was acutely aware of this, so he carefully planned a campaign of getting access to the finest painters in London, people who might be able to help him in his quest to be accepted as a student in the Royal Academy Schools.

His uncle Cobley who, it will be remembered, had spent some time in Italy and was consequently 'accustomed to the best society', gave Haydon a letter of introduction to a gentleman with the unlikely name of Prince Hoare, a painter who had travelled to Rome after joining the Royal Academy in 1772. When Haydon first met him, Prince Hoare was the Honorary Foreign Secretary to the Academy, and a fellow of the Royal Society of Literature. A man of extraordinary abilities, he had channelled his energies away from painting into the theatre and had become a successful writer of musicals and farces although he still wrote academic papers about art in his spare time.[17] He was, said Haydon, 'a delicate, feeble-looking man with a timid expression of face, and when he laughed he almost seemed to be crying'.

Around 47 years old in 1804, Prince Hoare was living in Buckingham Street, further down the Strand from Haydon, and he would have found the nephew of his friend Cobley to be an ardent and intelligent youth. Although Haydon was sincere in his desire to meet Prince Hoare his real objective was to gain access to the older man's connections, amongst whom were James Northcote and John Opie, two celebrated painters who had also studied in Italy and who were both now living in London. After reviewing and commenting favourably upon Haydon's drawings, Prince Hoare gave him letters to both Northcote and Opie. 'Northcote being a Plymouth man,' said Haydon, 'I felt strongly a desire to meet him first.'

James Northcote was a successful painter in his fifties when, one day in late 1804, Benjamin Haydon walked into Argyll Place, south of Oxford Street, and knocked on the door of the artist's splendid house. Northcote had served as an assistant to Joshua Reynolds himself and was a member of several impressively named European Academies – the Imperial Academy at Florence and the Ancient Etruscan Academy at Cortona, for example. He was small in stature and had piercing eyes – the artist Henry Fuseli, about whom we shall hear more, famously said that Northcote looked 'like a rat who has seen a cat'.[18]

'I was shown first into a dirty gallery,' said Haydon, 'and then upstairs into a dirtier painting room, and there... stood a diminutive wizened figure in an old blue-striped dressing gown, his spectacles pushed up on his forehead.' Northcote had, said Haydon, 'shining little eyes' and spoke in the broadest Devon accent. After reading the letter, he asked Haydon what sort of painter he wanted to be and Haydon replied that he wanted to be an historical painter. 'An historical painter!' exclaimed Northcote. 'Why, you'll starve with a bunch of straw under your head.' After delivering this portent, Northcote returned to the letter. He looked up, pushed his spectacles onto his head and commented upon the fact that Haydon was studying anatomy. 'That's no use,' said Northcote. 'Sir Joshua didn't study it.' 'But Michelangelo did, sir,' responded Haydon. The incredulous artist pointed out that Michelangelo had nothing to do with painting in London in 1804, and that the only realistic prospect of earning money in London was to paint portraits; but Haydon had long ago dismissed this idea out of hand. Although Haydon's visit to Northcote was not an unqualified success, he had nonetheless made a new friend and valuable ally.

It was just a short walk from Argyll Place to Berners Street where Haydon's next contact, John Opie, lived. A servant, or possibly Opie's wife, the poet Amelia Opie, showed Haydon into a 'clean gallery of masculine and broadly painted pictures'. After a while, a 'coarse-looking intellectual man' entered the room. Opie had been a mathematical prodigy as a child (he had opened an evening school in arithmetic and writing when he was only 12 years old) but had always been interested in art. He had come to London as a youth to paint portraits of the nobility and such was his brilliance that he became known as 'The Cornish Wonder'. With advice and encouragement from Sir Joshua Reynolds himself, Opie had prospered and, of more interest to Haydon, had developed a fine reputation as an historical painter. He was by now a middle-aged man of 43 and about to be elected Professor of Painting at the Royal Academy.[19]

Haydon handed him the letter of introduction. 'He read my letter,' said Haydon, 'eyed me quietly and said: "You are studying anatomy – master it – were I your age, I would do the same".' Haydon's heart leapt at this encouragement. After discussing his plans with Opie, he returned to his lodgings on the Strand – to his plaster casts and his drawings of flayed corpses – with a renewed sense of purpose.

***

Haydon's visits to Northcote and Opie became regular after these first encounters. In their houses in Argyll Place and Berners Street respectively, he absorbed their conversations, studied their paintings and accepted their letters of introduction to other artists. In this way he gradually became accepted as a minor player in London's artistic community. Meanwhile Prince Hoare continued to take an interest in Haydon's career and arranged for him to meet Henry Fuseli, one of the most imaginative painters currently working in England and a very important contact for Haydon because he had just been elected the Keeper of the Royal Academy, the overseer or controller of the students. Noted for his brilliance in his youth, Fuseli had rapidly developed a reputation as having a fiery and original mind. 'His glance is lightning,' said a friend, 'his word a storm... He cannot breathe the common air...'[20]

Fuseli was yet another member of the clique who had settled in Rome in the 1770s and now lived on the fringes of London's Soho. During his time in Rome he had developed a deep and abiding love of Michelangelo's work and had spent weeks studying the ceiling of the Sistine Chapel. He had learned French, English, Italian, Greek and Latin, and a friend once said of him that he had devoured *all* of the major poets. He passionately believed in the synergy between poetry and painting and the artist he admired above all others, with the possible exception of Michelangelo himself, was Shakespeare. Fuseli's most famous work was, and still is, *The Nightmare*.

'Fuseli had a great reputation for the terrible,' wrote Haydon, '...I had a mysterious awe of him. Prince Hoare's apprehensions lest he might injure my taste or hurt my morals, excited in my mind a notion that he was a sort of gifted wild beast.' Haydon was understandably nervous the day he walked up to Berners Street, where Fuseli was a neighbour of Opie, and knocked on the great man's door. The maid showed him 'into a gallery or showroom, enough to frighten anybody at twilight'. He found himself surrounded by pictures of devils, 'malicious witches brewing their incantations', Satan and Lady Macbeth. 'Humour, pathos, terror, blood and murder,' said Haydon, 'met one at every look.'

> I expected the floor to give way – I fancied Fuseli himself to be a giant. I heard his footsteps and saw a little bony hand slide round the edge of the door, followed by a little white-headed lion-faced man in an old flannel dressing-gown... all apprehension vanished on his saying

in the mildest and kindest way: 'Well, Mr Haydon, I have heard a great deal about you from Mr Hoare.'[21]

After looking at some of the drawings that Haydon proffered, and advising him to continue studying anatomy, Fuseli invited Haydon to come and see him at Somerset House. The letter of introduction had finally served its purpose – the ambitious young artist was about to become a student at the Royal Academy of Art.

***

Haydon's first term of study at the Royal Academy Schools was to begin in January 1805 and run through to March. One memorable evening in January he attended a students' welcome gathering during which Fuseli introduced himself. The students will have been shown round the Academy's facilities – for example, its Antique Room, where it housed an impressive collection of plaster casts from ancient marble statues. The casts were in many different poses and various states of repair, but elaborately arranged in a sumptuous room with ornate plaster cornices, a wooden floor and fine ceiling decorations. They were carefully lit by lamplight to accentuate the perfect features of the ancient athletes and statesmen they represented. A group of students would sit on the floor and draw them, also by lamplight, while an Academy tutor wandered through the shadows, looking over their shoulders, making helpful and critical comments. There was also the Life Room where models would sit for hours being drawn by the students, and the Lecture Room where lectures on perspective, anatomy and architecture took place. (J.M.W. Turner would become Professor of Perspective in November 1807.) Haydon had entered a rarefied intellectual world, a world apart from the sparkle of commercial activity in London, and a world away from the bookshops and streets of Plymouth. He felt completely at home in Somerset House, mingling with artists and scholars of the highest ability, studying the classics of Greece and Rome, and discussing the merits of Michelangelo, Titian, Raphael and Tintoretto.

As we saw earlier, Sir Joshua Reynolds had dared to hope that some four centuries after the Italian Renaissance had spread along the banks of the Arno in Florence to reach its height in Rome, a second, perhaps even more colourful Renaissance could begin on the grey, smoky banks of the Thames in London. As he wandered among the paintings and treasures of Somerset House, the 19 year old Benjamin Robert Haydon was determined to make Sir Joshua's dream a reality.

Chapter 2

The childhood shows the man, as morning shows the day.
John Milton: *Paradise Regained*

At around one o'clock in the morning of Sunday, 15 April 1804, a month before Benjamin Haydon took his lodgings on the Strand, a man called Thomas Keats was riding a horse down the City Road towards Moorgate. Lanterns hanging on fences and poles at irregular intervals burned a pale, clean-burning whale oil which cast a dim light into the road (the much brighter gas lights had already been invented but had not yet made their first appearance on the streets of London). When the horse passed out of the lamplight and into the shadows its progress would have been obvious to any criminals in the vicinity because of the sound of its hooves on the cobbles. The city was policed by a number of uniformed night watchmen and the nearest of them, a man called John Watkins, was stationed just to the north of the City Road.

Thomas Keats arrived at the gates of Bunhill Fields which even then was an old London cemetery and the final resting place of some of the great writers of dissenting literature – John Bunyan and Daniel

Defoe were already buried there and William Blake would join them in 1827. Laid to rest among them was one of Thomas Keats' own sons, Edward, who had died in infancy. The cemetery is still there, but these days on the opposite side of the road there is a black statue of John Wesley pointing his right hand towards the tombstones. The statue stands in the courtyard of a Wesleyan chapel which was opened in 1778 and so would have been relatively new as Thomas Keats approached it. He was a short, stocky, good-looking man around 30 years old. His wife was called Frances, and they had three surviving sons and a daughter.

Their two older sons, John and George, were boarding at a school in Enfield. They had been there for about six months, and both Thomas and Frances visited them regularly. Indeed, in the early hours of this Sunday morning, Thomas was returning home from a visit to the boys while Frances had remained at home. After leaving the school he had stopped for supper at Southgate, and since leaving Southgate had ridden about 16 miles. He was now just a few hundred yards from home, a roadside inn and stable called The Swan and Hoop that he managed with the help of Frances and her father. It was a thriving business located adjacent to the London Wall, an ideal place from which to cater for the merchants and traders who travelled daily into and out of the city. A busy city trader might take breakfast on his way to work, or dinner on his way home while his horse was being rested and groomed. Thomas may have been thinking that in just a few minutes his own horse would be stabled and he would be reunited with Frances. Doubtless the two younger children would be asleep, but Frances would almost certainly be waiting up for him to ask him about John and George, how they appeared, whether they were eating properly.

At almost exactly the place at which the black statue of John Wesley now points, something occurred that caused Thomas Keats to fall heavily from his horse. The animal may have been startled by someone emerging from the shadows or it may simply have slipped on the cobbles. Whatever happened, the panicked and riderless horse clattered some 400 yards back up the City Road towards the watchman, John Watkins, who later gave testimony that he ran down to the cemetery and found a man sprawled on the ground. He was unconscious but even in the dim light of the oil lamps Watkins could see blood seeping from his head. A local surgeon was summoned, but the man could not be roused.[22]

In the silence of the night, Thomas Keats was carried the last few hundred yards of his journey to the Swan and Hoop. The prayers of his wife and servants can only be imagined as the devoted father and husband was placed in his bed and nursed until dawn. He died without ever regaining consciousness.

***

It would hardly be an exaggeration to say that, with her husband's death, Frances Keats' world fell apart. She inherited the management of The Swan and Hoop because her father, John Jennings, was the proprietor – he had purchased the lease 30 years earlier in 1774. It proved to be a sound investment because it made old John Jennings a wealthy man. After 28 years of service he had retired in 1802 to a life of ease and prosperity at a village just outside London called Ponders End. It was a suitable rural retreat for a retired gentleman but the old man had kept the lease on the inn because he had wanted the business to remain in the family. When Frances married Thomas Keats it was arranged that her new husband would manage the business on the old man's behalf. Thomas in his turn had become well off, leaving £2000 at the time of his death, and this at a time when a family could live comfortably on £100 a year. With such an inheritance a widowed mother in Frances' position could be expected to have severe emotional, rather than financial, problems but in her case things were not straightforward. On 27 June 1804, just ten weeks after Thomas' death, Frances Keats and a man called William Rawlings entered the pale, classical portico of the fashionable St George's Church near Hanover Square and took their matrimonial vows. William Rawlings was a bank clerk, a young man who seemed not to have any financial assets or property of his own.[23]

Incredible though it may seem to us now, a woman marrying in the early nineteenth century became *legally* subservient to her husband and almost everything she owned became his. The enormity of Frances' sacrifice becomes apparent when we remember that, once married, it was almost impossible to get divorced because divorce could only be sanctioned by Parliament, an avenue closed to all but a select few. For the lifetime of the marriage (a lifetime in the literal sense) the husband became the undisputed owner of all the property his wife possessed, whether it was real estate, jewellery, money or anything else. If a married woman chose employment, then her wages belonged to her husband. If she bought some furniture, it belonged to him. So whatever Rawlings' reasons for marrying Frances Keats (and they may have been entirely honourable), he must have thought that, in material terms at least, he had struck gold.

It is inconceivable that Frances had not had a personal relationship with Rawlings in the weeks and months leading up to the marriage. Perhaps he had been a friend of an employee at the inn, or an acquaintance of someone in the neighbourhood. To Frances' parents and children, however, he must have seemed to have come out of nowhere. We can only wonder how the Keats children felt as their new step-father familiarised himself with what remained of their father's life – his investments, his personal possessions and his marital bed. A comparison with Shakespeare's Hamlet is unavoidable.

So what sort of a woman was Frances Rawlings? By all accounts, she was good-looking and, before her second marriage at least, a devoted mother and wife. The only independent character sketch we have of her is by an unreliable witness, Richard Abbey, about whom we shall hear more later. He wrote that her

> ...passions were so ardent... that it was dangerous to be alone with her. – She was a handsome, little woman – Her features were good and regular... She used to go to a grocers in Bishopsgate Street, opposite the Church, probably out of some liking for the Owner of the Shop, – but the man remarked that Miss Jennings always came in dirty Weather, & when she went away, she held up her Clothes very high in crossing the Street, & to be sure, says the Grocer, she has uncommonly handsome legs. – He was not however fatally wounded by Cupid the Parthian –[24]

Despite all appearances to the contrary, William Rawlings had not in fact married well. The lease on the Swan and Hoop was £44 a year and due to expire in 1805. Thomas Keats' legacy of £2,000 invested at a then acceptable three per cent would only produce an income of £60 a year, not enough to cover a new lease and the running costs of the inn.[25] There were practical problems, too. It is thought that Thomas Keats had been John Jennings' liveryman before marrying his daughter, so he would have been very familiar with the management of a stable. If he had experienced any problems with the inn-keeping after his marriage he would have been able to call on his new father-in-law for expert advice. The latest master of the Swan and Hoop knew a lot about ledgers and accounts (being a former bank clerk) but probably knew little or nothing about stabling horses or the day-to-day business of keeping an inn. The potential consequences of this lack of management expertise must have been obvious, but Frances was probably relying upon her now retired father to offer his help.

We know that Frances' mother, Alice Jennings, actively disapproved of her daughter's hasty remarriage and although the views of her father are not recorded, they can readily be discerned from his will. On the old man's death the following year, his substantial fortune of £13,000 was distributed around his family but Frances was bequeathed an annuity of just £50. With Thomas' legacy of £60 a year, this may have been just enough to keep the Swan and Hoop afloat (perhaps that was the old man's intention), but Frances and her new husband, feeling they had been rebuffed, took the matter to Chancery (the court which presided over disputed wills), and in so doing ended any chance of friendly advice or practical help from the rest of the Jennings family.

Frances and William Rawlings' personal relationship is a mystery; we don't know whether they were happy together or not, but we do know that their post-marital problems soon became insurmountable. Perhaps it was the hostility shown to the couple by Alice Jennings, perhaps the resentment of the Keats children or the non-cooperation of the staff at the Swan and Hoop, but for whatever reason, the marriage failed and in early 1805 Frances ran away. (It was rumoured that she had set up with 'a Jew called Abraham' in Enfield and was drinking heavily.) In just two years she had lost her first husband, her home, her financial security and the goodwill of her family. And as if that were not enough, her children were taken into the care of their grandmother. With that single act, the tragedy of Frances Rawlings was almost, but not quite, complete.

***

The Keats children were now to all intents and purposes orphaned and Alice Jennings tried her best to compensate. Nearly 70 years old, she was a relatively wealthy woman who had maids to help with the domestic chores, but she was approaching the end of her life when she effectively became the mother of four young children. After her husband's death she had moved house and now lived near to the doctor who had nursed her husband through his final illness, in Church Street, Edmonton. The doctor was a respected gentleman called Thomas Hammond, 'a surgeon of aristocratic bearing', and he was to play a major role in the life of Alice's eldest grandson, John Keats. But, for now, the children tried their best to adjust to their new environment. John was nine, George eight, Thomas (hereafter called Tom) was five and the youngest, Fanny, was just two years old.

Edmonton in 1805 was a rural village scattered along a road some six miles north of London. Most young children living in a rural situation will find excitement and fun in their environment, and the Keats children were very ordinary in that respect. As the trauma of their father's death and their mother's abandonment receded, they began to explore their new surroundings. They harvested wild fruits which their grandmother mixed into cakes; they fished in the river Lea, catching minnows, dace and 'ticklebacks' and they trapped mice which the boys presented to their sister as pets. As the years passed and the seasons cycled, these activities instilled in the children a deep sense of the harmony and wholeness of the English countryside which John, in particular, was to treasure for the rest of his life.

For the time being, Alice decided that John and George should continue their education at the boarding school in Enfield where they were fortunate in the quality of their education and the progressive philosophy of the people who taught them. Many boisterous children in the early 1800s were taught by rote and beaten into silent submission, a situation highlighted half a century later by Dickens in his novel *Hard Times*, but the headmaster at Enfield, John Clarke, and his son, Charles Cowden Clarke (who was his father's teaching assistant), adhered to a philosophy of education based upon self-improvement. They did this by encouragement and example. They were nonconformist intellectuals and political liberals in a time of war and oppression, and they were unusually kind and benevolent even when compared to the other nonconformist schoolmasters of the day.

Of the two Keats boys studying at Enfield, George was the younger but he was also the wiser and more easy-going. John had a reputation for fighting which suggests that the loss of his parents may have affected him more deeply. He needed guidance and Charles Cowden Clarke set about providing it. The teacher was about eight years older than his pupil and befriended the clearly disturbed boy in a manner that placed him somewhere between an elder brother and a badly-needed father figure. Sophisticated and cultured, widely read in history and the composer of some original poetry, he fell into the role with gentlemanly ease. With Clarke as a role model, the transformation of John Keats from a disturbed and pugnacious schoolboy into a scholarly young man now began. Many years later, Clarke wrote:

> In the early part of his school-life John gave no extraordinary indications of intellectual character; but... a determined and steady spirit in all his undertakings...[26]

One thing that was often said of John Keats was that he was extraordinarily beautiful in his physical appearance. He was very short but, like his father, he had a well-proportioned, compact body and wide shoulders – the physique one might expect of a young boxer. We can get a very good idea of what he looked like from various pictures of him drawn and painted by professional artists, as well as a plaster cast life mask.[27] These show his nose to have been strong and somewhat crooked in profile, with large nostrils. His mouth was wide, and the upper lip protruded slightly. He had a mass of red-brown curling hair which complemented his luminous hazel eyes. Years after his death, many of those asked to describe his physical appearance would emphasise the lustre of his eyes, recalling that they seemed to glow with vigour and intellectual curiosity. All in all, there was something alert and radiant in John Keats' face, and it seems he was the sort of boy that other boys, even the most intellectual, were drawn towards.

As he matured, his personality, too, became extremely attractive. Clarke talked about his

> ...high-mindedness, his utter unconsciousness of a mean motive, his placability, his generosity... I never heard a word of disapproval from anyone, superior or equal, who had known him.[28]

Later, we find an example of the type of eulogy Keats was to attract from his friends and colleagues for the rest of his short life:

> Had he been born in squalor, he would have emerged a gentleman. Keats was not an easily swayable man; in differing with those he loved his firmness kept equal pace with the sweetness of his persuasion, but with the rough and unlovable he kept no terms – within the conventional precincts, of course, of social order.[29]

***

After abandoning her children in 1805, Frances Rawlings became a mysterious figure. If it is true that she was living in squalor in

Enfield (or perhaps in Edmonton) with someone called Abraham, then she would have been geographically close to her children but there are no accounts of her visiting them. After four years of absence, in the early part of 1809, she walked back into her mother's life and asked for sanctuary. She had fallen victim to consumption, and Alice Jennings immediately took her in.

It has been estimated that in 1815, one quarter of the population of England was stricken with consumption in one or other of its forms, and all too often it was a death warrant. At the time when Frances contracted the disease, almost nothing was known about it beyond the fact that it killed large numbers of people, and although it was not widely known to be infectious (although some medical authorities suspected this to be the case), it had been feared for millennia. The Hebrew scribes stated that consumption was a punishment from God:

> The LORD shall smite thee with a consumption, and with a fever, and with an extreme burning, and with the sword... and they shall pursue thee until thou perish. (Deut. 28.22 KJV)

and Shakespeare referred to the horrors of consumption several times in his plays, in *King Lear*, Act IV, Scene 6, for example:

> There's hell, there's darkness, there is the sulphurous pit –
> Burning, scalding, stench, consumption...
> Give me an ounce of civet, good apothecary,
> to sweeten my imagination.

The Keats children could only watch with horror as their mother succumbed to the cruel disease. Its unfortunate victims would begin to lose weight, at first gradually, but later to such an extent that it seemed they were being eaten, or consumed. As the bones began to show through the skin, the patient would take on a skeletal appearance, with sunken eyes shining bright with fever, and the teeth taking on the appearance of a smile, but it is the smile of a cadaver, as Aretaeus the Cappadocian put it. 'One may not only count the ribs, but trace them to their terminations... the shoulder blades are like the wings of birds.'[30]

The local doctor, Thomas Hammond, began to administer to Frances, while John, the son to whom she had been most devoted in earlier years, became her nurse. This must have been an appalling ordeal for a 14 year old boy and there's little doubt he would have consulted Hammond about the best way to care for his mother, what medicine and food she required. A friend later wrote that he was very assiduous in his duties – preparing and administering the medicine, cooking her food and reading to her in quiet intervals while she tried to rest. He would have been desperate to learn more about her, and no doubt about his father, too.

***

Whether he was trying to please his dying mother, or had become frightened and shaken by the precariousness of life, Keats began to mature at an astonishing rate. Education – or rather, *knowledge* – seemed to offer him the constancy and the strength he needed to make sense of his fragile world. With that 'determined and steady spirit' he displayed in all his undertakings, he began to devote his spare time to reading. It is no exaggeration to say that he carefully and systematically tried to read through the whole of the school library, shelf by shelf, and that this self-imposed course of study soon became an obsession.

It was noted by his contemporaries that he arose early in order to have more time for reading, and that he ate his meals while turning pages. His school friends and masters must have looked on in wonder as he immersed himself in geography and history books, in books of exploration and in novels. He studied the Classics – including Virgil's *Aeneid* – and a range of books about Greek and Latin mythology – the *Polymetis*, the *Pantheon* and most importantly, the *Bibliotheca Classica* or *Classical Dictionary* which had been published in 1788 by the school teacher, John Lemprière. Keats was said to have learned its contents almost by heart and he had a copy with him throughout the rest of his life. He also began to read Shakespeare, possibly with Edward Holmes, an intelligent boy who was later to write the first biography of Mozart in English.

When he wasn't caring for his mother, Keats began to form a system with which to connect his readings about exploration, history and mythology into an integrated whole, much as his contemporary Percy Bysshe Shelley had been advised to do at Eton by his mentor, a brilliant but eccentric teacher called Dr James Lind. But Keats had embarked on his intellectual journey alone, and the astonishing results of his endeavours soon became apparent, not least to Charles Cowden Clarke. He began to win prizes and we can imagine the pride with which his dying mother received the news.

The Pursuit of Beauty and Truth

As the autumn of 1809 turned to winter, Frances Rawlings continued to hang on to life, but precariously. Her father's will was still being contested in Chancery (it will be remembered that John Jennings had died in 1805) and Frances must surely have doubted that she would live to receive her meagre inheritance. Keats continued to nurse her during the holidays, either directly or indirectly under Thomas Hammond's guidance. Then, one terrible day in March 1810, he was taken aside at school and told that his mother had lost her struggle for life. Tough and resolute as he was, there was no defence against the news. He was utterly crushed.

Frances' funeral took place on 20 March 1810, and in the ensuing weeks and months Keats was drawn closer than ever to his brothers and his sister. In the summer of 1810, still aged 14, he left Clarke's school and was apprenticed to his mother's doctor as an apothecary (at that time a newly apprenticed apothecary, or what we might now call a pharmacist, carried out some medical duties while serving as a doctor or surgeon's assistant). Whether the suggestion that he pursue a medical career was Hammond's, Alice Jennings' or Keats' himself, we do not know, but the fact that he took his apprenticeship seriously and carried out his duties with diligence and purpose is beyond doubt.

***

Thomas Hammond's surgery adjoined his house, a fine Georgian block set back from the road in Church Street, Edmonton, a site now occupied by a row of nondescript shops. Keats was given lodgings in the attic rooms over the surgery. As an apprentice to an early nineteenth-century doctor he would at first have helped his master with the simplest of duties – cleaning, sweeping and washing – but the science of medicine was still little more than medieval and Keats would have progressed to some fairly distasteful and even gruesome duties. There were innumerable (what we would now consider ineffectual or even 'quack') medicines and 'cures' for everything from gout to corns, colic to venereal disease, and Keats would have been instructed in their preparation and administration. He would have been taught how to bleed a patient using leeches and how to bandage all manner of cuts, burns and blisters. He was instructed in the mechanics of dentistry, a particularly dreadful procedure before the advent of anaesthetics, requiring brute force and a strong stomach. He would also have attended and assisted with childbirths and watched post mortems. And, of course, he would have become even more familiar with the diagnosis and treatment of consumption. In short, he became intimately acquainted with the bodies, ailments and deaths of the people of Edmonton, and they with the short, well-proportioned, bright-eyed youth who was devoting his working hours to the alleviation of their suffering.

In his spare time, in the garret of the surgery, Keats continued with his literary studies. He had begun a translation of the whole of Virgil's masterpiece, *The Aeneid*, while still at school and he continued with this formidable task whilst simultaneously starting to grapple with the complex language and imagery of Shakespeare. His former school teacher Charles Cowden Clarke had by now become a personal friend, and he made it clear that Keats was very welcome to return to the Enfield school whenever he had some spare time, to use the library and discuss the books he was reading.

The kindly young schoolmaster gave of his time generously, and spent many hours with Keats who would walk the two miles or so from Edmonton to borrow books, read them, and converse about them.[31] Between the school garden and the adjacent fields was an enclosed area, an arbour, where master and pupil – Clarke aged 22 and Keats aged 14 – would sit, read and talk, away from the distraction of the schoolboys who not only ran around playing and shouting as boys will do, but who were also encouraged to grow fruit and vegetables in the school's garden and do practical experiments in their endeavours to understand Newtonian mysteries such as centrifugal force and gravity.

As we have seen, Keats' childhood with his grandmother at Edmonton had made him acutely aware of the beauty of the English countryside, and images recalled from this time dovetailed perfectly with the sylvan scenes and characters from the ancient European mythologies he had taken to heart in Lemprière's *Classical Dictionary* – the woodland groves, nymphs and dryads, all under the ever-watchful eyes of the gods. It was just this kind of amalgamation of real and imaginary landscapes that found perfect expression in the book to which Clarke was now to introduce him, *The Faerie Queene*, by the sixteenth-century English writer Edmund Spenser. The effect of this upon Keats was so dramatic and so central to the story of his short life that it is necessary to take a fairly detailed look at it.

The Faerie Queene is both an allegory and a romantic epic, the first of its kind in England. It is a vast and complex work, rich in symbolism, inspired by Homer and Virgil, designed to rival or even surpass the epics of the Italian Renaissance. The poem is divided into six books, and each book contains the tale of a person who represents one of the aspects of virtuous conduct; thus, Book One is entitled, 'The Legende of the Knight of the Red Crosse or Of Holinesse' and Book Two, 'The Legende of Sir Guyon or Of Temperaunce' and so on. The characters in the poem have symbolic names – for instance, Abessa (the Church), Charisma (grace), Fidelia (faith), Sans foy (faithless), Sans loy (lawless) and Una (the 'one'). Among the gods is Morpheus, the god of dreams, and among the magicians, Merlin. The setting is a faerie-land of fields, woods, rivers, quicksands, caves and seas which is populated by all manner of real and imaginary animals – bears, bulls, 'leathery bats', owls, night-ravens, serpents and sea monsters.

The poem opens with a knight called Red Crosse embarking on a mission given to him by Gloriana, The Greatest, Glorious Queene (readily identifiable as Spenser's beloved Queen Elizabeth I). Red Crosse must go and slay the monster Error. He meets a wizard called Archimago who is disguised as a holy man:

> ...An aged Sire, in long black weedes yclad,
> His feet all bare, his bearde all hoarie gray,
> And by his belt, his booke he hanging had;
> Sober he seemde, and very sagely sad...

This gives a mere flavour of the poem's style and subject matter, but it is the sheer beauty of the language, the word painting, which initially impresses anyone new to the poem and which so enthralled Keats. Spenser uses a wide range of technical devices to beautify the imagery; for example, alliteration:

> The **b**lazing **b**rightnesse of her **b**eauties **b**eame…

> In homely **w**ise, and **w**ald with sods around,
> In **wh**ich a **w**itch did dwell, in loathly **w**eedes,
> And **w**ilfull **w**ant, all carelesse of her needes…

and repetition:

> Some <u>feard</u>, and fled; some <u>feard</u> and well it faynd…

We can easily imagine Keats' feelings when he came to the following stanza. It not only applied to his own vocation as an apprentice apothecary, but would have resonated with the memory of his mother's tragic death. It is set in a hospital, where seven 'Beadmen' do godly things. The fifth (fift):

> The fift had charge sicke persons to attend,
> And comfort those, in point of death which lay;
> For them most needeth comfort in the end,
> When sin, and hell, and death do most dismay
> The feeble soule departing hence away…

Back in the garden of the school at Enfield, as Clarke read and discussed *The Faerie Queene* with him, Keats found himself in a world of scholarship that he never wanted to leave. It was as if he had come home to himself, had found his true vocation. He wanted to raise himself to the status that his teacher enjoyed, that of an erudite literary man, a man of letters. Considering how this was to be done, he knew he had an advantage over most people – he could hear, see and feel things in poetry that most other people apparently couldn't. The most cited example of this phenomenon is Keats' reaction to the following stanza from Book Two of *The Faerie Queene*:

> Most ugly shapes and horrible aspects,
> Such as Dame Nature selfe mote feare to see,
> Or shame, that ever should so fowle defects
> From her most cunning hand escaped bee;
> All dreadfull pourtraites of deformitee:
> Spring-headed Hydraes, and sea-shouldring Whales,
> Great whirlpooles, which all fishes make to flee,
> Bright Scolopendraes, arm'd with silver scales,
> Mighty Monoceros, with immeasured tayles.

The language of these lines may be a little obscure to us now, but under the tutelage of Cowden Clarke, Keats quickly became familiar with the structure and technical details of this verse, its nine-line stanza invented by Spenser himself (the Spenserian stanza); its eight iambic pentameters and one alexandrine; and its distinctive rhyme scheme – a, b, a, b, b, c, b, c, c. (aspects, see, defects, bee, deformitee, Whales, flee, scales, tayles). He would also have known that the Hydra was a many-headed sea monster, that the Scolopendra was a fabulous fish that vomited, then reswallowed, its viscera, and that the Monoceros was a kind of whale which had a large, spiralling tusk.

Keats' reaction to the verse made such an impression upon Clarke that he remembered it more than 50 years later:

> ...he especially singled out epithets for that felicity and power in which Spenser is so eminent. He hoisted himself up, and looked burly and dominant, as he said, 'what an image that is – "sea-shouldering whales!"'[32]

***

With Cowden Clarke's guidance and encouragement, John Keats now began to realise that he himself possessed extraordinary poetical gifts. Though the exact chronology is a little obscure, two events occurred in late 1813 or early 1814, around his eighteenth birthday, which were to change the direction of his life. One was that he quarrelled with Dr Hammond and moved out of the lodgings above the surgery, of which more later; the other was that he moved beyond just reading poetry, and started writing it himself. His first poem to survive and be handed down to us is called *Imitation of Spenser*. It is of course a juvenile production, but it reveals an astonishing facility for a first attempt, and an unusual richness of imagination. Written in the form of a Spenserian stanza, with its concomitant rhyme scheme, it begins:

> Now Morning from her orient chamber came,
> And her first footsteps touched a verdant hill,
> Crowning its lawny crest with amber flame,
> Silvering the untainted gushes of its rill,
> Which, pure from mossy beds, did down distil,
> And after parting beds of simple flowers

> By many streams a little lake did fill,
> Which round its marge reflected woven bowers
> And, in its middle space, a sky that never lowers.
> There the king-fisher saw his plumage bright
> Vying with fish of brilliant dye below,
> Whose silken fins and golden scales light
> Cast upwards through the waves a ruby glow...

Keats' images are vivid and full of movement — we can clearly imagine the scene he is portraying, and there are the first faint glints of Shakespearean influence in the beds of simple flowers ('simple' having medicinal overtones). There is also a careful use of colour throughout the poem — there are heraldic overtones where the kingfisher's blues and greens vie with the brilliant golds and rubies of the fish below.

Although, as we have already noted, this is necessarily a juvenile and fanciful poem, the *Imitation of Spenser* contains intimations of where Keats himself thought his intellectual development was taking him. He wrote:

> Ah! could I tell the wonders of an isle,
> That in that fairest lake had placèd been,
> I could e'en Dido of her grief beguile,
> Or rob from aged Lear his bitter teen...

'Ah, *could* I tell...' Conscious of the beauty in this, one of his first attempts at writing poetry, Keats is already comparing his work as an apothecary with his first attempt at writing verse. On the one hand he can attempt to heal the sick body with herbs and medicine, on the other he can explore the possibility of easing the pained soul with poetry. For the time being, however, the 18-year-old apprentice had to put his thoughts about literature aside in order to concentrate upon his work in Dr Hammond's surgery – washing floors, bleeding people and pulling teeth.

Chapter 3

Poema pictura loquens, pictura poema silens.
(Poetry is a speaking picture, painting a silent poetry.)
Simonides of Keos

In the years between his election as the first president of the Royal Academy in 1768 and his death in 1792, Sir Joshua Reynolds was an imposing and authoritative figure in London's artistic community. He was undoubtedly a talented painter and an eloquent writer, but the true secret of his success lay in the fact that he was mindful of his limitations: In his famous *Seven Discourses*, he wrote:

> A portrait painter... when he attempts history, unless he is on his guard, is likely to enter too much into detail... Thus an habitual practice in the lower exercises of the art will prevent many from attaining the greater. But such of us who move in these humbler walks of the profession are not ignorant that, as the natural dignity of the subject is less, the more all the little ornamental helps are necessary to its embellishment.[33]

History painting – the Grand Style – was, he believed, the most sublime and demanding form of the art so it followed that the greatest history painters were the most noble and gifted of artists. Reynolds publicly pronounced that he was not among them, even if he was the President of the Royal Academy. The truth behind his *Discourses* was that he considered history painting to be a poetical phenomenon which required greater powers of imagination than landscape or portrait painting. Of course, such basic skills as draughtsmanship, the ability to draw perspective correctly and the judicious use of colour are required in every genre but, according to Sir Joshua, these technical devices are merely the language of painting, just as words, metaphor and alliteration form the language of poetry. It is not proficiency in the use of this language which marks out the great artist but the uses to which it is put (many people can write a lively and interesting letter, but very few can write a great poem).

Benjamin Robert Haydon was determined to become an expert in the language of painting and devoted most of his time and intellectual energy to the pursuit, even if it meant ignoring Sir Joshua's stricture that:

> A facility composing a lively, and what is called a masterly handling [of] the chalk or pencil are, it must be confessed, captivating qualities to young minds... By this useless industry they are excluded from all power of advancing in real excellence.[34]

Haydon simply didn't care that most of his fellow students in the Academy were aspiring to excellence in what Sir Joshua called the humbler walks of the profession, viz., the painting of landscapes, scenes from everyday life and portraits (in which genre the Dutch were the acknowledged masters), because Haydon was determined to rise above them all. He knew he was in a minority and he could not hide his exasperation:

> I prefer the delights of Virgil and Homer to the imbecile, tiresome, technical nonsense of dutch connoiseurship [sic], 'how cleverly that is painted,' &c, &c, – after dinner one takes a candle and walks over to an insipid Jan Mieris, of a Woman and a Boy, with cabbages, Potatoes, & red herrings, a cat, a brass pan, and some carrots, – then all are in raptures, 'what an exquisite imitation, look at the carrots, look at the herrings, well we must take that down'… then my Lord and my Lady, and Master and Miss, all crowd around this inimitable carrot Picture, lost in rapture & delight… To hear terms that would be applicable to the highest beauties of Art applied to a tame, insipid, smooth, flat, mindless imitation of carrots – Good God, is this the end of Art, is this the use of Painting?[35]

Haydon's ambition was no less than to rival or even surpass the great Italian artist Raffaello Sanzio (Raphael of Urbino, 1483–1520) as an historical painter. It was a vast and bold ambition, but he believed that if he devoted all of his artistic genius and seemingly endless energy to the pursuit, then his historical and religious paintings would come to adorn the greatest buildings in London, and history would place him alongside the great painters of the High Renaissance as an acknowledged master of the genre. He did have a problem, though, and it was a wholly prosaic one. It would be several years before he was in a position to sell a great painting, so in the meantime, how was he to earn his living?

The news came from Plymouth that his father was gravely ill. After the requisite visit home (during which he advanced his knowledge of anatomy by procuring some bones and muscles from the Plymouth hospital), Haydon returned to London knowing that his family's financial support was no longer guaranteed and that his only option was to become marketable in his artistic pursuits. Unfortunately, there was as yet no National Gallery in England so the demand for large-scale historical paintings was limited to the whims of a few wealthy patrons. The question was, how did one catch the eye of a wealthy patron? A young man called John Jackson would provide the answer.

***

By his own admission, Haydon was not much fun in the Academy Schools. While others played, he worked. Perhaps he was conscious of his lack of experience – it was clear that a new arrival called Wilkie was a far better draughtsman than he. Haydon could still call on Opie, Fuseli and Northcote for gentle encouragement and professional advice (which he accepted or rejected according to his own estimate of its correctness and value) but clearly he also needed people of his own age with whom he could share his studies and youthful dreams.

The first friend he made was John Jackson, later to become a respected portrait painter and Royal Academician. It is often said that friends are attracted to those with personality traits that accentuate their own; if this is true, then Haydon and Jackson chose well. Just as Haydon's most notable characteristic was a seemingly limitless reserve of energy, Jackson was possessed with a tendency to indolence that was so congenital it was almost comical. The friendship came about one morning in Somerset House, when Haydon began talking to a man dressed all in black:

> He made a shrewd remark or two, and when we left we walked home together, as he lodged in the Strand not far from me. I showed him what I was trying: he said to me, 'Sir George Beaumont says you should always paint your studies'. 'Do you know Sir George, Sir Joshua's friend?' 'To be sure I do.' I was delighted. 'What is your name?' 'Jackson.' 'And where do you come from?' 'Yorkshire.' 'And how do you know such a man?' 'Know him,' Jackson answered, bursting into a laugh. 'Why Lord Mulgrave is my patron, and Sir George is his friend.'[36]

Haydon instantly knew that Jackson was to be his entrée to the hallowed halls of patronage. He was sure that if Jackson mentioned Haydon's ambition to the stalwart Tory, Lord Mulgrave, or Mulgrave's friend, the kindly Sir George Beaumont, their interest in him would certainly be aroused. An historical painter? He must be a very talented man.

After establishing a friendship with Jackson, Haydon lost no time in similarly cultivating Wilkie, the gifted newcomer to the Academy. Even at this early stage of his career it was clear that Wilkie's talent as an artist was exceptional. He was just two months older than Haydon but was far more advanced in his art as he had already been a student for five or six years.

David Wilkie was a tall, thin, rustic Scotsman who loved to observe and paint ordinary people. As a student in Edinburgh, one of his pleasures had been to walk around the wharves and quarries near Leith, studying the expressions and physical postures of the native fishermen and quarrymen. One of his very early paintings was of the inhabitants of a village mingling around a market under a cloudy sky. Now in the Scottish National Gallery, it is called *Pitlessie Fair* and was at the time considered to be an extraordinary effort for so young a student because Wilkie had faithfully captured the faces and gestures of many of the villagers. (It was said that he did this by sketching them during church services before transferring their likenesses into the pre-painted market square; if so, this was a clever innovation.)[37] Soon after completing *Pitlessie Fair* Wilkie travelled to London and entered the Royal Academy Schools where Haydon quickly noticed him:

> [Wilkie] was tall, pale, quiet, with a fine eye, short nose, vulgar humorous mouth, but great energy of expression… After drawing a little he rose up, looked over me, and sat down. I rose up, looked over him, and sat down… The next day I brought the book of anatomical studies, which I had done in Devonshire. The students crowded round me, but Wilkie was not there.[38]

Once the two students began talking they found each other congenial, and one evening they set off to dine together at an eating-house in Poland Street. It was a London ordinary, a place where less affluent members of the community could enjoy a cooked dinner at a fixed price. (In an essay called *On the Want of Money*, the journalist

William Hazlitt, about whom we shall hear more, wrote, 'One may dive into a cellar, and dine on boiled beef and carrots for tenpence, with the knives and forks chained to the table'.) Over dinner, the short, handsome, intellectual Englishman and the tall, pale, talented Scotsman would converse about their art and aspirations.

Around this time, ostensibly for his health, and possibly to save money, Haydon moved to new lodgings at 3 Broad Street, now the western side of Broadwick Street (just around the corner from the Poland Street ordinary). Meanwhile, Jackson stayed in the Strand and Wilkie was lodging 'in a front parlour' at 8 Norton Street, now called Bolsover Street. The newly formed trio of friends would sometimes dine at a chop house in St Martin's Court, and at other times in John o'Groats of Rupert Street. In the late spring of 1805, Jackson replied to a letter from Haydon:

30th May, 1805

Dear Haydon,

You say you have been drawing in Indian ink; that is a practice I should rather be disposed to dissuade you from. Though you may certainly acquire the knowledge of the anatomy as well in that manner as in any other, yet why not use the tools by which your reputation is to be acquired? Depend upon it, my dear fellow, there is more real difficulty in successfully handling the brush than some people are aware of; therefore the sooner we begin to use it the better... I have been advised by Sir George Beaumont, since I last saw you, to paint all my studies at the academy in black and white...

This letter is interesting because it reveals Jackson to be in disagreement with Haydon's method of study. He is imploring Haydon to move on, to cease his seemingly endless pursuit of drawing and to begin painting. He was aware that Haydon was obsessed with anatomy so he held out a very tempting offer to his new friend:

> ...I have had the great pleasure, through the kindness of an old medical friend, to see many curious anatomies lately. I intend to have a subject for my own dissection. Will you join me? Only, for Heaven's sake, let us be sure that he is not murdered, and that he is quite dead.[39]

It is not known whether Haydon responded to this invitation, but a few months later, at a surgeon's in Hatton Garden, Haydon was granted access to a corpse of his own and he began to dissect it with relish. In contrast to his studies back in Plymouth where he had been given some dislocated bones and muscles to dissect, Haydon was now peering at the bones and muscles *in situ* and working out how they functioned together, how they moved beneath the skin. He was still drawing with black and red ink, or sometimes with a grey and red wash, and many of these drawings survive. They show Haydon to have possessed an extraordinary technical facility. His new friend occasionally joined him, but drew so indolently, according to Haydon, 'that it hardly deserved the name of drawing'.

***

John Bell's *The Anatomy of the Human Body* with its illustrations of flayed corpses hanging by their necks was a remarkable book. Indeed, the Bells were a remarkable family because John Bell's younger brother, Charles, was also a surgeon and an accomplished draughtsman. In the summer of 1804, Charles Bell was working on a book of his own; when he left Edinburgh for London on the 23rd of November, he had the manuscript in his baggage. After descending from the coach at a coffee house near the Strand (the popular London Coffee House on Ludgate Hill), he immediately began to seek introductions to some of London's best known medical men, to ask for their assistance in getting established in the English capital. One of these was Astley Cooper, an eminent surgeon at Guy's Hospital in Southwark. The generous Cooper invited Bell to move into his own house but Bell knew that he needed peace and quiet to work on his book so he politely declined the offer and moved into temporary lodgings at 22 Fludyer Street, the site of which is now buried under the pale blocks of the government offices near Downing Street.

In the ensuing weeks and months, Bell laboured over his book, *Essays on the Anatomy of Expression in Painting*. It was a work in progress and Bell needed an income while he was writing it so he decided to rent a sizeable but inexpensive house from which he could teach anatomy to students. He soon procured a lease on 10–11 Leicester Street which at various times had been the home of a lord, a duchess and a Speaker of the House of Commons. Although the property was now totally dilapidated and reputedly haunted, an advertisement duly appeared for '…A Course of Operations on the Dead Body, superintended by Mr BELL, Five guineas.' The advertisement came to Wilkie's notice and he told Haydon about it:

...a Scotchman....came to town, and Wilkie taking considerable interest in his success, asked me if I would attend a class, were one to be got up, for a course of lectures on anatomy. I was delighted; we beat up sixteen pupils at two guineas each, and here I concluded my anatomical studies.[40]

Bell and his assistants worked tirelessly delivering two types of lecture – one for the surgical men and another for the painters. A comment of Haydon's that the latter lectures were incorporated into Bell's book, *The Anatomy of Expression*, suggests that the students looked on as the skin was removed from the faces of cadavers, and the underlying muscles were carefully twitched, drawn and catalogued.

The book, which came out in 1806, was printed in the quarto format, roughly ten by twelve inches, and was sold in both standard and luxury leather-bound versions. It is a remarkable testament to Charles Bell's erudition that in a preface or 'advertisement' for the book, he wrote:

> ...Anatomy stands related to the arts of design, as the grammar of that language in which they address us. The expressions, attitudes, and movements of the human figure are the characters of this language; which is adapted to convey the effect of historical narration... The art of the painter, considered with a view to these interesting representations, assumes a high and dignified character.[41]

Crucially for Haydon, Charles Bell, in talking about conveying the *effect* of *historical narration*, was making a connection between a successful return to the Grand Style of painting and an accurate representation of passion and emotion. He invoked the 'word paintings' of the greatest poets to bolster his case:

> In the Episode of Nisus and Euryalus, Virgil gives to the death of Sulmo all the horror of violent death... but in **painting** the death of Euryalus, **the poet** recurs to all the images of languid and gentle decline.[42] [My emphasis.]

To develop his argument further, he called upon Spenser's brilliant poetical–pictorial representation of the state of despair in Book One of The *Faerie Queene*:

> That darkesome cave they enter, where they find
> That cursed man, low sitting on the ground,
> Musing full sadly in his sullein mind;
> His griesie lockes, long growen, and unbound,
> Disordred hong about his shoulders round,
> And hid his face; through which his hollow eyne
> Lookt deadly dull, and stared as astound;
> His raw-bone cheekes through penurie and pine,
> Were shronke into his jawes, as he did never dine.[43]

Charles Bell was clearly in agreement with Sir Joshua Reynolds on the principle that finally became enshrined in the Horation declaration, '*Ut pictura poesis*' – 'As is painting, so is poetry'. But the surgeon-draughtsman and the President of the Royal Academy disagreed when it came to the question of what or whom one should study in order to capture the expressions of the heroes in an historical painting. Sir Joshua Reynolds was a defender of tradition, an advocate of the classical ideal. He had advised the Academy's students to study the heads of the white marble casts of Greek and Roman statesmen in order to acquire an appreciation of how the expressions of such great and dignified men conveyed their thoughts and passions. Charles Bell, on the other hand, believed that such a course of study would lead a painter into a 'tame and lifeless' style, and so advocated the scientific study of real men in real life (and, of course, death):

> Till [the painter]...can seize with intuitive quickness the appearances of passion and all the effects produced upon the body by the operations of the mind, he has not raised himself above the mechanism of his art, nor does he rank with the poet or the historian...[44]

In conveying these ideas to David Wilkie, the clever painter of ordinary people, Charles Bell was preaching to the converted (according to Haydon, Wilkie actually produced some of the drawings for Bell's book). Haydon, however, was still wavering between Reynolds' idealism and Bell's realism, endlessly drawing the beautiful casts in the Academy then picking over the bones and muscles of corpses in the mortuary. Jackson, in the wings, as it were, was becoming more and more exasperated because Haydon was still not venturing upon his first attempt at a painting. What Haydon really needed was a commission for an historical picture, someone who would pay him to put his years of study to good use. In the meantime, Haydon retreated into himself, immersing himself in his intellectual pursuits, becoming, as he admitted to himself, 'perhaps too remote and peculiar'.

***

Some good news finally came for Haydon. It was in a letter from David Wilkie dated 9 September 1806:

> It will perhaps give you pleasure to hear that you are not unfrequently the subject of conversation. It seems Mr Jackson has spoken very highly of you, several times, to Lord Mulgrave... Sir George [Beaumont] has expressed a desire to call upon you, when he returns to London, and Lord Mulgrave has desired me to transcribe a few lines from a subject which he seems to wish to have painted, as he admires it for its grandeur. He wishes also to know, if you think it would suit your ideas, although he would not wish to put any restraint upon your inclinations...[45]

Two years and four months after his arrival in London, after having spent many hundreds of hours perfecting his drawing technique, studying Sir Joshua Reynolds' *Discourses*, poring over the Bell brothers' various treaties on anatomy and memorising huge tracts from the great poetry of antiquity, the ambitious and scholarly Benjamin Robert Haydon had finally landed a commission for a painting. And it was indeed to be a painting in the Grand Style because the 'few lines from a subject which [Lord Mulgrave] seems to wish to have painted' were the lines relating to the death of the famous Roman soldier and statesman, Dentatus, as related in Nathaniel Hooke's *The Roman History*. We have seen that the death of Dentatus was already on Haydon's list of subjects to paint, so it is no surprise that he immediately began researching and planning the picture.

The scene was to be set in Italy around 454 BC. Sicinius Dentatus had delivered a moving and influential speech to the people in support of a more equitable distribution of land. He had challenged the ruling elite, the Patricians, to relinquish some of their land rights to the Plebeians; but the challenge was to cost him his life. Tricked by one Appius to help quell an incursion by hostile forces, Dentatus was given the task of setting out a new camp in enemy territory but, en route, his own guards murdered him in a mountain pass.

From his student lodgings on the second floor of the house in Broad Street, Haydon carefully studied the account of the treacherous guards as described in *The Roman History* (an edition of which had been published in four volumes in 1770):

> [Dentatus] no sooner perceived their base design, but setting his back against a rock, that he might not be attacked behind, he received them with a courage that struck terror into the boldest of them. Calling up all of his ancient valour, he slew several of the assailants, and wounded others: And not one of them durst venture near him: They stood at a distance, and threw their darts at him. But, as even this did not effect their purpose, the villains climbed up to the top of the rock, and thence knocked him on the head with stones.[46]

In Hooke's *Roman History*, Dentatus is portrayed as a caged animal, a noble one, stoned to death by a military mob. Haydon was going to paint Dentatus fighting, drawing his sword, ready to thrust it into one of the aggressors with an expression of grim determination while above him a cowardly soldier raises a large rock. It was an enormous challenge for a first painting and Haydon was initially overwhelmed by it, not least because he knew it could make or break his reputation as an emerging historical painter. The man commissioning the painting, Lord Mulgrave (Henry Phipps, 1st Earl of Mulgrave and Viscount Normanby), was a distinguished soldier, a friend of Pitt and a formidable debater who was shortly to be appointed First Lord of the Admiralty. Although on the opposite side of the political spectrum to Dentatus (as far as the comparison goes), and unlikely to be murdered in a mountain pass, he may have identified with the heroic soldier and statesman.

Wisely, Haydon decided to postpone the commencement of *Dentatus* in order to practise painting on a less demanding picture. He chose a subject that had already been painted divinely by (among others) Caravaggio in 1596–7: *Joseph and Mary Resting on the Flight into Egypt* and it was clear that he had listened carefully to Sir Joshua Reynolds:

> The subject I had chosen was a pretty one if poetically treated, and I had so treated it. In the centre was Joseph holding the child asleep, the ass on the other side; above were two angels regarding the group, and in the extreme distance the pyramids at the break of day.[47]

With his first painting designed, the canvas purchased and brushes prepared, everything was now in place. Buoyed up by the knowledge that he had been recognised by a distinguished patron, and genuinely believing he was about to create a new era in English art, Haydon picked up one of his paintbrushes on the morning of Wednesday, 1 October 1806, and, after praying for success, 'dashed down the first touch'.

***

Haydon's meteoric rise in London society now began. First, Wilkie brought Sir George and Lady Beaumont to Haydon's lodgings. The aristocratic couple peered at the six by four foot painting as the proud artist studied them. After a pause came the verdict: 'Very poetical,' Sir George pronounced, 'and quite large enough for anything.' Sir George was tall and handsome, Lady Beaumont young for her age, and graceful. Haydon noted what each was wearing and also committed to memory everything they said. His observations were sent back to Plymouth – to his mother and father, sister Harriet and uncle Cobley – where the report was received with rapture. In the midst of all this excitement came an invitation to dine at the Beaumonts' lavish home at 29 Grosvenor Square. Wilkie called to find Haydon

> …shaving until my chin was half skinned – washing until I was quite in a heat – and dressing and redressing until my back ached – brushing my hair – looking behind me in the glass – putting the glass on the floor and then opening the door – bowing and talking to myself and wishing my mother could see me! I was ready and away we drove, I in a cold perspiration.[48]

The Beaumonts' soirées at their magnificent home in the most fashionable and sought-after part of London (they had another, even grander, home in the countryside) were attended by some of the most distinguished artists, writers and scientists of the day. Among the guests when Haydon made his debut were Humphry (later Sir Humphry) Davy, the brilliant chemist and professor at the Royal

Institution, and George Dance, the architect and portrait painter. With the effortless grace and panache for which the Beaumonts were renowned, Haydon was made to feel completely at home in a world that was, in fact, entirely new to him. When he found himself the centre of attention he rose to the occasion, being 'quite entertaining' as he talked about his plans for Lord Mulgrave's picture.

Sir George Beaumont is remembered today for being a kindly patron and a wealthy collector of art who was instrumental in the foundation of London's National Gallery. What is less well-known is that he was himself a proficient amateur artist whose great love was to paint landscapes. A few days after the dinner he called again at Haydon's modest lodgings to watch him work and to listen to his erudite and informed conversation. He then took the enthusiastic young painter to see an art collection belonging to one of his aristocratic friends, Lord Ashburnham.

Haydon's first painting, *The Flight into Egypt*, was a triumph. It took him six months to paint and was bought by Thomas Hope of Deepdene, another wealthy and well-known patron of the arts (unfortunately, this picture is now lost). Haydon then turned his attention to Lord Mulgrave's commission, *The Assassination of Dentatus*. Everyone who knew Haydon believed in the young man's abilities and Lord Mulgrave was no exception. He genuinely appreciated Haydon's ardour, erudition and conversational skills. As the picture progressed and began to take shape, Haydon was regularly invited to dine at Lord Mulgrave's table, sometimes at the Admiralty in the company of various aristocrats and an ambassador or two, and sometimes alone with Mulgrave at his home to talk about politics and history.

After dining with Lord Mulgrave, or perhaps with the Beaumonts in Grosvenor Square, Haydon would return to his lodgings to continue with his studies and his painting. He was a perfectionist. He painted the head of his hero, then rubbed it out, then painted it again, then rubbed it out again. The work was, as expected, difficult and demanding, but it slowly became apparent to Haydon that it was much *more* difficult and demanding than even he, who had spent years preparing for just such a commission, had anticipated. Frustratingly, despite having mastered technical drawing and gained expertise in anatomy, despite his attendance at Charles Bell's lectures and his close study of facial expressions, he still couldn't seem to capture the expression he needed – that of a great and noble warrior fighting for his life.

After a spell back in Plymouth earning some much-needed money by painting portraits (necessity having temporarily forced him into 'the humbler walks' of his profession), he moved into grander lodgings on the first floor of 41 Great Marlborough Street, just off the bustling Swallow Street. From here he continued to wrestle with the figures of the hero and his combatants. It was not just their facial expressions that were proving problematic, but their physical postures, the arrangement of their limbs and muscles. Even the drapery he had painted – the red cloak sailing across Dentatus' shoulder – looked too solid (to emphasise the point, Fuseli drew a prop under it.)

At the height of these difficulties, early in 1808, a seemingly innocuous event was to transform not just Haydon's view of his art – but his whole life. An invitation arrived from Wilkie to view some antique sculptures which had been hammered and levered from the Parthenon frieze in Athens and transported to England by sea. Almost nonchalantly, Haydon went along with his friend. It was in a ramshackle shed in the back yard of Gloucester House, 137 Piccadilly, that he came face to face with the Elgin Marbles. For Haydon, the encounter was momentous, his very own 'Road to Damascus'. In a single, breathtaking moment, he saw that the anatomy of men and animals had been *perfectly* captured by the artistic geniuses of Greece more than 2000 years before he, Haydon, had even begun to contemplate the subject. And it was abundantly clear that the Greeks had perfected their art by studying nature itself rather than the paintings or statues of any previous civilization. Even more importantly, Haydon knew that he, as a student at the Royal Academy of Art and an expert in anatomy, was almost uniquely qualified to appreciate the value of this achievement and to learn from it. (In this, he was largely correct; he was almost alone in his veneration of the Marbles at that time.)

With Wilkie alongside him, Haydon focused upon the wrist of one of the female figures, and saw that the radius and ulna were depicted 'in a female form'. 'I was astonished,' he wrote, 'because I'd never seen them hinted at in any female wrist in the antique.' He looked up to the elbow, and there was the 'outer condyle'. The arm was in repose, and the soft parts were in relaxation. 'My heart beat!' he continued, 'If I had seen nothing else, I had beheld sufficient to keep me to nature for the rest of my life.'[49]

***

Haydon began to dream about the Elgin Marbles (he once went sleepwalking and woke up in his cast room at 3am). With the help of Lord Mulgrave's considerable influence, he received permission to draw the Marbles in Lord Elgin's shed. It was a makeshift, cold and damp environment in which Haydon would labour for up to 15 hours a day – by candlelight at night – until the porter came and ushered him out. He would then wearily trudge the mile or so back to his lodgings, spread his drawings out on the floor and sip tea while his damp clothes steamed in front of the fire. Often, in the early hours of the morning, he 'pondered on the change of empires and thought that I had been contemplating what Socrates looked at and Plato saw'.[50]

Some time in the summer of 1808, Haydon began to keep a diary and it quickly became a necessary part of his intellectual life, a place where he could pour out his observations and wrestle with his thoughts. What is most noticeable from the diary is that after the long daily routine of staring at, measuring, drawing and interpreting the Elgin Marbles, he almost always turned to literature for relaxation:

> ...walked and came home, drank tea & passed my time laxly in reading Boswell's Johnson... There is no resisting this book...[51]

> Read Homer, in English, to stir up my fancy... any fine passage I went to the Greek immediately...[52]

Read Virgil; understand it and can make it out pretty well...[53]

As the summer passed away into the autumn and winter, as Haydon discovered more and more about the Elgin Marbles and became increasingly conscious of their perfection, he began to feel despondent. He knew that he had a mountain to climb before he could apply the principles of the Marbles in the service of painting and the resultant wane in his enthusiasm affected his progress with *Dentatus*. Earlier, he had recorded in his diary that people had said to him, '...you can't be expected in your second picture to paint like Titian & draw like Michel Angelo...', '...but I do expect it,' he had responded, 'and I will try...'. Finally, sitting by his fire in January 1809, surrounded by the innumerable drawings he had made of the Elgin Marbles, his seemingly irrepressible spirit began to sag:

January 19. Thursday. Idle.
January 20. Friday. Did little.
January 21. Saturday. Did nothing.
January 22. Sunday. Nothing.
January 23. Monday. Less.

***

It wasn't until Friday, 31 March 1809 that Haydon finally added the finishing touches to *The Assassination of Dentatus*. He laid down his paintbrush and claimed that he had produced the first English painting to conform with the aesthetic policy of the ancient Greeks. It was a very large picture, and a fine one for so young an artist, so it was hung in a prominent place in the main gallery at Somerset House.

However, for reasons that are now obscure, it was subsequently moved to the ante-room. This still formed part of the main exhibition space so the re-positioning was in no way a statement about the quality of the work, but the ante-room was undoubtedly a less prominent gallery. Haydon had by now a complex mix of emotions; he was elated because he was exhibiting at the Royal Academy again but anxious about the forthcoming critical response to the painting, and completely exhausted by the effort it had taken to finish in time for acceptance by the Academicians. Unfortunately, he took the removal of his painting to the ante-room as a gross and deliberate insult and such was his (totally misplaced) disappointment and hurt pride that he chose to pick a quarrel with the Academicians themselves.

One very early consequence of Haydon's self-confidence was that he had raised the expectations of his friends and patrons to a clearly unattainable level. He often publicly compared himself with, and identified with, the very greatest artists in history. Here are just three of many examples that can be found in his diary (several of his friends had access to his diary and some even wrote it for him when he was worn out with work or when, as happened often, his eyes became tired and distressed):

> As I walked along Fleet Street, I felt hungry and went into Peele's coffee house to have some soup... I shrunk in, blushing, fearful to look up for fear of meeting the eyes of Michel Angelo's spectre crying, 'Haydon, Haydon, you Idle rascal, is this the way to eminence?'[54]

> I knelt down last night surrounded by the works of Raphael, and prayed God fervently & from my soul, to grant I might be as great or greater before I left this World, to enable me to supply his deficiencies and rival his beauties.[55]

> Passed an acute & miserable morning in comparing myself with Raphael. At my age he had completed a Vatican Room.[56]

This state of mind was noted and commented upon by many other people – all of Haydon's friends, for example, habitually compared him with Raphael. It was certainly a bold effort and showed a prodigious talent, but *The Assassination of Dentatus* was an inferior work when compared with any painting of Raphael or Michelangelo. The hero's face was too grim and determined and his massively muscled legs seemed slightly disjointed from his body. As the public, the patrons and the Academicians pondered the picture – their expectations having already been raised to a pitch by the painter himself – they concentrated upon these relatively minor defects and instead of applauding Haydon as a new and genuine talent, they began to murmur about his deficiencies. He came to be seen as a failure and the consequences were predictable. Before *Dentatus* was exhibited, he had often been the centre of attention at Lord Mulgrave's or Sir George Beaumont's dining tables, but after the exhibition he found himself 'out of favour' and Wilkie once again became the artist about whom everyone was talking.

Shortly after Lord Mulgrave had commissioned *Dentatus*, when Haydon's reputation had still been fully intact, Sir George Beaumont had offered his own money and encouragement by commissioning a painting on any scene or subject from Shakespeare's *Macbeth*. But after the muted response to *Dentatus*, Sir George began to have second thoughts about the commission and used the size of the painting as the issue upon which he could attempt to withdraw from his obligation. Haydon was to go through agonies of indecision over whether to hold Sir George to his original request for a full-length painting, in other words on a canvas so big that it would hardly fit into the artist's painting room, or whether to accede to Sir George's revised request for a smaller picture, more suited to the patron's drawing room. This would be a crucial moment in Haydon's career for surely he could ill afford to ignore such a powerful patron's wishes?

One day, he received what was now an increasingly rare invitation to dine at Lord Mulgrave's house:

> ...Lord Mulgrave in the kindest manner after dinner said: 'Haydon, if you consent to oblige Sir George you will please us all.' I looked at Sir George across the table, but his face expressed rigid indifference. Lady Beaumont chatted away to Lady Mulgrave. Wilkie and Jackson cast down their eyes and said nothing... Lord Mulgrave, apparently astonished at the whole affair, changed the conversation. At leaving, Lord Mulgrave shook me kindly by the hand and whispered, 'Yield,'...[57]

Haydon knew that his intellectual ability was greater than that of both Lord Mulgrave and Sir George Beaumont, and that when it came to matters of art he had more technical knowledge than either of them. After all, he was a professional artist, whereas Lord

Mulgrave and Sir George Beaumont were merely amateurs and connoisseurs. So when Lord Mulgrave took his hand and implored him to yield, Haydon decided to ignore him. It was a decision that would have disastrous consequences.

***

At this crucial juncture in his career, with both the Academicians and his patrons questioning his talent and his judgement (Lord Mulgrave paid Haydon over £200 for *Dentatus* but without a great show of enthusiasm), Haydon momentarily lost confidence in his own abilities. As he prepared to begin work on Sir George Beaumont's commission for *Macbeth*, this was manifested in an almost obsessive return to his studies. The pages of his diary for this period are filled with observations about human nature, art, scenery and, more than ever before, poetry. Here is an entry he made when he and Wilkie set sail for a holiday in Devonshire, in June 1809:

> Evening approached, the Sun set, and as we wafted with the breeze, the Moon, apparent queen, unveiled her peerless light, and glittered on the sails of the distant shipping. Every thing now seemed hushed, except the rippling and bubbling of the waters as we gently divided them... There was a strong dewy breeze, and as I looked towards the north, I saw the white cliffs of Portland, standing as it were, alone and solitary... Nothing could be more poetical. Every thing Homer, Shakespeare, Milton and Virgil had said of morning rushed into my fancy...[58]

Haydon's claim to be intimately familiar with the works of Homer, Shakespeare, Milton and Virgil was no idle boast because he loved books just as much as – perhaps even more than – he loved painting. With his reputation as an artist beginning to falter he could have discreetly changed careers; his knowledge of literature and the quality of some of the writing in his diary demonstrates that he could have become a significant literary figure, perhaps a novelist, an essayist or journalist. But as the weeks and months passed, with the huge, dark canvas of *Macbeth* standing neglected, he clung on to his 'vaulting ambition' to be a great painter. Just as his contemporary, the German philosopher Arthur Schopenhauer, struggled all of his life to promulgate his own ideas and gain a small readership, so Haydon doggedly continued to develop, discuss and expound his philosophy of art, its connection with poetry and his growing understanding of the importance of the Elgin Marbles. In the midst of all this agonising over his future he was once again invited to dine with Lord Mulgrave. On 17 December 1809, he wrote:

> ...there was something very delightful in the illuminated gay splendour of Lord Mulgrave's apartments, which together with his affable manners and amusing conversation, spread a calm over my troubled soul I had not felt for months...[59]

As 1809 gave way to 1810, the 24-year-old Haydon at last began to make progress with his painting of *Macbeth*. He was still ignoring Sir George Beaumont's concerns about its size but had offered a compromise of sorts – to paint it life-size (or something very near to it) and allow Sir George to renege on the commission if he wasn't happy with the result. But Sir George, with one eye on posterity in terms of his own judgement, was already unhappy; Haydon's lack of tact and understanding in this matter is displayed in a diary entry from early 1810:

> Sir G.B. is a man whom I consider as playing a deep game, and all the World his opponents, he is a man of rooted meanness of heart, who would as soon have blood rung from him as money – and this he tries to conceal from the world, by wishing to appear a liberal patron of Art...[60]

As Haydon's position over the size of the *Macbeth* painting became more and more entrenched, he was increasingly shunned by Sir George and, inevitably, by Sir George's close friend, Lord Mulgrave. These two very wealthy and influential men had believed in Haydon and offered him nothing but kindness, encouragement and employment. And more than anything else, Haydon now needed employment. So why was he so obstinate? Why did he risk complete alienation by insisting upon painting such a large picture? The answer lies in his eyes.

The house in which he lived, 41 Great Marlborough Street, was large, but his own rooms were small. His landlord, Henry Perkins, was a grocer or tea-merchant and the house was a property investment that had been divided up in order to maximise its potential rental income. Haydon had a painting room and a cast room in which he spent most of his working life surrounded by the appurtenances of painting. He used a variety of turpentines and spirits but had very little ventilation so, quite apart from the fire risk, the solvent vapour would have dried out his eyes, possibly creating painful corneal abrasions. As his eyesight deteriorated, he painted larger and larger pictures so that he could paint in the detail that he required. Eventually, he would wear more than one pair of spectacles, lifting them up in turn as he moved around his painting.

Haydon's lack of money was by now becoming a serious problem. Although he lived frugally with very little furniture and few possessions, he was nevertheless living in the heart of London's retail district and his rent was accordingly high (nearby Swallow Street was soon to be demolished to make way for the ever-fashionable Regent Street). He claimed that he was a 'virtuous and diligent youth', that he never touched wine, dined at reasonable chop houses, lived in his study, and did little but work, think, paint and draw. By necessity, however, he spent large amounts of money on materials and models. On one occasion he nearly killed a model – 'a black, a native of Boston, a perfect antique figure alive' – by encasing him in plaster in order to obtain a cast of his musculature. When the plaster set, the model could not breathe and it took a huge effort to break the mould from the man's body and save him from suffocation. The model had been engaged for a month and his encasing had required seven bushels (56 gallons) of plaster. This all cost money that Haydon could ill afford.

Late in 1810 came news that would drive Haydon inexorably towards the charity of his friends and acquaintances. (The cold, uncharitable clutches of the moneylenders were to be avoided at all costs.) Haydon's still ailing father wrote from Plymouth to inform him that he could no longer provide even a semblance of financial support. At first, Haydon turned to his friends. He borrowed money from Charles Bell, from Wilkie and from a friend of Wilkie called Peter Cleghorn. His landlord, in an astonishingly generous gesture, agreed to forego his rent until the painting of *Macbeth* was complete (and sold). Meanwhile, for his own peace of mind, Haydon resolved to keep his living expenses to an absolute minimum while he concentrated all his efforts upon his painting. He was confident that *Macbeth* would have a good chance of winning the 300 guinea prize that would be awarded to the painter of the best historical picture by the British Institution (widely known as the British Gallery because of its exhibition gallery in Pall Mall). This award would be made during the 1812 season, and if he won the competition, Haydon could pay the prize money to his growing number of creditors. Such a public success would increase the chances of selling the painting, either to a placated Sir George Beaumont or to some other collector of art. Haydon calculated that if the picture received favourable reviews in the many newspapers that reported upon the London art exhibitions, he could expect to get around 500 guineas for it, making a total gain of 800 guineas.[61]

In late 1811, as *Macbeth* approached completion, the now 25-year-old Haydon should have been preparing the way for success by effecting a reconciliation with the critics of *Dentatus* in the Royal Academy. The Academy was, after all, a rival institution of gentlemen and scholars whom the British Institution would not wish to offend. But in a single act of breathtaking arrogance, he was to completely destroy any remaining support he had at the Royal Academy.

***

Back in 1805, a man called John Hunt and his younger brother, Leigh, had established a newspaper called, simply, The News. John was the newspaper's general manager and Leigh was its theatre critic. Both Wilkie and Haydon were regular theatre-goers and had enjoyed reading Leigh Hunt's lively reviews. Soon after his reputation as an artist had been established, David Wilkie had been introduced to Leigh Hunt and had in turn introduced Hunt to Haydon. John Hunt had brought out a new publication in 1808 – a respectable and cultured, but anti-government Sunday newspaper called *The Examiner* – and had invited his younger brother to join him as chief writer and editor. It was a role for which Leigh Hunt was singularly qualified. Haydon had thought him

> …with his black, bushy hair, black eyes, pale face and 'nose of taste', as fine a specimen of a London editor as could be imagined; assuming yet moderate, sarcastic yet genial, with a smattering of everything and mastery of nothing; affecting the dictator, the poet, the politician, the critic and the sceptic, whichever would at the moment give the air to inferior minds of being a very superior man. I listened with something of curiosity to his republican independence, though hating his effeminacy and cockney peculiarities.[62]

With his *Macbeth* well advanced but his aristocratic patrons still effectively cold-shouldering him, Haydon decided he had nothing to lose by contributing an essay to such an anti-establishment newspaper as *The Examiner*. His first article appeared in November 1811 and was 'considered perfectly immature and unintelligible', but his second, ostensibly aiming 'to expose the ignorance of a powerful patron', was mature, intelligible and disastrous. He entitled the piece, *To the critic on Barry's works in the Edinburgh Review, Aug 1810* and Leigh Hunt, sensing its potential for igniting a debate, published it. 'The critic' was a man called Richard Payne Knight and he can't have been the only reader of *The Examiner* who wondered why a response to an article he had published in August 1810 was appearing in January 1812.[63]

Haydon's motives in this matter are obscure but discernible. He admitted that he had been 'animated by a desire to write' in early life because Sir Joshua Reynolds had waited until very late in his career to produce his *Discourses*. Haydon, despite the murmurings about *Dentatus*, was still anticipating future fame as an artist and wanted to make his debut as a writer and commentator in the early part of his career. The aim of his *Examiner* article was to promulgate his ideas about High Art and the Grand Style in such a brilliant and eloquent manner that it would establish his reputation as a serious scholar and ameliorate the critical response to *Dentatus*. (The painting had received a prize from the British Institution in 1810 but this had arrived too late to thwart the damage to its reputation.)

To the critic on Barry's works was well-written, erudite and scholarly. It was full of observations about Rubens, Rembrandt, Raphael, Titian and Michelangelo, and contained learned commentaries on Pliny, Phidias and the Greeks. But it was deeply insulting to Richard Payne Knight. Almost from the start, the author, 'An English Student' (as Haydon signed himself), talked of Payne Knight's 'absurdity and pernicious sophism'. He inferred that the Academicians (for in attacking Payne Knight he was pointing his pen obliquely at the Academicians) were imbeciles who delay painting '...till they have been to Rome and been to Vienna, till they have got French brushes and Indian lake, and all those innumerable accessories, under which idleness and imbecility they are sure to take refuge, as an excuse for the greatest of all difficulties, *commencing to think*...'[64]

One wonders what Haydon himself was thinking at this time, sitting at his table in Great Marlborough Street, writing such invective. 'That uneducated impudence should go out to Rome,' he continued, 'and return as ignorant as it came, – full of *morbidezza* and *bozzo*, and all the technical nonsense of connoisseurs, – is surely a just subject of contempt.' At one point he said rather ambiguously to Payne Knight, who was not only a well-known and respected antiquarian, but a wealthy landowner and former Member of Parliament, 'You praise the picture of Rembrandt, Sir, as all men praise such pictures who know they are in a lower rank, in spite of their wishes.'[65]

The article went on to say much, much more in a similar vein. It ran in *The Examiner* over three issues, those of the 26th of January, the 2nd of February (in which appeared: 'But, Sir, instead of doubtfully sneering at the Grand Style you sneered at the palpable absurdities of the Exhibition, at the girls feeding chickens and boys feeding pigs... you would have shown greater feeling for the taste of your country') and the 9th of February.

In penning the article (and handing it over to Leigh Hunt for publication), Haydon had made a monumental error of judgement.

He had thought the article would be viewed as an attempt by a brilliant young man to successfully engage a respected critic in an intellectual duel. But far from raising his profile as a scholar, its effect was to destroy any credibility he had left with his patrons and the Academicians. He quickly came to realise the folly of his actions:

> All the patrons were in a fury. Who could it be? Who was this English Student? The Sunday following, the attack on the Academy followed [i.e. the second instalment of the article], and never since the art was established were its followers in such a hubbub of fury and rage... From this moment the destiny of my life may be said to have changed. My picture was caricatured, my name detested, my peace harassed...[66]

Haydon now knew that he had ruined any chance of the directors of the British Gallery awarding him the 300 guinea prize for *Macbeth*. Surveying the wreckage of his ambition – his paints, palette, plaster casts, prints and his now unsaleable painting of *Macbeth* – the clearly shaken 26-year-old wondered what to do next. He knew that Benjamin West, one of the few celebrated historical painters living in England (he was connected to Leigh Hunt's family by marriage), had in recent years sold a painting of *Christ Healing the Sick* to the British Institution for the astonishing sum of 3000 guineas. Even though Haydon's reputation was in tatters, and even though his patrons had all but abandoned him, he convinced himself that with an Herculean effort he could paint such a picture. He believed that he could exhibit it far away from the Royal Academy and the British Gallery and sell it privately to a wealthy collector. He *had* to believe this, because his debts were now £616.10s and he had no way of repaying them.

One day while walking down Haymarket – past the theatres and the prostitutes – worrying about a debt he could not pay, Haydon bumped into Prince Hoare. The older man warned his young protégé that his already infamous 'Payne Knight article' would cost him dearly because any picture he painted in future would be unsaleable. Prince Hoare knew what he was talking about. He was a member of the group of Academicians who had studied in Rome in the 1770s (he had studied briefly with Fuseli and Northcote under Anton Raphael Mengs, at that time considered one of the greatest artists in Europe) and was now a respected academic and authority on matters of art. Indeed, it is to Hoare's credit that he was not personally offended by Haydon's *Examiner* article and that he continued to offer him support.

Haydon argued that if he painted a picture of great merit the public would make it popular and its very popularity would make it saleable. Prince Hoare shook his head. 'What are you going to paint?' he said. 'Solomon's Judgment,' said Haydon. 'Rubens and Raphael have both tried it,' said Prince Hoare. 'So much the better,' said Haydon, 'I'll tell the story better.' Prince Hoare smiled and put his hand on the younger man's shoulder:

> How are you to live?
> Leave that to me.
> Who is to pay your rent?
> Leave that to me.
> Well, I see you are ready with a reply. You will never sell it.
> I trust in God.[67]

Haydon ordered an enormous canvas, approximately 15 feet long by 13 feet high, so large that it could not be set up vertically in his painting room and had to be tilted against the wall. ('The gentlemen of this country...' Sir George Beaumont once wrote to Haydon, 'have neither houses to receive, nor money to spare for such works as you have in contemplation.') The canvas was duly delivered on Friday, 3 April 1812 and the very next day Haydon began drawing in the background and the lines of perspective.

As expected, the British Institution did not award *Macbeth* their 300 guinea prize and Haydon's friend Charles Bell, to whom Haydon owed money, wrote to express his sympathy. Haydon had already begun to sell and pawn his possessions, his clothes, his beloved books, his furniture and prints. There was a huge market for second-hand clothes and other household goods in London at this time and he would have had no trouble in selling even his shoes. It was particularly painful for him to have to sell his watch, 'a keepsake from an uncle', but he was now desperate and all thoughts of sentimentality had to be ignored. Many years later, Haydon reflected upon his life at 41 Great Marlborough Street during the painting of *The Judgment of Solomon*. His recollections are extremely vivid:

> What I suffered in those apartments! Painting a picture that filled up one complete side of my room, all the lower part of which I was obliged to do lying on my side on the floor, for I could not move it up a half an inch – continually sitting in the stench of paint, and after painting 8 & 10 hours, cleaning my brushes and palette till I almost fainted, with the sickly, soapy smell, and then sitting down in it to read

or prepare drawings for the next day, my outer room stuffed with casts so that one could scarcely walk through them, and sleeping inside in a little paltry apartment, close to the window, so that once in the intense winter I lost my voice during the night, the frost was so severe that it chilled my very breath... Here I lived, here I painted... here I was blind & starving... How often have I returned home from dinner, my room all in disorder, drawings, cloths, brushes, palettes, lying here and lying there, & my Picture across the room with a head newly and successfully painted; how often have I sat down by the chimney and losing myself in a train of speculation by the light of the fire, settled the most difficult principles of Art... and then the Servant wondering why I had not rung for candles, has come up and found me quite gone & insensible to everything, and she has roused me by 'Lord, Mr. Haydon, you are always conjuring'.[68]

Haydon's capacity for convincing people that he was destined for greatness now came to the fore. He was desperately (and very evidently) impoverished, even lacking 'the common necessaries of life'. As noted above, he sometimes dined at the John o'Groats Tavern, 61 Rupert Street, Haymarket, where a good dinner of potatoes, various meats and vegetables, followed by a fruit pie, might cost around two shillings. The proprietor, John Seabrook, had become accustomed to having the well-known painter and writer dining in his tavern and deferring payment until a later date (being 'trusted' to pay). Haydon would enjoy several dinners without paying and then settle with his benefactor the next time he managed to borrow some money or sell one of his dwindling stock of possessions.

One day, however, Haydon had extended his credit beyond the normal bounds and was fearful he might be refused a dinner and humiliated in front of the other customers. Seabrook simply took him to one side and assured him that he could dine at John o'Groats for free so long as he was working on *Solomon*. Similarly, in a typically generous gesture, Henry Perkins said he would continue to forego his rent for as long as it took Haydon to paint his new picture (which was clearly going to be years rather than months).

For the whole of the two years that it took to paint *The Judgment of Solomon*, no matter how distressing his circumstances, no matter how demanding his accruing debts, Haydon adamantly refused to paint portraits for money. His attitude towards what he considered a noble, even heroic, venture was perfectly summed up in a diary entry he wrote towards the end of this period, in late 1813:

> I feel the want of kindred spirits – there is not an Artist to whom I can pour out the enthusiasm of my soul, who will listen and participate...[69]

He then added a few lines from Spenser's *The Faerie Queene*:

> The noble heart that harbours virtuous thought
> And **is with child of glorious great intent,**
> Can never rest untill it forth have brought
> The eternal brood of glorie excellent.[70]
> (The emphasis is Haydon's)

After two years' work, in February 1814, Haydon finally completed his painting of *The Judgment of Solomon*. Even his harshest critics must have been affected by his condition. He was pathetically thin, physically trembling and his eyes had broken down completely.

His oculist, William Adams, set off to visit him in Great Marlborough Street, only to find an apothecary leaning over the emaciated patient, knife in hand, about to open his temporal artery. Adams warned, 'If that's done, he will be blind...'. The operation was stopped, and Haydon afterwards maintained that Adams saved his eyes.

***

Haydon's health was broken when he exhibited *The Judgment of Solomon* at the Water-Colour Society exhibition in Spring Gardens, a quiet residential area between Lord Mulgrave's former residence at the Admiralty and the busy junction of Charing Cross. The exhibition opened in stages – to royalty and the aristocracy first, then to the nobility and finally to the ordinary public. Richard Payne Knight came to the first opening with Caroline, Princess of Wales. The painting was huge and imposing, depicting King Solomon seated high on his throne over two women who were laying claim to the same baby. The king's expression portrayed a seriousness of intent, the swordsman nearby watching his face, ready to execute an order to slice the baby in two. There was shock, horror and eager anticipation in the faces of the witnesses. Haydon had taken great pains to ensure historical (or biblical) accuracy, even down to the clothes and jewellery of the spectators.

Payne Knight, knowing the artist to be the man who had so insulted him in *The Examiner* and recalling the criticism of *Dentatus*, dismissed the painting as 'distorted stuff' and the Princess agreed with him. This worried the president and officials of the Water-Colour Society, but Haydon, 'thin and hectic, hands trembling', bravely told them not to worry; the public, he said, would love the picture. When the nobility were admitted, the picture was found to be 'very large' and it seems that not much more was said about it. Finally, on Monday, 2 May 1814, the exhibition proper opened.

Now, finally, Haydon had his reward. The public loved the picture. People crowded around it, everybody was talking about it. A gentleman offered him £500 on the spot but his debts amounted to £1100 and he could not afford to accept. The price he was willing to accept was 660 guineas, a considerable sum for the fourth painting of a controversial non-Academician (it must be remembered that *Macbeth* was still on Haydon's hands as he had not been able to sell it). The gentleman who had offered £500 then invited Haydon to dinner and agreed to pay the asking price, only to be overruled by his wife. 'But my dear,' she said, 'where am I to put my piano?'[71]

Later, however, as Haydon walked into the exhibition hall, he found that a 'Sold' sign had been placed on the painting. 'I really thought I should have fainted,' he said. The buyers, who had paid 700 guineas, were a partnership of Plymouth banker Sir William Elford and his colleague, one J.W. Tingecombe. Sir George Beaumont had tried to buy the painting for the British Institution but had arrived too late, just as the 'Sold' sign was being applied. Haydon must have found this news exquisite in the extreme. Lord Mulgrave, Sir George and Lady Beaumont and a whole host of other dignitaries now fêted Haydon, invited him to dinner, swore that his picture was as fine as anything painted by Raphael and left cards at his lodgings. ('When I came home my table was covered with cards of fashion – noble lords, dukes, ladies, baronets, literary men.')

With the exhibition of this single painting, Benjamin Robert Haydon had taken a huge step forward in his quest to be at the vanguard of a renaissance in English art. When the painting was reviewed in the periodicals, he found himself to be the most famous and talked about historical painter in England. His theories about art and anatomy, his worship (this is not too strong a word) of the Elgin Marbles, and his analysis of the contemporary artistic establishment in *The Examiner*, had all been proved right. Surrounded by friends old and new, with his fame and fortune seemingly guaranteed, the completely exhausted Haydon returned to his lodgings in Great Marlborough Street and began to plan his next picture. It was to be a truly monumental effort called *Christ's Entry into Jerusalem*.

Chapter 4

> *...to hope till Hope creates*
> *From its own wreck the thing it contemplates...*
> Percy Bysshe Shelley: *Prometheus Unbound*

Some time around the year 1814, when he wrote the *Imitation of Spenser*, John Keats had a serious argument with Dr Thomas Hammond and moved out of his lodgings above the Edmonton surgery. Bearing in mind the comments that his friends were later to make about his 'high-mindedness, his utter unconsciousness of a mean motive, his placability...', such a confrontation seems to have been entirely out of character. But we can recall that Charles Cowden Clarke attached a caveat to his description of his young protégé:

> Keats was not an easily swayable man; in differing with those he loved his firmness kept equal pace with the sweetness of his persuasion.

The rent for Keats' rooms was included in the cost of his apprenticeship, so in vacating them and moving to new rooms he was effectively paying twice for his lodgings. But why? A few years later he talked of having 'clenched his fist' at Hammond, which suggests that he, Keats, had been the offended party, that he had been angered by a perceived injustice. Other than that we know nothing about the argument, so can only speculate.

There may be a clue in the description of Hammond as a man 'of aristocratic bearing', a phrase said to have been current soon after his death when local people still remembered him. Hammond was a man to whom Keats owed a debt of gratitude – as we have seen, he had nursed Keats' grandfather and then his tubercular mother through their final illnesses and after his mother's death had taken the boy under his professional wing. But how did the doctor's treatment of Keats compare with the kind and benevolent treatment he had been accustomed to at Clarke's school in Enfield?

Hammond lived with his family in a fine house called 'Wilston'. It was situated in its own gardens in Church Street, Edmonton and, being the house of a successful doctor, would have been furnished to a high standard. The dining rooms of similar houses at this time were lit by delicate chandelier-type oil lamps, while the dinner tables were further brightened with ornate candelabra. (Although a few of London's streets were by now lit with gas, houses generally were not.) Sheraton and Hepplewhite's elegant furniture designs were popular and Wedgewood's vases were in vogue, with tastes having recently moved to neoclassical lines. Simply put, the house would have been comfortable and refined.[72]

The surgery, by contrast, would have resembled a workhouse. This was located in a separate, plain brick building close to the main house with an attic serving as lodgings for the apprentices. In fact, as an apprentice in Regency England, Keats was to Hammond little more than a paying (not *paid*) servant. During the day, Keats would have been responsible for taking the coats and hats from the patients, boiling water, assisting with medical procedures, disposing of old bandages and washing down the floors and work surfaces in the surgery. A home visit would occasionally be needed and on one such visit to Enfield, Keats was left outside in the snow to look after the horse. A schoolboy from Clarke's school threw a snowball at him, probably not realising that his target, the stocky young man, had only recently been admired at the school for his fighting prowess. This anecdote has an air of ignominy about it, and it is one of the very few to have survived from the period.

Although it is likely that Keats was treated kindly enough by Dr Hammond – that he was invited to share in family meals, for example – it is undeniable that his status as a sort of surgery houseboy would have been menial. This is important because everything we know about Keats in later life tells us that he rebelled against and hated the voguish middle classes with their superior attitudes, their dull conversation and fastidious table manners. This is an extract from a letter he wrote to his brothers in December 1817, after dining with a set of literary men:

> ...These men say things which make one start, without making one feel; they are all alike; their manners are all alike; they all know fashionables; they have all a mannerism in their very eating and drinking, in their mere handling a decanter. They talked of Kean [a famous actor of the day] and his low company. 'Would I were with that company instead of yours,' said I to myself![73]

His contempt for these men and their mannerisms is clear. So it may be that he found the doctor of 'aristocratic bearing' equally unbearable. Perhaps Hammond reprimanded him or embarrassed him in front of a patient, or even a dinner guest.

***

Hammond's influence over and supervision of Keats was now restricted to their working hours only. When the day's work was done, Keats went to his own home. We can be sure that his new lodgings were modest, almost certainly just a room or two in his new landlord's house, with breakfast served in the mornings. It is likely that he spent most of his evenings pursuing his love of poetry, that's to say, when he had time away from his medical books. He would have been pleased with his *Imitation of Spenser* and he took care of it, but as far as we can tell he didn't show it to anyone – not even to Charles Cowden Clarke, the man who had introduced him to Spenser in the first place.

Keats was particularly interested in the 'musicality' or melody of poetry – a friend once said that his sense of melody was 'quite exquisite'.[74] One of the poems that he wrote in his new lodgings appears to have been experimental in this context. It is called *Fill for me a brimming bowl* and it is thought to have been inspired by a woman he saw during a break from his work, when he visited a fairground-style pleasure garden at Vauxhall, south of the Thames:

> Fill for me a brimming bowl,
> And let me in it drown my soul;
> But put therein some drug, designed

> To banish Woman from my mind.
> For I want not the stream inspiring
> That heats the sense with lewd desiring;
> But I want as deep a draught
> As e'er from Lethe's wave was quaffed...

This jaunty little poem points to themes of vocational devotion and amorous distraction which Keats would take up with much more thought, imagination and intellectual depth in the future.

***

Keats was still living in Edmonton so he remained close to his grandmother's house, the only house he and his brothers and sister could collectively call a home. With both his father and his mother now dead it is likely that he visited his grandmother very often. She died in December 1814 but Keats must have continued to pass the house many times in the following weeks and months. He had always been deeply attached to his grandmother and he was acutely conscious of the sacrifices she had made for himself and his siblings.

Alice Jennings was buried in the now demolished St Stephen's church in Coleman Street, a church which was just a stone's throw from the Swan and Hoop and had become all too familiar to Keats. His father's funeral (when he was eight), his grandfather's (when he was nine) and his mother's (when he was fourteen) had all been held at St Stephen's. But away from the public mourning, when he wanted to say a private, heartfelt goodbye to his grandmother, it was to poetry that Keats turned. On 19 December 1814, he wrote a sonnet called *As from the darkening gloom a silver dove*. It is not considered to be one of Keats' better poems, even among his early ones, but the love and gratitude that he felt for his grandmother shine through it:

> As from the darkening gloom a silver dove
> Upsoars and darts into the Eastern light
> On pinions that naught moves but pure delight;
> So fled thy soul into the realms above,
> Regions of peace and everlasting love...

Once again, it appears that he kept the poem to himself because he was lacking the confidence to show it to other people, not even to the brothers with whom he habitually shared his innermost feelings.

As December 1814 gave way to January 1815, Keats was fighting an overwhelming sense of loneliness and an understandable uncertainty about his future. It is possible that his brother Tom actually shared his lodgings with him, but he saw much less of his other brother, George, and his little sister, Frances, both of whom were now under the care of a guardian who had been appointed by Alice Jennings, a city tea merchant called Richard Abbey. For reasons known only to himself, Abbey made sure that the Keats children were kept ignorant of the true extent of their Jennings family inheritance (which was considerable). How Abbey felt about John being condemned to remain in his rented rooms with few possessions and little money can only be surmised, but there was certainly something unusual about Abbey's harsh and unfeeling attitude toward his young ward, and something unsavoury about his feelings towards the young man's mother. Abbey was the one who left the account of Frances Keats crossing the road with her skirts held high.

We don't know very much about this part of Keats' life, the time that he was serving his apprenticeship with Thomas Hammond and living in lodgings. None of his letters from this period survive and he didn't keep any sort of diary (as far as we know). Official records of his activities are practically non-existent. We can deduce at least some of his feelings and concerns from the poetry that he wrote, at least the small amount of poetry that has survived. Some time around February 1815, for example, he wrote a revealing poem called *To Hope*:

> When by my solitary hearth I sit,
> And hateful thoughts enwrap my soul in gloom,
> When no fair dreams before my mind's eye flit,
> And the bare heath of life presents no bloom,
> Sweet Hope, ethereal balm upon me shed,
> And wave they silver pinions o'er my head.

In the second stanza he talks about his battles with loneliness and depression as he walks into the local woods 'at the fall of night', and in the third he confronts the real prospect that he will be disappointed in his literary endeavours. In the fourth stanza he remembers his parents and his grandparents:

> Whene'er the fate of those I hold most dear
> Tells to my fearful breast a tale of sorrow,
> O bright-eyed Hope, my morbid fancy cheer;
> Let me awhile thy sweetest comforts borrow...

The fifth stanza, however, is the most revealing. He calls his parents 'cruel', but cruel only in the sense that they died early and 'abandoned' him, leaving the fate of himself and his siblings in the hands of people who had no loving, familial interest in them (Thomas Hammond, Richard Abbey and various lawyers). As had the final stanza of *Imitation of Spenser*, this fifth stanza of *To Hope* contains the kernel of an idea which Keats was about to develop, that the greatest poetry is akin to the greatest philosophy – its beauty and wisdom being medicine for a troubled soul:

> Should e'er unhappy love my bosom pain,
> From cruel parents, or relentless fair,
> Oh, let me think it is not quite in vain
> To sigh out sonnets to the midnight air!

We know that Keats had long ago taken to heart a philosophical poem called *The Minstrel*, by James Beattie. It is little known today, but it is worth taking a closer look at this poem because it helped sustain Keats through his loneliness and hardships. Indeed, its themes echo throughout his writing – both his poetry and his prose – for the rest of his short life.

The poet James Beattie was born in Laurencekirk, Scotland, in October 1735 and he died in 1803. As had Keats, Beattie lost his father in childhood and relied upon his mother for his emotional security. As a boy Beattie, too, had shown a deep love and respect for classical literature (including Virgil's *Aeneid*, which as we noted in chapter 2, Keats spent years translating as a schoolboy and thereafter). When he left school at the age of 14, Beattie went to

Marischal College in Aberdeen where he excelled as a Greek scholar, and during the next few years he gained a reputation for being something of a poet. Beattie became the schoolmaster in the rural parish of Fordoun where he was considered eccentric because of his habit of wandering through the countryside from nightfall until dawn. He contributed poetry to a magazine (*The Scotsman*) before taking up an appointment at a grammar school in Aberdeen. On account of his intellectual gifts (with a sprinkling of patronage), he soon returned to his old college, Marischal, this time as the Professor of Philosophy.

Beattie initially found fame as a writer of philosophical essays, particularly an *Essay on the Nature and Immutability of Truth*. The success of this propelled him into Scotland's higher literary circles, but it was a poem that he published anonymously in 1771, when in his mid-thirties, that made him 'famous' in the ordinary sense of the word. Suffused with philosophical wisdom and captivating natural images, this was a small volume entitled *The First Book of The Minstrel* and such was its favourable reception with the public (though not necessarily the critics) that he published a second canto in 1774, this time under his own name.

It is a measure of the influence of Spenser on later poets that *The Minstrel* was written in the Spenserian stanza. Beattie wrote:

> I have endeavoured to imitate Spenser in the measure of his verse, and in the harmony, simplicity and variety of his composition. Antique expressions I have avoided...[75]

Keats, of course, had done exactly the same thing with his first poem, the *Imitation of Spenser*. Just how successful Beattie was, how closely he listened to Spenser, can be gleaned from the following comparison ('antique expressions' aside):

From The Faerie Queene:

> Then for her sonne, which she to Locrin bore,
> Madan was young, unmeet the rule to sway,
> In her owne hand the crowne she kept in store,
> Till ryper yeares he raught, and stronger stay:
> During which tyme her powre she did display...

And Beattie's imitation, from *The Minstrel*:

> The rolls of fame I will not now explore;
> Nor need I here describe, in learned lay,
> How forth the Minstrel fared in days of yore,
> Right glad of heart, though homely in array;
> His waving locks and beard all hoary gray...

that last line instantly reminding us of *The Faerie Queene's* seeming sage, Archimago, whom we met in chapter 2:

> ...An aged Sire, in long black weedes yclad,
> His feet all bare, his bearde all hoarie gray...

Beattie's minstrel is initially a boy-poet who is full of fanciful thoughts and imaginings but who, through an intense study of the natural world and the philosophic teachings of a hermit, becomes a Minstrel. This is a sacred figure, not just an itinerant poet and musician, but a philosopher and sage, and we shall come to see just how powerful an effect this idea – that poetry and philosophy are analogous arts – had upon Keats. Crucially, any attempt to understand Keats' love of *The Minstrel* must also include the observation that Beattie achieved recognition as a poet *despite* his childhood difficulties. We cannot compare Keats and Beattie beyond youth and early adulthood because Keats died too young, but the two men must have shared many emotional and intellectual qualities, even if they were separated by two generations.

***

Perhaps rather surprisingly, Keats' younger brother George was confident, socially active, and had an interest in those 'fashionables' that Keats viewed dimly in the letter we saw earlier. From his place of work (Abbey the tea merchant's counting house in Pancras Lane), George would regularly have walked through Cheapside, at that time a major retail street in London. At the other end of Cheapside was Goswell Street (now called Aldersgate Street), the home of a wine merchant called Mathew.

At some point, George Keats met the wine merchant's daughters, Caroline and Anne Mathew, and they became friends. The girls had a cousin called George Felton Mathew who fancied himself as something of a literary man, so it wasn't long before George, acutely aware of his older brother's isolation and loneliness, introduced Keats to this lively family.

Caroline and Anne Mathew came to delight in Keats. When they went to Hastings on holiday they sent him a copy of a poem and a little gift, a 'curious shell'. His response was to write them a thank-you poem called *To Some Ladies*, and another poem to their cousin,

George Felton Mathew, called *On Receiving a Curious Shell and a Copy of Verses from the Same Ladies*. In the first two stanzas of the latter poem, which are for once wonderfully lively and spirited, we are reminded of what made Keats' *Imitation of Spenser* such an auspicious beginning:

> Hast thou from the caves of Golconda a gem,
> Pure as the ice-drop that froze on the mountain,
> Bright as the humming-bird's green diadem,
> When it flutters in sunbeams that shine through a fountain?
>
> Hast thou a goblet for dark sparkling wine,
> That goblet right heavy, and massy, and gold
> And splendidly marked with the story divine
> Of Armida the fair and Rinaldo the bold?...

The poem has even more of that vividness, that real, almost tangible physicality that we noted in the *Imitation of Spenser*. In the first stanza the images are mainly crystalline – pure, frozen, bright, shining. The contrasting image of the humming-bird's jewel-like plumage as it 'flutters in sunbeams' on the other side of a fountain can be held in the imagination and enjoyed. In the second stanza, there is a deliberate switch of imagery. The goblet is heavy and unwieldy and full of dark sparkling wine. The story with which it is marked, of 'Armida the fair and Rinaldo the bold', is from a poem called *Jerusalem Delivered* by the influential sixteenth-century Italian poet, Tasso. In it, a soldier called Rinaldo is charmed into indolence by a beauty called Armida. Keats referred to it because it mirrored his own situation at this time. As lonely as he was, he wanted nothing more than to spend his spare time among his books, pursuing his studies. He did not want to be distracted by attractive young women, even the young women to whom he was now writing poetry. (The idea that a seductive woman can charm an active man into insouciance was the theme in *Fill for me a Brimming Bowl* above.) In the sixth stanza, however, in a moving and very revealing phrase, he acknowledges that the poem that accompanied the gift of a 'curious shell', a poem called *The Wreath and the Chain*, had the effect:

> Of charming my mind from the trammels of pain.

In writing such poems to George Felton Mathew and his cousins, Keats revealed that he was starting to gain a little bit of confidence, starting to feel able to show his poetry and express his feelings to his friends. Though *On Receiving a Curious Shell* is still very much in the realms of Keats' earliest attempts at writing poetry, it has a richness and fluidity that we will see develop as his thoughts mature and his craftsmanship evolves.

***

On Sunday, 1 October 1815, one month before his twentieth birthday, John Keats began the process that would finally release him from his work in Dr Hammond's dull, brick-built garden surgery. On that day, he enrolled at one of the most advanced and admired teaching hospitals in early nineteenth century Europe – Guy's and St Thomas' Hospital, in Southwark. From now on we do not have to rely so much upon Keats' poetry to try and tease out the circumstances of his life; we can see his life and surroundings much more clearly because as an apothecary at Guy's and St Thomas', his activities were officially documented. Also, his activities were more regularly commented upon in the letters he began to write, and in those of his friends and colleagues.

If Edmonton was a largely unspoiled early nineteenth-century pastoral landscape just five or six miles away from the heart of London, then Southwark, directly opposite the City on the south bank of the Thames, epitomised the urban squalor that was slowly spreading through the emerging Industrial Revolution. Originally a Roman bridgehead to the new city of Londinium, Southwark was a crowded area of wharves, warehouses, foundries, workshops, breweries and taverns. The air stank of chimney smoke and brewery hops, the streets were quagmires of mud and, in common with many areas of London bordering the Thames, the water was filthy and infectious. The borough's houses and workshops ejected their waste and sewage directly or indirectly into the river and the water company simply drew it out again for domestic water supplies. In addition, the area had an unenviable reputation for crime. Some of its narrow streets and propped-up alleys (many of which had changed little since Elizabethan times) were notorious as hideouts for London's thieves and miscreants, even if there was a significant number of prisons in Southwark, including the King's Bench and the Marshalsea (the infamous Clink had already been burnt down in the Gordon Riots of 1780).

Right at the heart of this squalor and pestilence stood the combined hospitals of Guy's and St Thomas', an array of grand Palladian buildings with courtyards, parks, statues and avenues. With his belongings, which would have amounted to little more than his clothes and his precious books, Keats arrived here and took up residence in his new lodgings during the first week of October 1815.

Outside the confines of the hospital, industrial Southwark was a great shock to him. It was, he said, using an adjective that has lost much of its power today, a 'beastly place'. He did not mean that it was merely disagreeable or unpleasant, he meant that it was brutish and bestial. He clearly felt confined in Southwark but the option to walk into the countryside and 'muse' under the trees by moonlight was no longer available to him. Quite simply, he was now a full-time medical student at one of the world's great teaching hospitals. Despite his misgivings, perhaps in memory of his long-suffering mother, or to refute some criticism of Hammond's, he was determined to succeed, to be one of the students who would pass the very demanding examination of the Society of Apothecaries.

Keats wrote a verse epistle called *To George Felton Mathew* just a few weeks after his arrival in Southwark. It informed his friend that Keats' medical studies would in future limit the time he would have available for poetical pursuits and it borrowed a phrase from Milton – *Lydian Aires* – to lament the loss of that musicality in poetry he had wanted to continue studying. In any case, even if he could have given some of his time to poetry, his new surroundings were not conducive to it:

...Far different cares
Beckon me sternly from soft 'Lydian airs'...

...But might I now each passing moment give
To the coy muse, with me she would not live
In this dark city, nor would condescend
'Mid contradictions, her delights to lend...

On 31 October 1815, Keats was twenty years old. With his brothers visiting him whenever they could, with George Felton Mathew still encouraging him to write sentimental pastiches, and with the girls of the curious shell flirting on the sidelines, he was about to learn just *how* dark was the city, and how brutal its contradictions.

***

Astley Cooper was a celebrated surgeon, perhaps the most famous in England. His speciality was anatomy. He had been the professor of comparative anatomy at the Royal College of Surgeons but had relinquished the chair on account of the burden of a private practice which, in 1813, had brought him the astonishing sum of £21,000. Cooper lived in fashionable St Mary Axe with his wife who was the daughter of a successful merchant and – long before the Anatomy Act of 1832 imposed licensing upon practitioners – he had installed a dissecting room in his house where he could practise anatomy. His wealthy wife must have sanctioned these activities and may even have become her husband's assistant.

Astley Cooper moved in the highest scientific circles and was, by all accounts, a delightful and generous companion (it will be remembered that he offered Charles Bell, on his arrival in London from Scotland, lodgings in his own house). Having the gift of remembering the names and circumstances of almost everyone he met, he was a master of both his working relationships in the hospitals and the small talk he enjoyed at the many parties and gatherings he attended. Cooper's fame rested on the scientific methods he used; he was among those late eighteenth and early nineteenth-century surgeons (including the brilliant luminaries John Hunter and the Bell brothers) who built the bridges between post-medieval quackery and modern science. Several parts of the body and one or two medical conditions are still named after him.

Cooper was something of a showman, and the lecture theatre's podium was his stage. Wearing a black coat and short knee-breeches, he always arrived at his classes in St Thomas' Hospital with a flourish, smiling and nodding at the students who would line the corridors to welcome him. His lectures on the surgery of bones and fractures were delivered with clarity and cheerfulness (he was said to be the country's leading authority on the subject of fractures). One of his more famous quotations was that a surgeon should have:

An eagle's eye, a lady's hand and a lion's heart.[76]

This is a very apt statement considering that Cooper and his colleagues were performing medical surgery in an era before anaesthetics had been discovered. A man, woman or child would be held down and literally strapped to a wooden table to have a fracture set or limb amputated. Eighty percent would die of shock or infection and, acutely aware of this terrible loss of life, Cooper once remarked, 'It is the surgeon's duty to tranquillize the temper, to beget cheerfulness and to impart confidence of recovery'.[77] On one occasion, however, he couldn't help weeping when a child smiled up at him from the operating table.

***

Astley Cooper took a personal interest in John Keats and arranged lodgings for him, perhaps because Cooper's home in St Mary Axe was near the Swan and Hoop, so the surgeon may have known John and Alice Jennings and been aware of their daughter's tragedy. In any case, Keats moved in with Cooper's dresser at 28 St Thomas' Street, directly opposite St Thomas' Hospital (which was later demolished and rebuilt to make way for London Bridge Station). Cooper's interest in the career of Keats continued into early 1816, when the surgeon promoted the young student to the position of dresser, an important position in the surgical hierarchy. The dressers ranked below the hospital's surgeons, but above its apothecaries (who were the general practitioners, the persons with whom the patients had day-to-day contact). This time Cooper must have been rewarding Keats for his own efforts, demonstrating the truth of Cowden Clarke's comment that Keats showed 'a determined and steady spirit in all his undertakings'. We shall see that Keats' rapid promotion did not go down well with some of his fellow students.

Keats attended lectures in anatomy and physiology with Astley Cooper and Henry Cline, the surgeon to whom Cooper himself had been apprenticed. The lectures were held in a small, cramped operating theatre at St Thomas' hospital (an example of which survives in its original condition).[78] At Guy's hospital Keats studied chemistry and the theory and practice of medicine. The compulsory lectures in anatomy began in October and ended in May when it became too hot for dissection. There was a high demand for corpses to dissect, so Southwark was known for an even less salubrious industry than its breweries and stinking waterworks – the sourcing, collection and sale of human corpses robbed from graves by the notorious 'resurrection men'. The industry was strictly speaking illegal, but it was rife with officials (doubtless including the watchmen) who were paid either to turn a blind eye or assist in the digging up of fresh, and not so fresh, bodies. The Borough Hospitals had their own contingent of resurrection men and they formed a veritable caricature of a rogue's gallery. Ben Crouch (the gang's drunken leader, a former prize fighter and the son of the carpenter at Guy's Hospital) was aided by Bill and Jack Harnett and others.

These men monitored the funerals in London's less conspicuous, more out-of-the-way burial grounds. When the dead had been lain to rest, the men stole the bodies before they became too putrefied to be of much use to the medical students. They would descend on the grave at dusk having paid the sexton or watchman to look the other way, and dig down to its head where, working by lamplight, they knocked in the end of the coffin. The corpse was extracted but the shroud left in the grave because it was a felony to steal this (it was a mere misdemeanour to steal the body). The whispers and grunts can easily be imagined as the corpse was lifted out and trussed in a sack, possibly with two or three others, then taken by cart or even Hackney cab to the hospitals. Occasionally, the resurrection men would be disturbed and the body simply dropped in the street while they made their escape, but more often than not it would arrive intact at the hospital where someone was waiting to pay around four guineas for it, plus another four shillings for the man in the dissecting room whose job it was to clean it up. These gruesome activities were organised by the surgeons and doctors themselves. They had an Anatomical Club as a vehicle to regulate the trade and they met for dinner at a tavern to administer it. There was a subsidiary trade in teeth but the doctors didn't get involved in this because human teeth were very much in demand for dentures and they would already have been extracted from the mouths of the corpses by the resurrection men.

Keats was absolutely committed to his apprenticeship, his medical studies and his work in the alleviation of suffering, but when he was exposed to the grave-robbing trade he began to recoil from its horrors. He was, in fact, already becoming disillusioned with his life in the Southwark hospitals and as a result became less engaged with the people around him. It is clear that he struck at least some of them as pretentious and among those who misunderstood him at this time was a fellow lodger called Henry Stephens. Acutely aware of Keats' literary interests (in a letter of 1847, he referred to someone as a classical scholar, 'as was Keats'),[79] Stephens nonetheless looked down upon Keats with a sneer of sarcasm:

> [Keats] attended Lectures and went through the usual routine, but he had no desire to excel in that pursuit. In fact, Medical Knowledge was beneath his attention... No, Poetry was to his mind the Zenith of all his Aspirations – The only thing worthy the attention of superior

minds. All other pursuits were mean and tame. He had no idea of Fame, or Greatness, but as it was connected with the pursuits of Poetry, or the Attainment of Poetical excellence. The greatest men in the world were the poets and to rank among them was the chief object of his ambition. It may readily be imagined that this feeling was accompanied with a good deal of pride and conceit, and that amongst mere Medical students he would walk & talk as one of the Gods might suppose to do, when mingling with mortals. This pride had exposed him, as may readily be imagined, to occasional ridicule, & some mortification.[80]

He also said, just to make his point clear:

> [Keats] did not generally make the most favourable impression upon people where he visited. He could not well unbend himself & was rather of an unsociable disposition, unless he was among those who were of his own tastes, & who would flatter him...[81]

When Stephens and at least one of his friends failed the examination of the Society of Apothecaries and Keats passed it, nobody was more surprised than Stephens. After he had recovered his balance he said, sniffily, that it was only because Keats happened to be good at Latin.

***

The poet William Wordsworth had brought out a new, two-volume edition of his poems in 1815 and Keats bought a copy some time that autumn. Wordsworth was not, in 1815, the giant of English poetry that he would later become. He was both the Comptroller of Stamps for Westmorland and the writer (in collaboration with Samuel Taylor Coleridge) of a book of poetry called *Lyrical Ballads*, a book that was now 16 years old. Wordsworth's poetry had always been read with ambivalence by the critics because on the one hand it was sometimes unfathomable – plain, abstruse and rustic – but on the other it contained some beautiful sentiments. Wordsworth's deep love of the natural world (and his almost mystical connection with it) shone though.

One of Wordsworth's poems which Keats read and remembered was a *Prefatory Sonnet*:

> Nuns fret not at their Convent's narrow room;
> And Hermits are contented with their Cells;
> And Students with their pensive Citadels:
> Maids at the Wheel, the Weaver at his Loom,
> Sit blithe and happy; Bees that soar for bloom,
> High as the highest peak of Furness Fells,
> Will murmur by the hour in Foxglove bells:
> In truth, the prison, unto which we doom
> Ourselves, no prison is: and hence to me,
> In sundry moods, 'twas pastime to be bound
> Within the Sonnet's scanty plot of ground:
> Pleas'd if some Souls (for such there needs must be)
> Who have felt the weight of too much liberty,
> Should find short solace there, as I have found.

This poem is a Petrarchan Sonnet (of which more later), and very much more weighty, more profound than anything Keats had read with George Felton Mathew and his cousins. It was a different type of poem when compared to anything he had read with Charles Cowden Clarke. It was different from *The Minstrel* – if anything, it was more philosophical even than that, the poem of a professional philosopher.

Wordsworth's *Prefatory Sonnet* is introspective and meditative. It has a powerful message, the message imparted by all the great religious and philosophical thinkers of antiquity, that we must live our lives fully focused on the present moment, that we must discover eternity not in some future life after death, but here and now. If we try, we can achieve spiritual fulfilment even in the most mundane work. Nuns in their narrow rooms; hermits in their cells; maids at the wheel; weavers at the loom; even bees murmuring in foxglove bells – none are imprisoned, none are trapped, none are fretful, none are harking after an irretrievable past nor dreaming about a possibly non-existent future. All are contented and fulfilled merely by living in the present moment. Wordsworth himself is doing exactly the same thing – living within the confines of his sonnet, its 'scanty ground' ready to be sown with the ideas that he is formulating in his mind. The very process of writing the sonnet is a peaceful and fulfilling one. He finds solace in it, and he hopes that in the future someone with a busy, fretful, discontented life, a life of too much liberty, will pause and find solace in it too.

Keats read this poem not long after he had started living and working in Southwark, when he was still coming to terms with the terrible pain and suffering and squalor he found there. At some point he would have read the Supplementary Essay that Wordsworth included in the first volume of the poems:

> With the young of both sexes, poetry is, like love, a passion; but, for much of the greater part of those who have been proud of its power over their minds, a necessity soon arises of breaking the pleasing bondage...[82]

Keats would have recognised this sentiment immediately, for it was the sentiment he himself had expressed in the lines:

> Far different cares
> Beckon me sternly from soft 'Lydian airs'...

Wordsworth continued:

> Poetry then becomes only an occasional recreation; while to those whose existence passes away in a course of fashionable pleasures, it is a species of luxurious amusement. In middle and declining age, a scattered number of serious persons resort to poetry, as to religion, as a protection against the pressure of trivial employments, and as consolation for the afflictions of life.[83]

Poetry 'as consolation for the afflictions of life' was exactly what Keats had been thinking about even before he had arrived in Southwark. Here, in Wordsworth, Keats was discovering a kindred spirit, a poet with the depth and gravity that Keats himself aspired to. Wordsworth goes on to discuss the role of the critic in the appreciation and dissemination of new poetry. He says that only those people whose youth is behind them have the experience and knowledge required to judge poetry on its merits:

> When a juvenile Reader is in the height of his rapture with some vicious passage, should experience throw in doubts, or common sense suggest suspicions, a lurking consciousness that the realities of the

muse are but shows, and that her liveliest excitements are raised by transient shocks of conflicting feeling and successive assemblages of contradictory thoughts – is ever at hand to justify extravagance, and to sanction absurdity.[84]

Juvenile readers, says Wordsworth, are delighted with shows, conflicting feelings, contradictory thoughts and absurdities in poetry because they expect them, because they think they are the 'realities of the muse'. The juvenile mind considers poetry to be nothing but an occasional recreation, a mere diversion. But to the poet who aspires to provide consolation to the afflicted, a more mature, thoughtful and philosophical approach to poetry (that's to say, to its subject) is required.

After having bought and read Wordsworth's new book, Keats decided to write a poem about his life of solitude and confinement in Southwark. The new poem reveals just how much he had assimilated from Wordsworth's poetry and its accompanying essay. It is much more mature and sophisticated than anything he had written before and, once again, it demonstrates his innate gift for emulation (the tone of the poem is recognisably Wordsworthian).

In the octave of the poem, *O Solitude, if I must with thee dwell*, Keats expresses a desire to escape from his life of solitude among 'the jumbled heap of murky buildings' in Southwark to a life among the hills and vales of the countryside. The sestet is a caveat, an acknowledgement that he would rather spend his time not in solitude, but in 'sweet converse' with 'an innocent mind'. Solitude, of course, is the state of being alone, but *a* solitude is a remote and solitary place, the type of place about which Wordsworth wrote so eloquently. It must be the height of human happiness, Keats concludes, when two kindred spirits can flee there together:

> O Solitude! if I must with thee dwell,
> Let it not be among the jumbled heap
> Of murky buildings; - climb with me the steep,
> Nature's observatory - whence the dell,
> Its flowery slopes - its river's crystal swell,
> May seem a span: let me thy vigils keep
> 'Mongst boughs pavilioned; where the Deer's swift leap
> Startles the wild bee from the foxglove bell.
> Ah! fain would I frequent such scenes with thee,
> But the sweet converse of an innocent mind,
> Whose words are images of thoughts refined,
> Is my soul's pleasure; and it sure must be
> Almost the highest bliss of human kind,
> When to thy haunts two kindred spirits flee.

Keats already knew that he had an innate gift for emulation, for seizing upon the essence of great poetry and re-creating it in original poems of his own. This latest poem was another example of this, and it established his abilities beyond doubt. Now, for the first time in his life, he began to think of publication. The question was to whom should he send the poem? There were so many newspapers and periodicals in London at this time, so many outlets for publishing poetry, that the choice was bewildering.

Keats had been an avid reader of Leigh Hunt's *Examiner* for many years – he had almost certainly been introduced to it by the Clarkes at their school in Enfield – and he had the same sort of enthusiasm for its lead writer and editor, Leigh Hunt, as had hundreds of other poets, writers, theatre-goers and artists in London at the time. (We can recall Benjamin Robert Haydon thinking Hunt, 'as fine a specimen of a London editor as could be imagined'.) In the early part of 1816, Keats sent his *Solitude* sonnet to Leigh Hunt and Hunt was sufficiently impressed that he published it in the *Examiner* on Sunday, 5 May 1816. From that moment Keats was a published *poet*, and his life would never be the same again.

Chapter 5

"About this time I met John Keats at Leigh Hunt's, and was amazingly interested by his prematurity of intellect and poetical power."
Benjamin Robert Haydon: *Autobiography*

"Very glad am I at the thoughts of seeing so soon this glorious Haydon and all his creation."
John Keats: *Letter to Charles Cowden Clarke*

After having passed his examination at the Society of Apothecaries in the summer of 1816, Keats decided to leave the Southwark lodgings he shared with Henry Stephens and look for a new home. He would be 21 years old at the end of October, legally old enough to make up his own mind about the course of his career. By now he was harbouring doubts about his dream of becoming a poet because he was devoting so much of his time to medicine. He knew that he must make a decision and that he needed time away from London for reflection, so he booked a passage to Margate on the south east coast of England. His younger brother, Tom, was to go with him for company.

The sailing ships, or 'hoys', which had for years plied between London and Margate had recently been displaced by a new and comparatively luxurious mode of transport, the steamship, but it has been estimated that more than 23,000 Londoners still travelled to Margate by sailing ship in 1815.[85] It is likely that Keats went by sea because the journey was shorter, cheaper and much less arduous than by road and Keats could hardly fail to have known this. After the seven-hour journey down the Thames and around the coast to the Isle of Thanet, Keats and Tom would have disembarked with their books, writing implements and clothes at Margate harbour, then joined the other passengers as they made their way along the new stone pier and into the centre of town to look for lodgings. The scene was described by Mrs Pilkington in her book about Margate, published in 1813:

> The tide was up, two packets had just reached the harbour; the parade and pier were crowded with pedestrians; streamers were floating from a number of sailing barges, whilst on the smooth surface of the sea, which scarcely appeared agitated by the evening breeze, a variety of vessels were discerned as far as the eye could reach.[86]

By 1816, Margate was an established and bustling seaside resort for the middle classes (seaside holidays were not yet affordable for the lower classes, the cost of transport and lodgings being prohibitive). The seaside towns did not, of course, feature the flashing lights, coloured plastic and loud music of today's coastal resorts; they relied upon bathing, gambling and theatrical entertainments to entice people from the cities. Margate had plenty of bathing machines and music rooms, and at least two libraries and a theatre, with these genteel attractions being separated off from the more squalid parts of town. A rope-works, owned by the Cobb family of shipbuilders, brewers and bankers, spoiled the view of the sea, even from the fashionable area, and anybody losing their way and finding themselves between the London Road and the Old Parade would be subjected to the stench of the town's raw sewage. As for the townspeople themselves, the 'lower orders', said a near-contemporary writer, were 'cunning, avaricious, disrespectful and somewhat malevolent'.[87] Of more interest to Keats, perhaps, there were 'several good surgeons and apothecaries' in the town.

Keats may have found his way to the Fountain Inn (another Cobb family business) because many Londoners booked into the 'Fountain' upon their arrival before beginning their search for lodgings. There were several lodging houses to choose from, some more elegant than others, and although we do not know where Keats stayed, we do know that soon after his arrival he settled down to write a poem to his brother George. He talked of the wonders he had seen since leaving London, including what was very likely his first sight of the sea:

> ... with its vastness, its blue green,
> Its ships, its rocks, its caves, its hopes, its fears,
> Its voice mysterious, which whoso hears
> Must think on what will be, and what has been.

Keats was to stay in Margate for nearly two months, 'thinking on what will be', writing, reading and walking along the cliff tops. He admitted that he found much of what he saw to be dreary and uninspiring (as we noted earlier, Keats was not as socially active as his brother George and much of the entertainment in the music rooms and gambling houses would not have interested him). He desperately wanted to write more publishable poetry, but he was simply bereft of ideas. When on occasion he did find himself inspired to write, it was because something beautiful or dramatic had kindled his imagination – a lightning storm at sea, for example. One evening he watched the moon disappear behind the 'waviness of whitest clouds', and on another occasion he contemplated the 'night's mysteries' while lying on the grass, staring up at the stars.

As the days passed into weeks, Keats' thoughts turned to the future. Despite his misgivings in Southwark, he remained firm in his desire to become an erudite literary man, a man of letters. His aim remained to emulate his friend and former teacher, Charles Cowden Clarke, even if this were to be achieved amid the contradictions and constraints imposed by working at the London hospitals. Keats had almost lost touch with the kindly Clarke since moving to Southwark, but George was still in touch with him and talked about Clarke in the letters he sent from London.

Musing upon Clarke's encouragement and kindness in former years proved to be a turning point for Keats. Why not write a poem to Clarke? Why not tell him how much his kindness, encouragement and support had been appreciated? Why not explain that only now, free from the distractions of London, had he the time to think about and appreciate the debt he owed to his early mentor?

Whene'er I venture on the stream of rhyme;

With shatter'd boat, oar snapt, and canvass rent,

I slowly sail, scarce knowing my intent;

Still scooping up the water with my fingers,

In which a trembling diamond never lingers.

By this, friend Charles, you may full plainly see

Why I have never penn'd a line to thee:

Because my thoughts were never free...

Keats wrote this poem, *To Charles Cowden Clarke*, and posted it to his brother George back in London. When it was finally in Clarke's hands, the now former schoolteacher resumed his generous, gentlemanly role of providing praise and encouragement. He decided to show the poem to his friend Leigh Hunt – the same Hunt whom he knew had already published one of Keats' poems, but who knew very little about the young Southwark poet who had so eloquently written about his desire for solitude. In doing this, Clarke was in effect introducing Keats to Leigh Hunt.

***

In Southwark, a dark and dank tunnel called Stainer Street runs directly underneath the platforms of London Bridge Station. In 1816 Stainer Street was called Dean Street and was open to the sky. The eastern side of the street contained a row of terraced houses with rear gardens; on the western side was a Baptist chapel and a large square by the name of Canterbury Square. It was a prosperous and busy residential neighbourhood, near to both Guy's Hospital and the extensive yards and wharfs which lined the south bank of the River

Thames. The world's largest brewery, the Anchor Brewery, was just a short walk away. On his return from Margate in early October 1816, a few weeks before his twenty-first birthday, Keats took lodgings in a terraced house at No.8 Dean Street, and the first of his letters to have survived was sent from this address. Written to Charles Cowden Clarke, it is dated Wednesday, 9 October 1816 and tells Clarke that 'the busy time' has now gone by so he is able to devote some time to 'the pleasure of seeing Mr Hunt'. He mentions that he has copied out some verses to take with him on the visit. Clarke was at the time living just across the River Thames in Clerkenwell, and a few days later, the two men set off for the walk to Hunt's cottage.

Leigh Hunt had not long been out of jail, having been sent there for printing and publishing a 'scandalous and defamatory libel' in the *Examiner* on Sunday, 22 March 1812. This had been written in response to an article that had appeared in a rival newspaper, the *Morning Post*, about a man whom the Post had described as the 'glory of the People', a 'Protector of the Arts' and an 'Adonis in Loveliness'. Hunt had retaliated that this 'Adonis in Loveliness' was 'a corpulent gentleman of fifty... a violator of his word, a libertine over head and ears in debt and disgrace, a despiser of domestic ties, the companion of demireps...'

Many of the *Examiner's* readers must have paused over their breakfast that Sunday morning, knowing this 'companion of demireps' to be none other than George Augustus Frederick, the Prince of Wales, who had assumed full Regency powers more than a year earlier and was certain to become the next King of England.

Hunt knew that such a tirade against the Prince Regent would lead to his being tried for libel with potentially serious consequences – certainly a heavy fine, possibly imprisonment – but he nevertheless chose to publish the article as a means to an end; not only to condemn a man he considered to be licentious, profligate and a disgrace to his nation, but also to assert the freedom of the press.

Leigh Hunt's actions came with a heavy cost. He had been tried, convicted and sentenced to two years in Horsemonger Lane Gaol in Southwark (its gallows being Surrey's principal place of execution) and now, having been free for about a year, his nerves were shattered and he was suffering from agoraphobia. He was living away from the centre of London in the relatively tranquil setting of the Vale of Health on Hampstead Heath. Despite the fresh and breezy inference of its name, this had been described by a contemporary as 'a stagnate bottom; a pit in the heath'.[88] Hampstead's Vale of Health had until recently been home to a varnish factory and a place where washerwomen would hang out their laundry but had subsequently been cleaned up and brought to the verge of respectability. Some small, terraced 'garden cottages' were built by a speculator, and it was one of these that Hunt rented and made his home.

In his youth, Hunt had often visited the home of a distant relative, the self-taught but eminent Neoclassical painter and president of the Royal Academy, Benjamin West. As had Sir Joshua Reynolds and Fuseli, Benjamin West had studied painting in Italy. Hunt had marvelled at the beauty of his house, describing it with loving detail. From the street it was large but unremarkable; it was the interior that created the impression of a miniature Italian palazzo. A corridor lined with pictures and graced with statues of Venus and Apollo led to a gallery and some 'loftier rooms' where several of West's famous paintings were displayed. The garden featured busts and statues arranged around a central lawn under an arcade and from this garden one could walk directly into a parlour lined with engravings and coloured prints by Rubens and Raphael. 'It is to that house,' wrote Hunt, 'that we owe the greatest part of our love for what is Italian and [what] belongs to the fine arts.'[89]

Heavily influenced by these childhood visits, Leigh Hunt now habitually surrounded himself with beautiful objects, many of which had a classical or Italian theme. His collection went with him around his various homes in London (he had always moved fairly regularly, even before his committal to prison) and wherever he lived, his house would feel more like that of a Florentine merchant during the Italian Renaissance than that of a London newspaper editor in the early nineteenth century.

Hunt loved buying objects to put on display, and was something of an expert on the array of shops that had made London one of the most vibrant cities in Europe. The butcher's and fishmonger's he found disgusting, with their 'blood-dripping sheep and crimped cod', while the poulterer's was a 'dead-bodied business with its birds and their lax necks'. The leather-cutter's, the shoemaker's and the stationer's shops he found boring, and he condemned the baker for having 'a very dull shop'. The tailor's shop made him feel melancholy and the hosier's worse, but the apothecary at least had a shop that looked well at night on account of its sparkling coloured glass. The music shop was a place of 'slumbering enchantment' but of all the shops in the street, the print-seller pleased him most. Here, said Hunt, you could enjoy fine engravings from Raphael and Titian and it was here that he spent a good deal of his time and money.[90]

***

On the day when Clarke and Keats were walking up from Clerkenwell to Leigh Hunt's house, Benjamin Haydon was also in Hampstead. He had taken a well earned break from his work in the Great Marlborough Street studio to rent a house in Pond Street where he could relax, breathe some fresh air and be near his friend Leigh Hunt. Despite his unwavering dedication to painting, Haydon's drift away from the aristocratic dining rooms of the Beaumonts and Mulgraves towards the libraries and parlours of Hunt and his circle reflected his growing interest in writing and literature. Haydon may have appeared to be a successful member of London's artistic community, but he was not actually earning any money through his art. He had been working continuously on *Christ's Entry into Jerusalem* since his *Solomon* exhibition two and a half years earlier, and was still a long way from finishing it. His only means of supporting himself during the progress of this monumental painting was in the manner he had supported himself during the painting of *Macbeth* and later *Solomon* – with loans and bonds that would be paid off once the picture was finally sold, and by means of the charity of his hapless landlord and many friends. He had developed a method of creative accounting, which, until recently, had kept him out of the clutches of the moneylenders.

Keats and Clarke arrived at Hunt's small, Italianate cottage carrying a sheaf of Keats' poems, some of which were heavily influenced by Hunt himself (he had recently published a poem called *The Story of Rimini*, based on the tale of Paolo and Francesca in Canto V of Dante's *Inferno*). It wouldn't have taken Hunt long to establish that Keats was an intelligent young man pursuing a medical career; that his parents were both dead; and that he was just a week or two away from his 21st birthday, the day on which he would no longer be reliant upon his sole guardian (Richard Abbey) to take care of his financial affairs. The fact that he was also a promising, bright-eyed young poet who had memorised Lemprière and translated Virgil would have virtually guaranteed his acceptance into Hunt's circle of friends. His poems were passed around and admired, his education and ideas were gently probed, and after making a very favourable impression, he was given an open invitation to visit Hunt's cottage.

Within a few days of this first visit, Keats returned to the cottage and was introduced to Benjamin Robert Haydon, the man whom Hunt in a recent sonnet had called 'fit to be numbered with sweet-souled Raphael'. At that stage, Keats would have been more familiar with Haydon's essays in the *Examiner* than with his huge paintings of *Macbeth*, *Dentatus* and *Solomon*. Keats may also have read a new, controversial essay by Haydon in a different publication called the *Annals of Fine Arts*. This was called *On the Judgement of Connoisseurs* and although it was ostensibly about the beauty of the Elgin Marbles, it was actually yet another attack on the nobility and their lack of artistic judgement, every bit as inflammatory as his earlier essay attacking Richard Payne Knight. Keats would have appreciated it but Lord Mulgrave, Haydon's former friend and patron, called it 'an indiscreet and abominable letter'. Luckily, after the success of *Solomon*, the public now appreciated Haydon's erudition and cleverness and the essay was widely distributed and appreciated. It even found a niche in the literary and artistic salons of Europe.

The painter and the young poet made favourable first impressions upon each other. Haydon was always ebullient and loud, priding himself on his patriotism, virility and masculinity, and possessing a booming laugh. After years studying at the Royal Academy and carefully cultivating a number of erudite friends in London's artistic community, after meeting aristocrats and diplomats at the dinner tables of Sir George Beaumont and Lord Mulgrave, and after having spent his leisure hours memorising great tracts of the world's greatest literature, Haydon had become one of the most interesting conversationalists of his generation. He could talk enthusiastically and with expertise on almost any subject. Art, poetry, history, religion, military matters (especially naval) and politics were all within his compass. He had the habit of quoting Shakespeare at every opportunity and a tendency to refer to the Christian God, in whom he believed with devotion, as the 'Great Spirit'. He could converse in French or Italian and read from any book in Latin or Greek. Keats, with his own aspiration to be an educated man of letters, would have listened to Haydon's conversation with deep interest and would have revealed the (admittedly shallower) depths of his own learning and the attractiveness of his personality.

Neither having very much money, both men were undoubtedly shabbily dressed by the standards of the day. Haydon at this time liked to wear square-toed boots (on account of his corns) and a broad-brimmed hat, and he wore his hair longer than was the fashion, in emulation of Raphael. Keats' look was deliberately 'Byronic', that is to say his clothes were loose and casual in the style of the most commercially successful poet of the day, the fabulously wealthy Lord Byron. Many years later, remembering this first introduction to Keats, Haydon wrote of him: 'He was below the middle size, with a low forehead, and an eye that had an inward look, perfectly divine, like a Delphian priestess who saw visions.'[91]

***

During this first meeting at Hunt's, Keats accepted an invitation to visit Haydon at his temporary lodgings at 7 Pond Street, which, despite its unpretentious name, was a row of fine Georgian residences built on a slope with a view over the countryside. Keats went along a few days later and was introduced to a young writer called John Hamilton Reynolds, of whom more later. He was then invited, along with Charles Cowden Clarke and possibly John Reynolds, to breakfast at Haydon's London studio once the painter was back in town. Keats eagerly accepted the invitation and wrote excitedly to Clarke about it, punning on the composer Joseph Haydn's *Creation* Symphony:

I will be as punctual as the Bee to the Clover – Very glad am I at the thought of seeing so soon this glorious Haydon and all his Creation.[92]

Haydon was temporarily back in town on Sunday 27 October and went back to Great Marlborough Street to take a look at his painting. He was very pleased with himself when he returned to Hampstead:

> My Picture today struck me when I was in Town as the most enchanting of all sights. There it was, silently speaking, full of beauty (pardon my vanity)… It came over [me] like a lovely dream… I felt its beauty, its superiority, to all temporary dispute & petty passion, & [I] rode back to Hampstead musing on the delights of my glorious calling, and will return tomorrow, adequate to its noble labours.[93]

The next Sunday, 3 November, Keats walked up the stairs to the first floor of Henry Perkins' house in Great Marlborough Street and entered Haydon's painting room for the first time. The huge canvas of *Christ's Entry into Jerusalem* was propped against the wall and, like *Solomon*, it was so large it had to be tilted in order to fit under the ceiling. The painter's rooms were sparsely furnished with fewer books, prints and expensive plaster casts than they had once held, but were still heady with the acrid aroma of the paints and spirits that had been so damaging to Haydon's eyes.

As there were no facilities for making breakfast in the rooms, this was usually brought in by one of Mr Perkins' servants. While breakfast was being arranged (tea and toast was typical), Keats would have had time to take in the paraphernalia lying around Haydon's studio. There were prints from Raphael, Michelangelo and various other masters of the Italian Renaissance, plus a portfolio of Haydon's own sketches from the Elgin Marbles. There was a collection of the anatomical drawings Haydon had produced in Charles Bell's classes, and the plaster casts of his models that he had procured at great expense. A part of the room would have resembled a small industrial workshop; one contemporary recipe for an oil called drying oil, an essential requirement for an artist, was as follows:

> [Take] 1lb of alum. Heat it in a shovel till white; powder it with 1lb of sugar of lead well powdered. Add a gallon of oil, linseed. Stir them together three or four times a day for a week; pour for use into a jar, large mouth. Cover with cloth, and expose to the sun.[94]

Haydon, typically, disagreed. He thought is better to boil the ingredients together. His store cupboard (a necessary piece of furniture before oil paints could be conveniently bought in tubes) would have resembled an apothecary's shop, full of jars of brightly coloured minerals (Cobalt Blue, Carmine Lake, Naples Yellow, Vermilion), sticky resins, translucent gums and clear oils along with a grindstone and some mixing vessels. His paint brushes included small red sable brushes made in England and large hog's hair brushes made in France ('I get all my brushes of that kind from Paris').

Both Keats and Haydon would have been aware that historically the relationship between the painter and the apothecary was a very close one; for hundreds of years, across the whole of Europe, apothecaries had supplied artists with their pigments and oils. In Renaissance Florence, the city of Haydon's dreams, the relationship was so close that the painters themselves belonged to the Guild of Doctors and Apothecaries (*Arte dei Medici e Speziali*). Keats had recently taken an examination in chemistry as part of his Society of Apothecaries qualification, and as a newly qualified medical man, he would have been aware of the toxic chemicals, the lack of ventilation and the unhealthy air in Haydon's painting room. Haydon's 'colourman' (his supplier of artist's materials) was Charles Smith, an 'experimental chemist' of 211 Piccadilly.

As interesting as Haydon's drawing collections and artistic materials were, of all the objects in Haydon's rooms, Keats would surely have been most interested in the library. Just a few years after this first visit from the poet, Haydon recorded that he owned single volumes for which he had paid £20, an astonishing sum considering the unreliable nature of his income and the precariousness of his finances. (To set this in context, Haydon states elsewhere that a porter at the Royal Academy supported his family on a wage of £50 a year.) It was common at this time to buy books unbound in quires, and then have them expensively bound by a specialist bookbinder. No doubt much of the expense of Haydon's collection was due to the fact that he would have his books bound in the finest materials – the best quality leather with gilt stampings. He would then stamp his own imprint on the title page: 'B.R. Haydon', with the year of purchase. He once wrote,

> I do not feel at home in my painting room without my books. I used to look up and see the books, and imagine (as each name came on my sight) I saw the author: Dante, Petrarch, Homer, Shakespeare, Milton, Spenser and Tasso… and my brain teemed with associations of their sublimity and charm.[95]

The Pursuit of Beauty and Truth

When Keats first went to Great Marlborough Street, Haydon's still impressive and expensive library contained his copy of *Albinus* with its pictures of flayed bodies, and John Bell's *Anatomy of the Human Body* with its corpses hanging from ropes around their necks. It contained Reynolds' *Discourses* and Haydon's copy of Wordsworth's poems. Haydon would surely have shown Keats his most treasured possession, an Italian edition of Vasari's *Lives of the Artists*. Reading Vasari's life of Raphael could literally move Haydon to tears.

As he took in his surroundings and sat down for breakfast, Keats may not have realised that, despite all appearances to the contrary, Haydon's life in those rented rooms was quite miserable. Despite the enormous success of *Solomon*, he had not had a single commission since the days of *Dentatus* and *Macbeth* (one reason, as we have seen, was that his paintings were simply too large) and he was perpetually in debt. For all his fame and his many friends, Haydon still felt misunderstood as an artist. He was lonely and he yearned for a like-minded companion. Now 30 years old, he had been living alone in various rented rooms since his first arrival in London back in 1804, and we can recall that nearly a decade later, in August 1813, when he was painting *Solomon* and already a member of the Hunt circle, he had written in his diary,

> I feel the want of kindred spirits – there is not an artist to whom I can pour out the enthusiasm of my soul, who will listen and participate…

There was something about Keats that answered Haydon's call for a 'kindred spirit'. The younger man's talent, enthusiasm and determination to succeed as a poet must have reminded Haydon of his own young self as an artist. For his own part, Keats was now much more aware of his intellectual gifts and he wanted to emulate Beattie and Wordsworth by turning his writing into a serious philosophical endeavour, just as Haydon had always wanted to elevate his art by creating the beginnings of a new Renaissance. (Keats will have learned by now that Haydon was a personal friend of William Wordsworth, and that Wordsworth had written a sonnet beginning 'High is our calling, Friend' for Haydon himself.) We can recall Charles Cowden Clarke talking of Keats' extraordinary efforts to educate himself when he was a schoolboy, in particular pointing to his 'high-mindedness'. Haydon, too, was largely self-educated, not having been to a university. He was later to say, 'Keats was the only man I ever met with who seemed and looked conscious of a high calling, except Wordsworth'.[96] After breakfast, as Haydon had another appointment, Keats was shown out but invited to come back and spend an evening at Great Marlborough Street, an occasion that was eventually arranged for about a fortnight later, on Tuesday 19 November.

After this first visit to Haydon's studio, Keats decided it was time to move out of Southwark. His brothers, George and Tom, were both working at Richard Abbey's counting house in Pancras Lane (Abbey was still their guardian) and were living together in an adjacent street, on the second floor at No. 76 Cheapside. It is likely that Abbey himself had found these rooms, although it will be remembered that the boys had friends in the Mathew family, the wine merchants from nearby Goswell Street, so they may also have helped.

The rooms were directly above a main thoroughfare in the commercial heart of the city, so much so that the view from the parlour window was of the decorated façade of the Mercer's Hall. There was a tavern around the corner called The Queen's Arms where the Keats brothers could buy cooked dinners, and doubtless they became well known to the tavern keeper and his clientele. When Keats left his solitary lodgings in Dean Street and moved in with his brothers, it was not just to spend more time with them but also to be nearer to Haydon and Hunt. (There appears to have been a policy of 'open house' at Cheapside because Charles Cowden Clarke once wrote that Keats had come home to find him 'asleep on the sofa, with a volume of Chaucer...')[97]

***

Tom celebrated his seventeenth birthday on Monday 18 November, soon after Keats had moved in. In the living room there was a sofa, a table and a coal fire. As Tom was quietly reading, Keats settled in front of the fire with pen and paper; he wanted to record this moment – his brother's birthday and their being together again in shared lodgings. The poem he wrote is now known simply as *To my Brothers*. It takes us to the very moment of its composition, to the hushed quietness inside the living room (and thus outside in Cheapside), to the crackling of the fire, its 'whispers' like those of the Roman household gods. Keats glanced at Tom and saw his eyes fixed on a page of the book he was reading, momentarily taking Tom away from his worries about the future. The poem tells us about Keats' love for his two brothers (which he once described as 'passing the love of women'), and his desire to live in peace with them, to find some happiness with them before the 'great voice', or God, or Haydon's 'Great Spirit' called them all away:

> Small, busy flames play through the fresh-laid coals,
> And their faint cracklings o'er our silence creep
> Like whispers of the household gods that keep
> A gentle empire o'er fraternal souls.
> And while for rhymes I search around the poles,
> Your eyes are fixed, as in poetic sleep,
> Upon the lore so voluble and deep
> That aye at fall of night our care condoles.
> This is your birth-day, Tom, and I rejoice
> That thus it passes smoothly, quietly.
> Many such eves of gently whispering noise
> May we together pass, and calmly try
> What are this world's true joys, ere the great voice
> From its fair face shall bid our spirits fly.

The next day, Tuesday 19 November, Keats went back to Great Marlborough Street to meet Haydon again. Despite his insistence that he was an abstemious man who lived for his work, Haydon kept a supply of wine in his rooms and enjoyed handing out bottles to his guests. This Tuesday evening would have been an education for Keats, a chance to learn more about Haydon and the Hunt circle, and about writing for the *Examiner* and other publications. As we have seen, Haydon already had an extensive network of friends and a busy social life so for him the evening would have been little more than a welcome distraction from his long hours of work, an opportunity for relaxed conversation with this keen, intelligent young admirer. Keats knew, of course, that Haydon had many friends, that he was a public figure, a man whose painting of Solomon had caused a sensation and whose writings were now known throughout Europe. The towering figure of Goethe in Germany was aware of Haydon's recent essay about the Elgin Marbles and 'a copy of it was found by Rumöhr upon the Ilissus in the Magliabecchian library at Florence'.[98] The Italian sculptor Canova, then at the height of his fame, had been introduced to Haydon during a visit to London in December 1815 and had become a personal friend. For all these international connections, it was Haydon's friendship with Wordsworth that impressed Keats the most.

Wordsworth's sonnet beginning 'High is our calling, Friend' had been published in a newspaper called the *Champion*. It was called *To B.R. Haydon, Esq.*, and was about the difficulties that all painters and poets must overcome if they are to achieve greatness in their chosen field:

> High is our calling, Friend! – Creative Art
> (Whether the instrument of words she use,
> Or pencil pregnant with ethereal hues,)
> Demands the service of a mind and heart,
> Though sensitive, yet, in their weakest part,
> Heroically fashioned – to infuse
> Faith in the whispers of the lonely Muse...

It went on to advocate persistence in the pursuit of the 'bright reward' and ended with the memorable line,

> Great is the glory, for the strife is hard!

Haydon had not only this but at least two other original sonnets in Wordsworth's hand, and the effect they must have had on Keats can readily be imagined.

He returned to his lodgings and mused over the evening. The very next morning, he wrote a letter to Haydon and had it delivered by messenger. 'My dear Sir,' it began, 'Last evening wrought me up, and I cannot forbear sending you the following…' He enclosed a sonnet which began with the line, 'Great Spirits now on earth are sojourning…'. The Great Spirits were Haydon (as always, compared with Raphael), Hunt and Wordsworth. (Clearly, Haydon's fastly held belief in the 'Great Spirit', was starting to creep into Keats' subconscious.) But there are other spirits, said Keats, who are 'standing apart', about to create works of art that will demand the world's attention, to attract the fame that Haydon, Hunt and Wordsworth had already assured for themselves. He, Keats, was one of them.

Haydon's thoughts returned to his painting, and in particular the expressions of the people who were prostrating themselves before Christ as he entered Jerusalem. The next day, Wednesday 20 November, he visited a workhouse or infirmary to study and sketch the expressions of the sick and dying. (Keats, or perhaps the surgeon Charles Bell may have helped Haydon gain access to the wards.) He also found time to receive, read and reply to Keats' letter, and promised to send Keats' 'Great Spirits' poem to Wordsworth. Keats wrote back on Thursday afternoon:

My dear Sir,

Your letter has filled me with a proud pleasure, and shall be kept by me as a stimulus to exertion – I begin to fix my eye on one horizon... The idea of your sending [the sonnet] to Wordsworth put me out of breath – you know with what Reverence I would send my Well-wishes to him...[99]

At the time he wrote these two letters to Haydon, Keats was still training at Guy's Hospital and had published just a single poem, *O Solitude*, in a London newspaper, a poem in emulation of Wordsworth. That was six month's earlier, but so much had happened in the interval that Keats must have been wondering whether Haydon was about to introduce him to Wordsworth himself.

***

John Hamilton Reynolds, 'Jack' to his friends, was 22 years old when he was introduced to John Keats at Haydon's temporary lodgings in Pond Street. Reynolds was the son of George Reynolds, a Shropshire man who was now working in London and was widely respected as a teacher, educational administrator and writer of textbooks. George Reynolds' family was comfortably off and lived in a large house at 19 Lamb's Conduit Street, Bloomsbury, a house which was to become very familiar to Keats in the coming months. Reynolds was almost universally described as very clever, good-looking and witty. After leaving school at 15 he had become a clerk in a newspaper office and from there went on to work as a clerk at the Amicable Society for a Perpetual Assurance in a back yard called Sergeants' Inn. This was right next to the Inns of Court off Fleet

Street and just around the corner from the house of a friend of Leigh Hunt called Charles Lamb.

The clerical work must have been dreary for a young man with Reynolds' intellectual gifts, sitting at a wooden desk for long hours every day, dealing with insurance matters, filing forms and writing everything by hand, but it was relatively well paid and during the six years he worked there he had ample time to pursue his other interests. He both attended the theatre and acted in amateur productions – the Reynolds family as a whole was very keen on amateur dramatics. He taught himself Greek (having already mastered Latin at school) and published book reviews in magazines. He even acted as a sort of London literary agent for a wealthy family friend in Shropshire.

In fact, by the time he met Keats, Reynolds was already a literary figure in his own right, and an established member of the Hunt circle. He had published a book of poetry called *Safie* when he was just 19 years old and his father had used his publishing connections to persuade John Murray, Lord Byron's publisher, to ask Byron to read it. Lord Byron quickly saw that Reynolds' 'Eastern tale', *Safie*, was very similar in style and content to his own hugely successful poem, *The Giaour*. (Reynolds openly acknowledged this; the poem was dedicated to Lord Byron.) An entry in Byron's journal in February 1814 reads:

> Answered – or, rather, acknowledged – the receipt of young Reynolds's Poem, Safie. The lad is clever, but much of his thoughts are borrowed… he has much talent, and, certainly, fire enough.[100]

Reynolds had followed *Safie* with a different type of poem, *The Eden of the Imagination*, which was another emulation of Wordsworth. He had also provided theatrical reviews for the *Champion* and then taken on some editorial duties at the newspaper. Finally, in April 1816, Reynolds had taken the significant risk of giving up his job at the Amicable to work full time as joint editor of the *Champion* (it was Reynolds himself who published both his own and Wordsworth's sonnets to Haydon; Reynolds may well have obtained his position at the newspaper through the influence of Haydon, who was a friend of the editor). By the time he met Keats in late 1816, Reynolds was in the process of publishing *The Naiad and Other Poems*, with yet another dedication to Haydon. Bearing in mind that Reynolds was just one year older than Keats – who had published almost nothing – Keats must have looked upon Reynolds as someone much more self-assured and successful then himself.

***

'I begin to fix my eye on one horizon', Keats had written to Haydon. He had been impressed by Hunt's example of hard work and literary achievement in the face of all opposition, fired up by Haydon's energy and ambition, and encouraged by the extraordinary achievements of one so young as Reynolds. If Keats' poem *O Solitude* had been the work that had first brought the young poet to the attention of Leigh Hunt, another poem he wrote around this time would earn him the genuine admiration of everyone in the Hunt circle. Hunt was to publish this poem in an article in the *Examiner* on 1 December 1816. The poem was called *On First Looking into*

Chapman's Homer and its impact was so significant that it is worth looking at its genesis in a little detail.

Back in October, Keats had spent an evening with his old mentor Charles Cowden Clarke in Clarke's lodgings at Clerkenwell, and just as the former teacher had spent many hours at school reading Spenser with Keats, he now brought to his attention another writer and another book, a 'beautiful copy of the folio edition of Chapman's translation of Homer', the property of a friend of Leigh Hunt, Mr Alsager of the *Times* newspaper. The book was a 1616 edition so was too valuable for Clarke to carry through the streets of London – which is why Keats had to travel to Clerkenwell to see it.

George Chapman, a classical scholar, dramatist and poet, was a contemporary of Shakespeare. As a dramatist, he had written comedies with such titles as *The Blind Beggar of Alexandria*, *The Gentleman Usher* and *The Widow's Tears*, while his tragedies included *The Tragedy of Chabot, Admiral of France*. He was also a poet and translator, and began publishing his translation of Homer's *Iliad* in instalments from 1598 onwards. His *Whole Works of Homer* finally appeared in 1616; it was the first English translation of the *Iliad* and the *Odyssey* and the one which Clarke was to share with Keats. This was written in a similar style of English to that used by Shakespeare, but Keats, familiar with both Shakespeare and Spenser, would have had no trouble in understanding it. We can recall from Chapter 2 that Keats could hear, see and feel things in poetry that most other people apparently could not, a fact which Clarke had noticed when the two of them were reading Spenser together:

> ...he especially singled out epithets for that felicity and power in which Spenser is so eminent. He hoisted himself up, and looked burly and dominant, as he said, 'what an image that is – "sea-shouldering whales!"'

Clarke tells us that something similar happened when the two men were reading Chapman together:

> One scene I could not fail to introduce him to [was] the shipwreck of Ulysses... and I had the reward of one of his delighted stares, upon reading the following lines:-
>
> Then forth he came, his both knees falt'ring, both
> His strong hands hanging down, and all with froth
> His cheeks and nostrils flowing, voice and breath
> Spent to all use, and down he sank to death.
> The sea had soak'd his heart through; all his veins
> His toils had rack'd t' a labouring woman's pains.
> Dead weary was he.[101]

Clarke continues,

> Chapman supplied us with many an after treat; but it was in the teeming wonderment of this [Keats'] first introduction that, when I came down to breakfast the next morning, I found upon my table a letter with no other enclosure than his famous sonnet, 'On First Looking into Chapman's Homer'.[102]

Clarke and Keats had stayed up all night reading Chapman, and the younger man hadn't left until daybreak to walk the two miles or so back to his lodgings. Clarke, like Haydon, had 'wrought him up' and once again Keats had responded with a poem. When Clarke came down to breakfast it was already waiting for him on the table, just as the 'Great Spirits' sonnet had appeared at Haydon's studio the morning after his evening with Keats. By the time Clarke was writing his account, long after Keats' death, he could use the phrase 'his famous sonnet' because *On First Looking into Chapman's Homer* had indeed been recognised as a very significant poem, one which signalled an enormous leap in Keats' confidence and abilities.

The poem is a Petrarchan sonnet, named after Petrarch, the fourteenth century Italian poet and Renaissance Humanist. It differs from a Spenserian sonnet in both rhyme scheme and structure. The first eight lines of the poem, the octave, state and develop the theme, then there is a natural break before the last six lines, the sestet, create the conclusion in a different rhyme scheme (the whole scheme is: a-b-b-a, a-b-b-a, c-d-c, d-c-d.). While at this stage of his development as a poet, Keats was slightly less familiar with the Petrarchan sonnet than he was with the Spenserian (his *Solitude* poem had been an early attempt at the form, copied, of course, from Wordsworth's *Prefatory Sonnet*), Keats was fully aware of the differences between the two and he knew that Clarke was, too.

Keats begins the octave by calling the world of Classical Greece the 'Realms of Gold' and points out that he had – through his studies – travelled widely in these 'western islands'. He had been familiar with the stories in the *Iliad* and the *Odyssey* (having read the books in another translation, that of Alexander Pope who wrote in the early eighteenth century, about a hundred years after Chapman) but had not fully understood their beauty and significance until he had been introduced to Chapman's translation. In the sestet, he gives his response to the octave. He feels like a 'watcher of the skies', an astronomer discovering a new planet, or like an explorer seeing the Pacific Ocean for the first time (he mistakenly uses the example of Cortez instead of Balboa). He had been enthusiastic but tired when he wrote the poem and the original manuscript contains some scratchy lines linking the octave's rhyme scheme together:

> Much have I travell'd in the Realms of Gold,
> And many goodly States and Kingdoms seen;
> Round many western islands have I been,
> Which bards in fealty to Apollo hold.
> Oft of one wide expanse had I been told,
> That deep brow'd Homer ruled as his Demesne:
> Yet could I never judge what Men could mean,
> Till I heard Chapman speak out loud and bold.
> Then felt I like some watcher of the Skies
> When a new Planet swims into his Ken,
> Or like stout Cortez, when with wond'ring eyes
> He star'd at the Pacific, and all his Men
> Look'd at each other with a wild surmise
> Silent, upon a peak in Darien.

Clarke was impressed when he read the poem over breakfast, particularly as he knew it had been produced in so short a time. He handed it over to Leigh Hunt who showed it to some other members of his circle, including William Hazlitt, of whom more later. Hunt decided to write an article about a new generation of poets, the 'Young Poets', as he was to call them. These were John Keats, Jack

Reynolds and another established member of the Hunt circle, the wild and aristocratic poet, Percy Bysshe Shelley. As we noted earlier, this article appeared in the *Examiner* on Sunday, 1 December 1816. Hunt talked of a 'new school' of poetry, but added:

> In fact it is wrong to call it a new school, and still more so to represent it as one of innovation, its only object being to restore the same love of Nature, and of thinking instead of mere talking, which formerly rendered us real poets, and not merely versifying wits, and bead-rollers of couplets.[103]

He went on to say that the object of the present article is:

> ...merely to notice three young writers, who appear to us to promise a considerable addition of strength in the new school. Of the first who came before us... we shall have no hesitation in announcing him for a very striking and original thinker. His name is PERCY BYSSHE SHELLEY...

> The next with whose name we became acquainted was JOHN HENRY [sic] REYNOLDS, author of a tale called Safie, written, we believe, in imitation of Lord Byron, and more lately a small set of poems... the principal of which is called the Naiad...

> The last of these young aspirants whom we have met with... is, we believe, the youngest of them all, and just of age. His name is JOHN KEATS. He has not yet published anything except in a newspaper; but a set of his manuscripts was handed us the other day, and fairly surprised us with the truth of their ambition, and ardent grappling with nature...[104]

There followed the poem, *On First Looking into Chapman's Homer*.

On that Sunday – 1 December 1816 – reading Hunt's article in the *Examiner*, the 21-year-old Keats understood that he was at a crossroads in his life. He was still working at Guy's Hospital and was still exposed to the squalor of Southwark and the nefarious activities of the Resurrection Men, but he was now being announced to the world as one of a new generation of poets, along with Reynolds and Shelley. Looking back over his poems, from the *Imitation of Spenser* through the 'curious shell' poems, *To Hope*, the Margate poems and others, he began seriously to consider publishing a book of his poetry using the contacts he had made in the Hunt circle, in particular a new acquaintance, Charles Ollier, who was just setting himself up as a bookseller and publisher. But it would take up a great deal of his time and energy to select and edit his poems, prepare fair copies and go through the process of publication. The question was, should he give up his medical work to concentrate on a new, literary, career?

Reynolds was working as a newspaper editor so at least had a fixed income, and Shelley was the son of a wealthy landowner and due an enormous inheritance. In pursuing their literary careers, neither was taking a risk of the sort Keats would face by abandoning his medical studies. Realising he had to be pragmatic, Keats decided not to talk to the men he knew would encourage him to give up medicine – Leigh Hunt, Jack Reynolds, and Benjamin Haydon – but rather to go and consult the man who was *least* likely to be sympathetic. This was the man who was still the guardian of his two younger brothers and his sister, the man who effectively held the purse strings of any inheritance Keats may have been due. He decided to talk to the tea merchant, Richard Abbey.

Chapter 6

The greatest Geniuses have always attributed every thing to God…
Benjamin Robert Haydon: *Diary*

Back in 1811, a painter called William Hazlitt had divided his time between his London lodgings and a cottage in a hamlet near the ancient city of Salisbury. He travelled by mail coach, a seven hour journey of some 80 miles at a cost of around four pennies a mile, between the White Horse Cellars in Piccadilly and a busy coaching inn called the Winterslow Hut on the Salisbury road. It was about a fifteen minute walk from 'the Hut' up a gently sloping hill to Winterslow, a village on the chalk downs that was divided into three parts. There was Winterslow itself, with a hilltop church and manor grounds (the manor house had burned down in 1774), and two nearby hamlets called Middle Winterslow and East Winterslow. The total population in 1811 was around 670 and this included a sufficient number of tradesmen to cater for most of the needs of the local residents. The village had its own baker, butcher and blacksmith and they could mingle with the other villagers in a tavern called the Lion's Head. In such a remote location this would have been a place where everybody knew everybody else and few strangers were ever seen. The lively city of Salisbury, with its theatre and concerts and assembly rooms, was about an hour's ride or two hour's walk away. The regional news, for those who took an interest in life beyond the village, was provided by *The Salisbury and Winchester Journal*.

Nine cottages bordered the main road through Middle Winterslow, each with a substantial garden for growing vegetables and keeping livestock. William Hazlitt and his wife, Sarah, lived in Middleton Cottage and the fact that it hasn't survived suggests that it was a typical thatched cottage built in 'chalk cob', a common building technique in old Wiltshire. (The naturalist Gilbert White noted that all such cottages in Selborne, also on the chalk downs, had been rebuilt in brick and stone by the time he published his famous *Natural History and Antiquities of Selborne* in 1789.)[105] The interior of the cottage was sparse because its structure had been improved in recent years and there had been little money left over to spend on decoration. However, the interior would still have had the usual furnishings and appurtenances found in all such cottages at this time. Curtains and bed linen, cutlery, candle holders and cast iron pots were valuable items and were taken good care of. In Hazlitt's cottage there was a collection of pictures around the walls, including some prints from Claude Lorraine and one of Hazlitt's own original paintings, a portrait of an old woman. There was also 'a parcel of rubbishy copies of old masters' and 'a bundle of manuscripts, exceedingly abstruse and unintelligible' as Hazlitt jokingly referred to his own print collection and papers.[106]

In summer, when the garden was colourful and the air warm and scented, Middleton Cottage would have been a very pleasant retreat for a man used to the unhealthy air and bustling crowds of London. But in winter, when the windows rattled with rain and the winds tore at the thatch, it would have been cold, damp and verminous. The windows of these Wiltshire cottages were invariably small and multi-paned so from early dusk the house was brightened by the fire and a few (relatively expensive) candles. The fire burned logs, not coal, so would have needed constant attention; Hazlitt and his contemporaries commented how they would have to pull their chairs close to the firelight in order to study a print, read a book or write a letter. With its air of intellectual pursuits, its paintings, books and scattered manuscripts, Middleton Cottage was a dull, rustic reflection of Leigh Hunt's picturesque cottage in Hampstead.

William Hazlitt was 33 years old in that summer of 1811, a slim man with unruly black hair and dark, expressive eyes. In such a small community, his neighbours would have known that his cottage had belonged to his wife's family and that Hazlitt himself, though ostensibly a painter, had also written some books but had no regular employment. On a practical level, Hazlitt was perfectly able to fend for himself, indeed he sometimes had to pick vegetables, cook a dinner, chop logs and clean out the fire because he lived alone at the cottage when Sarah went up to London to visit friends. He was, however, perfectly happy with a sedentary lifestyle. Here is how he once mockingly described himself in a letter to his friends (written in the third person). He was lodging in London at the time and recovering from an illness, but there is little doubt that it provides a glimpse of what he perceived to be his priorities in life:

> ...[he has] slept soundly for... twelve or fourteen hours... [then] every day about twelve or 1 o'clock he has got up, put on his clothes, drank his tea, & eat two plate-fulls of buttered toast... then sat for some hours with his eyes steadfastly fixed on the fire, like a person in a state of deep thought, doing nothing... growing tired from his sedentary posture, he has occasionally got up from his chair and walked across the room... At one time he turned the front of his great picture to the light, but finding the subject painful to him, he presently turned it to the wall again. Also, that he has twice attempted to read some of his own works, but has fallen asleep over them.[107]

The opinion of his neighbours was divided: some people regarded him as a gentleman (his wife's family had property; her brother was a lawyer who had once been the admiralty advocate of Malta), but others thought him a shabby 'low fellow'. He was indeed shabby in appearance, awkward in manner and painfully shy. The poet Samuel Taylor Coleridge famously described Hazlitt as 'brow-hanging, shoe-contemplative, strange'. Wherever he was living, he did not mix with the locals and he never went to church. The villagers of Winterslow probably knew very little about him except that he was a painter – they would have seen him take a canvas and brushes when he went for walks in the countryside. He would saunter through the local fields and woodlands with a hat on his head, a canvas under his arm, some brushes and paints in a bag and a piece of bread with a boiled egg or a bit of cheese in his pocket.

He would follow the ancient paths around the village, studying the landscape, before taking out his canvas and nailing it to a tree. Then he would sit and think about his favourite landscape artists, imagining the golden light in the blue skies, the waving trees and classical temples of Claude Lorrain. This is what he wrote many years later:

> There is a pleasure in painting which none but painters know... In tracing the commonest object, a plant or the stump of a tree, you learn something every moment... Patience grows out of the endless pursuit, and turns it into a luxury. A streak in a flower, a wrinkle in a leaf, a tinge in a cloud, a stain in an old wall or ruin gray, are seized with avidity as the spolia opima [the rich spoils] of this sort of mental warfare, and furnish our labour for another half day.[108]

But landscape painting was a mere diversion, a pastime, because for several years Hazlitt had been trying to earn his living as a portrait painter. He had once seemed destined for success, had received well-paid commissions from wealthy industrialists in the north of England. One of them had sent him to Paris to copy the Old Masters in the Louvre. Hazlitt took this work very seriously. He believed the best portrait painters were those who studied the smallest details in the faces of their subjects – the eyes, the imperfections in the skin, the very wrinkles and veins. In taking such pains he thought one was more likely to capture the essence of the person (the subject which had so exercised Sir Joshua Reynolds and Charles Bell, along with Haydon and Wilkie). Of course, the results were often less than flattering but when he painted a self-portrait, he perfectly captured his own features, his sorrowful eyes and somewhat condescending expression.

Despite mocking his own idleness, and sometimes sleeping soundly for twelve or fourteen hours a day, Hazlitt did have occasional bursts of energy. At these times he would travel around the country visiting the great houses of England to study the paintings in their galleries. He would gaze intently at the paintings of Claude Lorrain and Rembrandt, Titian and Vandyke, studying the technique of each artist, the draughtsmanship, brushstrokes and colouring. He later came up with some arresting phrases befitting the knowledge he had gained from these great masters; 'by the aid of the pencil,' he wrote, 'we may be said to touch and handle the objects of sight'[109] and 'the colours seem breathed on the canvas...'[110]

Hazlitt believed that the most sensible men were the painters, that the humblest painter was a true scholar and a student of human nature. The painter, he said, 'reads men and books with an intuitive eye'. Sadly, the very high standards that he set for himself (he aspired to paint like Rembrandt and Titian) eventually overwhelmed him so that his enthusiasm waned and people began commissioning portraits from him not so much for their intrinsic value, but out of little more than friendship. He finally, reluctantly, accepted that he could not earn his living by painting portraits but he did not altogether give up painting, which is why he could still be seen wandering into the fields around Winterslow.

What the people of Winterslow could not have known, because it was evident neither from his external appearance nor from his interaction with the villagers, was that their seemingly otiose and misanthropic neighbour was in fact one of the most learned men in Europe. The lawyer and diarist Henry Crabb Robinson, who knew a wide range of artists and intellectuals in both London and Germany, once wrote of Hazlitt:

> His bashfulness, want of words, slovenliness of dress, &c, made him sometimes the object of ridicule... He had few friends, and was flattered by my attentions... I recollect saying to my sister-in-law, 'Whom do you suppose to be the cleverest person I know?' 'Capel Lofft [an English lawyer and prolific writer], perhaps?' 'No...'
> 'I give it up.'
> 'William Hazlitt.'
> 'Oh, you are joking. Why, we all take him to be just the reverse.'[111]

Which is almost certainly what his neighbours in Winterslow would have said. In fact, Hazlitt was an extremely talented writer who had published several of his own works including a full-length book of philosophy, *The Principles of Human Action*. But after preparing and having rejected a series of essays on the English philosophers, and also a biography of Thomas Holcroft (the playwright), it became apparent that his subjects were not popular. In the self-mocking letter to his friends that we noted earlier, he remarked that he had written a number of books, 'but it does not appear they were read by anybody'. Surprisingly, for all his lack of worldly success, his shabbiness and his awkwardness in company, William Hazlitt was perfectly comfortable in his own skin. He was well aware of his superior intellectual gifts and often described himself as *a thinker*.

When a son was born in late 1811, Hazlitt decided to leave Winterslow and take his family back to London in order that he might try again to earn some money from his writing. He thought about giving a series of public lectures using the work he had already completed on the English philosophers (which, considering his shyness and awkwardness, gives a fair idea of his desperation). Having lived for many years in London he already had several friends there, including the painter James Northcote of Argyll Street (Haydon's friend) and the diarist and lawyer Henry Crabb Robinson (from whom we heard above, and who was at the time a compassionate and good friend of Hazlitt). There was also a clerk in the East India Company, a brilliant essayist called Charles Lamb, the friend of Leigh Hunt.

After writing to an educational establishment called the Russell Institution and asking permission to use their hall in Great Coram Street, Hazlitt rented rooms in his favourite lodgings, the Southampton Buildings in Chancery Lane. He entered the neoclassical edifice of the Russell Institution in January 1812, mounted the podium and began to deliver the first in a series of lectures on the *History of English Philosophy*. Although the introductory lecture was a disaster (Hazlitt had underestimated the amount of time he would have to deliver it and as a result had read it too quickly), the lectures improved as the series progressed and by the end they were well received.

Following the lectures, Hazlitt found that his friends had rallied together and managed to get him a job as a parliamentary reporter on a newspaper, the *Morning Chronicle*. This came about because Lamb, Robinson and others had worked hard on Hazlitt's behalf spreading the news that he had once written a book about great parliamentary speeches, *The Eloquence of the British Senate*. They also pointed out that he had a preternatural memory – he seemed able to remember everything he had read and heard, and would be able to listen to, record and recount any debate with ease.

The strategy met with success and Hazlitt was offered a job which came with an extremely generous salary of £220 a year. After establishing himself on the staff of the newspaper and completing the move from Winterslow to London, Hazlitt heard that Leigh Hunt of the *Examiner* had been sent to prison. As Hunt had been a regular guest at the home of Hazlitt's friend Charles Lamb, it is likely that the two men were at least acquainted. In any event, Hazlitt went along to Horsemonger Gaol in Southwark to offer moral support to the man who had risked everything to defend the freedom of the press. Within two years, the shy and socially awkward parliamentary reporter on the *Morning Chronicle* would become a major contributor to Hunt's *Examiner*.

Benjamin Haydon met William Hazlitt around the time Hazlitt was lecturing at the Russell Institution. Both men were visiting James Northcote at his studio in Argyll Street. It will be remembered that Northcote was one of the painters that Haydon had approached soon after his arrival in London, the man once described as looking like a 'cat that had seen a rat'. Hazlitt was very well acquainted with Northcote because, as had Haydon, he had sought out the Argyll and Berner Street set of painters (Northcote, Opie and Fuseli) in order to advance his career. Hazlitt had spent many hours in Northcote's studio enjoying conversations he found so stimulating that he eventually wrote a book about them.

During this initial encounter with Haydon at Northcote's house, Hazlitt had graciously praised Haydon's painting of *Macbeth* (which he had seen at the British Institution exhibition in Pall Mall). Haydon, delighted by the praise, invited Hazlitt to his studio in Great Marlborough Street. In the cramped painting room, discussing art and Shakespeare, the two men discovered a range of common interests and quickly became firm friends. Hazlitt once said of Haydon:

> I find him... well read up in the literature of the day, and never at a loss for subjects of conversation, whether of books, politics, men or other things. He talks well, too, on most subjects that interest one; indeed better than any painter I ever met... Haydon is more a scholar, and has a wider range and versatility of information. One enjoys his hearty, joyous laugh; it sets one upon one's legs as it were better than a glass of champagne...[112]

When Haydon was invited to attend a dinner for the Christening of Hazlitt's son, he went along to the new Hazlitt family home at 19 York Street, Westminster, and recorded a vivid account of the experience in his diary:

> I dined on Friday with a man of Genius, William Hazlitt. His child was to be christened, and I was desired to be there punctually at four. At four I came, but he was out! his wife ill by the fire, nothing ready, and all wearing the appearance of neglect and indifference. At last home he came, the cloth began to cover the table, and then followed a plate with a dozen large, waxen, cold, clayy, slaty potatoes. Down they were set, and down we sat also: a young mathematician, who whenever he spoke, jerked up one side of his mouth, and closed an eye as if seized with a paralytic affection… an old Lady of Genius with torn ruffles; his wife in an influenza, thin, pale & spitty; and his chubby child, squalling, obstinate and half-cleaned. After waiting a little, all looking forlornly at the potatoes for fear they might be the chief dish, in issued a bit of overdone beef, burnt, toppling about on seven or eight corners, with a great bone sticking out of it like a battering ram…[113]

More than three years later, on Sunday, 3 November 1816, Hazlitt visited Haydon in his studio at Great Marlborough Street in order to have his portrait sketched. Haydon, in the manner of the Italian Renaissance artists, was putting the portraits of his friends into his painting of *Christ's Entry into Jerusalem*:

> Hazlitt called in and sat for three hours, pouring out the results of a week's thinking… He said some fine things, which when he writes them will be remembered for ever. I gave him a bottle of wine, & he drank & talked, told me all the early part of his life, acknowledged his own weaknesses and follies. We then disputed about Art. I told him he always seemed angry on that subject because he had given it up… Hazlitt is a man who can do great good to the Art. He practiced

Painting long enough to know it; and he carries into Literature a stock which no literary man ever did before him…[114]

That Sunday, 3 November, was the same day Keats visited Haydon's studio for the first time, Hazlitt being Haydon's 'other appointment' that we noted earlier. Whether Keats and Hazlitt met at Haydon's that day, or soon after, is not known, but Hazlitt came to be the major influence upon Keats' mature thinking as a poet, a greater influence even than Spenser, Beattie, or Wordsworth had been. Indeed, Hazlitt became one of the people Keats admired most in the few short years of his life, not only because of his writings in the *Examiner* or the brilliant essays he was soon to begin publishing as an independent author and essayist, but also because of that early book of philosophy, the one Hazlitt claimed nobody had ever read – the *Principles of Human Action*. We shall learn more about its effect upon Keats later.

***

On Monday, 20 January 1817, Keats attended a dinner along with Haydon, Hunt, Hunt's wife and his sister-in-law, and the third of the 'Young Poets', Percy Bysshe Shelley. Haydon wrote in his diary that the dinner occurred at the house of Horace Smith, one of Hunt's wealthier friends. Smith was a stockbroker who lived in a spacious terraced house at Mayor's Row, on the Kensington Road near Hyde Park Corner. His house looked onto a busy thoroughfare along which he would drive his carriage the two miles or so to his office in Throgmorton Street, which was a short walk from the noisy and colourful spectacle of the Stock Exchange. Horace Smith was well connected and had many influential friends (including Haydon's former patron, Lord Mulgrave), but he had made his fortune independently by speculating on stock linked to government loans. In June 1815, three days after the Battle of Waterloo and before the outcome was officially confirmed in the newspapers, the stock rose dramatically on rumours of a Wellington victory and Smith had made a profit of several thousand pounds. His wealth was not the only, perhaps not even the main reason Smith was a friend of Hunt. The tall, handsome, witty and personable stockbroker had also penned *The Rejected Addresses*, a brilliant parody of several of the better known poets of the period. Written with his brother James, it was among the most successful books of the decade and had made the Smith brothers famous.

Smith had met both Keats and Shelley at Hunt's house before this dinner. He had read and admired Keats' work when Charles Cowden Clarke had first brought it to Hunt's cottage, and he had been struck by Shelley's deep knowledge of Plato's philosophy during a walk on Hampstead Heath.[115] On this occasion, though, Shelley left a less favourable impression upon his host, even though Smith has left us the following observation:

> Manifest as it was that [Shelley's] pre-occupied mind had no thought to spare for the modish adjustment of his fashionably-made clothes, it was impossible to doubt, even for a moment, that you were gazing upon a gentleman.[116]

The comment about Shelley's 'pre-occupied mind' is interesting in the context of another account of Shelley left by a printer called

Charles Richards. Shelley went to see Richards on business and the printer subsequently commented that 'he never had so strange a visitor':

> He was gaunt, and had peculiar starts and gestures, and a way of fixing his eyes and his whole attitude for a good while, like the abstracted apathy of a musing madman.[117]

Shelley was the son and heir of a wealthy landowner, the MP and aristocrat Sir Timothy Shelley of Warnham, near Horsham (Shelley hated his father, a pillar of the establishment – and the feeling was mutual). He was educated at Eton and for a time at Oxford and was thus one of the very few members of the Hunt circle to have had the benefit of a university education. A character sketch of Shelley in his student days has been left by his friend Thomas Jefferson Hogg, after he first walked into Shelley's rooms at University College, Oxford. He describes them as if they were the rooms of an abstracted scientist, perhaps a young professor:

> Books, boots, papers, shoes, philosophical instruments, clothes, pistols, linen, ammunition and phials innumerable, with money, stockings, prints, crucibles, bags and boxes scattered on the floor and in every place… An electrical machine, an air pump, the galvanic trough, a solar microscope and large glass jars and receivers were conspicuous amid the mass of matter.[118]

One day Shelley was found standing on a table connected to his 'electrical machine' with his long hair standing on end. Now, six years later, at 24 years old, his life was equally disorganised and chaotic, but in a much more serious and tragic way. He had recently learned that his former wife had committed suicide in London by drowning herself in The Serpentine, a lake in Hyde Park. Shelley had left her alone with their children while he pursued an affair with Mary Wollstonecraft who, as Mary Shelley (the marriage had already taken place), was in the process of writing her now famous novel *Frankenstein*. Of all the members of the Hunt circle, Leigh Hunt himself was the only one who truly liked the wild and eccentric, cruel, rich and brilliantly intellectual Shelley; he became 'infatuated' as Keats put it. And of all the members of the Hunt circle, it was Haydon who came to loathe Shelley the most.

At this stage of his life, Shelley had published very little – a few pamphlets, some poems and one small book, all at his own expense. The book was called *Alastor; or the Spirit of Solitude and Other Poems*. It had been published early the previous year and received little attention, but of the few reviews it did attract, the following was typical. It appeared in the *Monthly Review or Literary Journal* in April 1816 and the reviewer didn't even bother to sign it:

> We must candidly own that these poems are beyond our comprehension… and therefore we entreat [the poet] for the sake of the reviewers as well as of his other readers (if he had any) to subjoin to his next publication an ordo, a glossary, and copious notes, illustrative of his allusions and explanatory of his meaning.[119]

Shelley was in fact something of a social chameleon. Horace Smith saw a 'gentleman' sitting at his dinner table but in reality Shelley was a political radical who hated Smith's profession (he once wrote that he thought it odd that Smith, a stockbroker, should be generous) as he hated lawyers and judges. One of his early poems was called *The Devil's Walk* and it was squarely aimed at the wealthy establishment, the lawyers, judges and priests who in Shelley's eyes were only there to support the despised Tory government. Here's how it begins:

> Once, early in the morning,
> Beelzebub arose,
> With care his sweet person adorning,
> He put on his Sunday clothes.
>
> He drew on a boot to hide his hoof,
> He drew on a glove to hide his claw,
> His horns were concealed by a Bras Chapeau
> And the Devil went forth as natty a Beau
> As Bond Street ever saw.
>
> He sate him down, in London town,
> Before earth's morning ray;
> With a favourite imp he began to chat,
> On religion, and scandal, and this and that,
> Until the dawn of day…
>
> He peeped in each hole, to each chamber stole,
> His promising livestock to view;
> Grinning applause, he just showed them his claws,
> And they shrunk with affright from his ugly sight,
> Whose work they delighted to do.

This poem had been printed as a mere 'broadside ballad' back in 1812 and it is unlikely that Horace Smith had even heard of it.

Haydon was slightly late arriving at the dinner party and when he sat down he didn't know who Shelley was, except that he was a 'hectic, spare, weakly yet intellectual-looking creature… carving a bit of broccoli or cabbage on his plate, as if it were the substantial wing of a chicken'.[120] Dinner was usually taken in the late afternoon and at this time of the year it would already have been dark outside, so the meal would have been eaten by candlelight. The host being a wealthy man, the tableware would have been of fine quality, the wine perhaps a Chateau Margaux taken from glasses of crystal (at a later dinner this wine was specially brought in for Keats; his favourite drink was claret). These details were particularly important to Hunt with his aesthetic sensibility but they were also important to Haydon, hence his disgust at the cobbled-together 'Christening dinner' at Hazlitt's house.

After the introductions and the small talk, Shelley opened the conversation 'in the most feminine and gentle voice', with 'As to that detestable religion, the Christian…'.[121] Haydon was astounded but as he looked around the table and saw Hunt smiling and the women 'simpering', he realised he was being baited. As Haydon stared at Shelley, he must quickly have realised that this fellow guest was everything that he, Haydon, was not. Shelley was rich, tall, effeminate and softly spoken, and he was clearly an atheist. (He was also a vegetarian although the word had not yet been invented; people who didn't eat meat were said to employ a 'natural diet' or a 'Pythagorean' one.) It is true that outside of his family and friends Shelley's atheism was not yet well known, but this was only because his readership was almost non-existent. Hunt, too, was something of an atheist – Haydon said he had expressed an 'unfeeling, heartless and brutal ridicule of Christ and his divine doctrine', but Haydon and Hunt had long ago reached an accommodation, an agreement to disagree without malice. Shelley was different. He hated God even more than he hated his father, so much so that it had cost him his university degree and his family ties (he was evicted from Oxford on account of a pamphlet he wrote called *The Necessity of Atheism*. He took it to a local bookseller for publication and this was considered a serious offence by the university authorities because atheism was considered blasphemy, and blasphemy was a crime that could attract imprisonment).

Haydon's belief in God, or the Great Spirit, was genuine and deeply held. In a long but amicable letter to a friend in this same year, 1817, while discussing the likelihood that God would turn himself into a man and allow himself to be crucified for the sake of a moral doctrine, Haydon said he thought the idea no more absurd than that God, 'in the midst of his sublimities and endless world [should] give a heart and a liver to a flea'.[122] He accepted the supernatural elements of Christianity, the miracles and the resurrection, but he was not blind and unthinking in his belief: 'It is nothing to me,' he said, 'whether God created the world as related in Genesis or not, or whether evil came into the world by an apple'.[123] He was more interested in what he saw as the real and obvious benefits that Christianity had brought to mankind – charitable institutions, hospitals and the abolition of slavery.

In London's intellectual circles, Haydon was far more 'famous' than Shelley, indeed he was very much a public figure. Despite this, he may have felt intimidated by Shelley's provocation because he knew by reputation that Shelley's intellect was among the sharpest and most acute of all the members of the Hunt circle, perhaps even more brilliant than Hazlitt's. It would have been extremely bad-mannered to start a heated discussion over dinner while the servants were coming and going and the wine was being poured, so for the time being Haydon kept his peace. During the rest of the main course the conversation was about painting and poetry, which Keats, in particular, would have appreciated, but it was over dessert, when the servants had retired, that Shelley resumed the conversation about God. He said that the Mosaic and Christian dispensations were inconsistent. Hunt agreed with him. Shelley then pronounced that Shakespeare could not have been a Christian because of a particular dialogue in *Cymbeline* (the 'blindness' dialogue between Posthumous and the first gaoler in Act V, Scene IV in which, Haydon says, Shakespeare 'has put sophistry about men's state after death into the mouth of his gaoler'). Haydon worshipped Shakespeare almost as much as he worshipped God, or Raphael, or the Elgin Marbles, so he replied with the familiar argument that you might as well say that Shakespeare 'was in favour of murder' because some of his characters are murderers. He then quoted from Shakespeare himself, Marcellus in Act I, Scene I of *Hamlet* who says, 'Wherein our Saviour's birth is celebrated'. (In quotations of this sort, Haydon was indeed proficient and impressive.) The discussion continued until it became personal and they said 'unpleasant things' to each other. The embarrassment in the room must have been excruciating.

Haydon was in fact annoyed less by the statements about Christianity than by the manner in which they were put, as, for example, when Saint Paul was referred to as 'Mister Paul' and it was intimated that he was a 'cunning fellow'. 'I never heard any sceptic but Hazlitt discuss the matter with the gravity such a question demanded,' he said. (Hazlitt also knew Shelley as a member of the Hunt circle, and wrote a famous description of him: '[Shelley] has a fire in his eye, a fever in his blood, a maggot in his brain, a hectic flutter in his speech... I suspect he is more intent upon startling himself with his electrical experiments in morals and philosophy; and though they may scorch other people, they are to him harmless amusements...')[124]

Hunt appeared to be enjoying himself; '...when all discussion had ceased,' wrote Haydon, 'and the wine had gone freely round – when long talk of poetry and painting had, as it were, opened our hearts – [Hunt] would suddenly (touching my arm with the most friendly pressure) show me a passage in the Bible and Testament, and say..., "Haydon, do you believe this?"'[125]

According to Haydon's account, Keats kept his own counsel as the argument unfolded (he 'never said a word...'). Keats was in exactly the formal 'dinner party' environment he disliked and he probably didn't want to draw attention to himself. He was in fact self-conscious of his appearance – we noted earlier that he dressed in a 'Byronic' fashion – several of his contemporaries, including Henry

Stephens (with whom he shared the lodgings in Southwark), had noted that Keats dressed with his collar turned down and a ribbon tied around his neck instead of the usual neckerchief. The difference between Byron and Keats, of course, was that Byron could afford to wear the most expensive and beautifully made clothes in a casual manner, whereas Keats was too poor to wear anything but the most ordinary clothes. His mode of dress was a defiant and brave gesture designed to assert his 'poetic' identity and he knew it attracted attention.

It is also likely that Keats did not join in because he did not want to appear to be taking sides against Haydon, even light-heartedly. He was growing close to Haydon and he felt a debt of gratitude to him because he knew that three weeks previously Haydon had finally sent his 'Great Spirits' poem to Wordsworth and had informed Wordsworth that Keats was thinking of publishing a little book of his 'smaller productions' of poetry.

But there was another, more important reason that he did not join in the discussion: his views about Christianity were actually more in agreement with Shelley's than with Haydon's. Keats had written a poem, one of his 'smaller productions', five weeks earlier, on a Sunday morning when Charles Cowden Clarke was standing 'by his side'.[126] They were listening to some church bells, probably the 'Bow Bells' of St Mary le Bow, which were just a few hundred yards away from the Keats brothers' lodgings. Keats found the sound melancholy and he believed that the ensuing church service would be gloomy. He couldn't understand why people would leave their firesides where they could read poetry – 'Lydian airs' again – to go and listen to a church service. The bells kept tolling and were getting on his nerves, but he knew that they would not last forever. They, and by implication the church and the people attending the service, were wailing at their own coming demise. The poem was called *Written in Disgust of Vulgar Superstition*:

> The church bells toll a melancholy round,
> Calling the people to some other prayers,
> Some other gloominess, more dreadful cares,
> More hearkening to the sermon's horrid sound.
> Surely the mind of man is closely bound
> In some black spell, seeing that each one tears
> Himself from fireside joys and Lydian airs,
> And converse high of those with glory crowned.
> Still, still they toll, and I should feel a damp,
> A chill as from a tomb, did I not know
> That they are going like an outburnt lamp;
> That 'tis their sighing, wailing ere they go
> Into oblivion; that fresh flowers will grow,
> And many glories of immortal stamp.

So the argument about Christianity ended in embarrassed silence and hurt feelings. Keats was now aware that Shelley, for all his brilliance, could be a deeply disruptive figure and that a fissure was opening up in the close friendship between Haydon and Hunt. Keats' own friendship with each of them was bound to be affected.

***

The reason that Charles Cowden Clarke had been with Keats on that Sunday morning in December was because he was helping Keats in his latest attempt to get published. After receiving the sonnet *To Charles Cowden Clarke* which Keats had written at Margate, Clarke had come back into Keats' life at yet another important turning point: the young poet had recently told Richard Abbey that he had decided to give up medicine in order to try and make a living as a poet. He said to Abbey that he 'knew he had abilities greater than most men' and that consequently he was determined to make a living by exercising them. Abbey, knowing just how much time and money had been invested in Keats' medical apprenticeship and surgical studies, was incredulous. He had assumed that the eldest son of Frances Keats was destined to become a doctor like Thomas Hammond, a respected man with his own busy practice. He said that he thought Keats wouldn't last long as a writer.[127]

***

Back in 1810, a 22-year-old bank clerk called Charles Ollier had begun to take an interest in the London theatre. He wrote a theatrical review that was accepted by Leigh Hunt for publication in the *Examiner* and from then on he became a member of the Hunt circle. He was now, in early 1817, planning to go into business as a retail bookseller and publisher with his younger brother, James. The Ollier brothers put together a circulating library and set up shop, under the imprint of C& J. Ollier, in Welbeck Street. They faced a lot of competition, however. There were literally hundreds of booksellers, publishers, printers, bookbinders, engravers and stationers in London at this time, many of them having been in the same family for generations. Publishing was, of course, a gentleman's occupation, but printing was very much an industrial process, with almost everything done by hand. (The manual, cast iron Stanhope printer could produce 480 pages an hour though a much more powerful steam-driven printer was in operation at the *London Times* newspaper; it printed its first edition on November 29, 1814.)[128] A man employed as a printer may well have been a typefounder, too, with a furnace in a separate 'metal house' where lumps of lead and antimony were melted to make the typefaces. There were many fires in buildings leased by printers, some of them leading to fatalities.

Charles Ollier and his brother James knew little about the publishing business when they opened their shop in the middle of a terrace at No. 3 Welbeck Street, and they had very little capital. But they did have their connections with the Hunt circle, and Shelley quickly established a reciprocal relationship with them. He set up an account to buy their retailed books (for the library of a house he had just taken in Marlow, Buckinghamshire) and had them procure other books for him. He also requested that they forward his letters to his various friends and contacts in London. For these services they were paid on account. In return, Ollier would have Shelley's works printed, at Shelley's own cost, by Charles Reynell, a young man who worked in his family's printing business at 21 Piccadilly. Advertisements would then be placed in selected newspapers and the Olliers would take a commission on the sales. If the Olliers had had more capital, they might have chosen to buy the copyright of Shelley's poems outright. They would have published and printed them at their own expense and given Shelley a share of the profits, but as we have seen, Shelley was used to paying for these things himself. From Shelley's perspective, just having a publisher's imprint gave his writings more credibility so they could be posted to newspapers and magazines with more chance of being reviewed. Shelley's first publication under the C & J Ollier imprint was a political pamphlet that he wanted distributed to newspapers and Members of Parliament. It was called *A Proposal for Putting Reform to the Vote* and it sold for one shilling.

Keats was introduced to Charles Ollier at Hunt's house. Ollier knew that Leigh Hunt himself had endorsed Keats as one of a promising new generation of poets, so when it became known that Keats was seeking a publisher for his book, it was quickly agreed that it would come out under the C. and J. Ollier imprint and that it would be called, simply, *Poems 1817*. (The Olliers' business was growing rapidly at this time; as well as publishing Keats and Shelley, they were in discussion with William Hazlitt about printing a new book called *The Characters of Shakespeare's Plays*.) By the time Keats attended the dinner at Horace Smith's, his book was nearing completion and the process of preparing it for the press had already begun. Keats must have been both excited and nervous – he knew there were some fine poems in it (*Chapman's Homer*, especially) but he also knew that some of the poems were among his earliest (*Imitation of Spenser, To Hope*) and that some of them, including the 'Curious Shell' poem, might appear juvenile. But that wasn't all. *To My Brothers*, written on Tom's birthday, was undoubtedly sentimental and the

'Great Spirit' poem to Haydon could well be taken as sycophantic. Keats was worried about the reception these poems would get from the reviewers and the critics, so despite his misgivings, he discussed these concerns with Shelley.

The book, to be printed 'in boards' with a selling price of six shillings, was due to be published in March 1817. It is not known exactly how many copies were planned but the initial run was likely to be around 250 copies, with further editions to be printed if demand were sufficient. The cost involved in printing, binding and advertising a new book was considerable (as we have noted, it was still largely a manual and thus time-consuming process) and Keats must have found the money from somewhere; perhaps Abbey had relented and provided it for him because it was after all the Keats family money he was administering. The Olliers had the book printed by Charles Richards, the brother of a friend of Leigh Hunt (this was the same Charles Richards who described Shelley as being gaunt, with 'peculiar starts and gestures').

Keats knew that if the book was not a success he would find it very difficult to justify his decision to give up medicine in the face of Abbey's scepticism, and to continue as a member of the Hunt literary set. It could not have helped that when he had talked to Shelley, during a recent visit to Hunt's house, Shelley had read some of the poems and advised him not to publish. Keats was still young (21 to Shelley's 24) and Shelley believed the critics would give it unfavourable reviews, or worse, ignore it completely (as they had largely ignored Shelley's first book). Although Shelley seemed genuinely to like Keats, he did, in fact, have a low opinion of his poetry. When Hunt published a poem of Keats' called *The Floure and the Leafe* in the *Examiner* on Sunday 16 March, Shelley's wife, Mary, wrote to the Hunts that Shelley's friends were 'much scandalised' by the praise heaped upon it, and meant to 'petition' Hunt against publishing any more of Keats' work.[129] Considering the closeness of the Hunt circle, this comment may well have got back to Keats.

Keats knew, however, that Hunt had recently published a major poem, *Rimini*, and that Reynolds was publishing *The Naiad*. Haydon's latest essay was now being read throughout Europe. The Olliers had established their business, and were publishing both Shelley and Hazlitt. On light of all this literary activity, Keats felt that he could not risk being left behind, so he decided to ignore Shelley's advice. To use a phrase of his own, he leaped headlong into the sea.

Chapter 7

Beauty of form is but the vehicle of conveying Ideas,
but truth of conveyance is the first object.
Benjamin Robert Haydon: *Diary*

The day after Horace Smith's dinner party, Tuesday, 21 January 1817, Haydon spent a long time complaining in his diary about Hunt and Shelley's behaviour. He thought he had been treated appallingly and was clearly aggrieved. The following day, Wednesday, 22 January, he had an appointment with Francis Charles Seymour-Conway, the Earl of Yarmouth, known to Haydon as Lord Yarmouth, a fabulously wealthy man who lived in a large London mansion called Hertford House in Manchester Square, near Oxford Street.[130] It was rumoured that the Earl of Yarmouth would do anything for money and indeed that he had married for it. (His wife, Maria Fagniani, was said to be the illegitimate daughter of the 4th Duke of Queensbury. 'Old Q', as the duke was known, had left the pair a fortune when he died.) Of more interest and importance to Haydon, the earl was known to be a serious collector of art and had offered to show Haydon his paintings by the Renaissance Masters. The family art collection was passed down through the ensuing generations and is now known as the Wallace Collection; it is still housed at Hertford House.

It is unlikely that Haydon had been called to Hertford House just to see the art collection – he was, he said, 'introduced' to the earl. The very next day, Haydon was to be presented to the Grand Duke Nicholas of Russia at the British Museum, where the Russian noble was to view the Elgin Marbles. The Earl of Yarmouth would have wanted to discuss this event with Haydon because his father was Lord Chamberlain to the Prince Regent and thus the chief functionary at the court; the earl himself was a personal friend of the Prince Regent and had been his Vice-Chamberlain back in 1812. Haydon had initially been invited to meet Grand Duke Nicholas by the noble's drawing instructor, Alexander Sauerweid, who knew Haydon to be an historical painter and a leading expert on the Marbles. Haydon understood that, after the visit to the British Museum, Sauerweid intended to bring the grand duke to Great Marlborough Street to see the painting of *Christ's Entry into Jerusalem*.[131] The prospect was dizzying. If a commission were to follow, it would not only replenish Haydon's depleted finances, it would extend his influence beyond the borders of Europe and into the heart of the Russia Empire.

The Grand Duke Nicholas was a son of Alexander I, the Emperor of Russia, and would become emperor himself one day (he became Tsar Nicholas I in 1825). For now, though, he was a young nobleman doing 'The Grand Tour' of Europe after a stint of military service in France. Just 21 years old, tall, handsome, reserved and imperious, he was genuinely interested in European culture and had recently become engaged to a princess. For reasons known only to himself, he always appeared in public dressed in military uniform; Haydon was dazzled by the prospect of meeting him.

Following their acquisition for the nation, the Elgin Marbles were now housed in a temporary shelter in the garden of the British Museum at Montague House, a mansion on the site of the present British Museum in Bloomsbury. The more massive Marbles were arranged on plinths, with some of the smaller items being secured on mounts high up on the walls. On the appointed day, the Grand Duke was announced by the clatter of his approaching coach and Haydon was waiting to meet him. Always in awe of the grand occasion, there is little doubt that Haydon will have practised his best manners (it will be remembered how he had scrubbed himself, dressed in his finest clothes and spoken to himself in the mirror before his first dinner at Sir George Beaumont's house).

Amid the colourful crush of dignitaries and guests, Haydon was introduced to the grand duke by Alexander Sauerweid. 'I felt my heart swell,' he wrote, 'to think I was thus walking about with an elegant young Prince amid things [the Marbles] I had defended when they were lying covered with dust & dirt, unbought, unfelt and ridiculed.'[132] The grand duke looked at the muscular (but headless and armless) torso of the river god, Ilissus, and 'in a loud voice, as if giving the word of command, thundered out, "C'est un superbe fragment"'. Haydon replied, 'not in the gentlest voice', 'Oui, Altesse Impériale'.[133] It was a good start. Haydon, who was being closely observed by the other guests, had been publicly acknowledged by the grand duke as an expert on the Marbles – and had spoken in French.

Haydon then told the grand duke that he had a relative in the service of the emperor (his mother's younger brother, Thomas Cobley). The grand duke responded pleasantly that he knew the man, remarking 'Je le connais très bien; c'est un commandant distingué' and went on to mention that he had passed three weeks with him in Odessa. Alexander Sauerweid and another dignitary, a learned adviser to the Russian government by the name of Dr Hamel, leaned forward, trying to overhear the conversation. The grand duke then moved on to the next fragment of the Elgin Marbles and, once again, all the other advisers being unable to answer his questions, Haydon stepped forward, eager in his desire to impress this potentially important patron. At the end of the visit, the grand duke was swiftly escorted to his carriage, despite appearing to want another word with the erudite historical painter. But Sauerweid had already led Haydon away, all the time reassuring him that the grand duke would visit the studio in Great Marlborough Street to view *Christ's Entry into Jerusalem*.

Haydon was later informed by Dr Hamel that he had transgressed the rules of etiquette by talking so familiarly (about his uncle Thomas Cobley) before the grand duke had invited such informal conversation. This was a huge faux pas because Sauerweid, who valued his position as the Russian court's chief adviser on matters of art, had been annoyed by Haydon's audacity; he felt that Haydon had deliberately tried to steal the limelight and usurp his authority.

Sauerweid had only promised that the grand duke would visit the studio so that Haydon would wait and not try to contact him. Of course, the visit never happened. Haydon sent some of his drawings of the Elgin Marbles to the grand duke, but they were returned unopened.[134]

***

Early in March, Keats' book *Poems, 1817* was published and we can safely assume that copies were put on display in the window of the Olliers' bookshop in Welbeck Street. Keats had received an advance copy on Saturday 1 March and walked up to Hampstead to share his success and excitement with the man to whom the book was dedicated, Leigh Hunt.

It was an exceptionally mild day and when Hunt had poured out glasses of celebratory wine they went out into the garden. There, in the manner of the ancient poets and the those of the Italian Renaissance, Hunt 'crowned' the newly published Keats with laurel and Keats reciprocated by placing ivy on Hunt's head. However, the younger man quickly realised (and ever after felt) that he and Hunt were acting in a foolish, rather immature fashion; he was beginning to see that Hunt was rapidly becoming a posturing dilettante and no longer the influential and authoritative writer Keats had once considered him to be.

Hunt, meanwhile, who it will be remembered had been to prison and been ruined for his principles, had more important things on his mind. He was deeply in debt and was in the process of temporarily moving his family into Shelley's new home at Marlow in

Buckinghamshire. Despite being charmed by Hunt's extraordinary gifts for friendship and hospitality, Keats knew that his friend had always lived beyond his means and may also have known that Shelley was giving him money (Shelley once gave Hunt £1,400, a small fortune at the time.)[135] Disappointed that Hunt's friendship and patronage (and, by extension, publication in the *Examiner*) could now seemingly be bought, it was from around this time that Keats began to spend more time with Haydon, and to seek Haydon's advice and opinions instead of Hunt's. He had plenty of time to reflect upon these things when he left Hampstead and walked the four miles of lanes and fields to the outskirts of the city. It was another two miles down the Hampstead and Tottenham Court Roads, then left through Holborn and along Newgate Street before he finally arrived back at his own relatively drab lodgings in Cheapside. The very next day, Sunday 2 March, he met Haydon and the two men went to the British Museum to see the Elgin Marbles. The museum was not open to the public on Sundays, so it is likely that Haydon was granted the privilege of taking Keats to a private viewing.[136]

As we have seen, there were few people in the whole of Europe more qualified than Haydon to explain the importance of the Elgin Marbles. He always felt directly connected to the past when he was studying them and habitually referred to them as 'the ruins of Athens'. When he took Keats to view them on that Sunday in March, a few weeks after his ill-fated meeting with the Grand Duke Nicholas, Haydon would have been keen to impress upon Keats that they represented (in Haydon's view) perhaps the greatest achievement in the history of Western art, if not the history of Western civilisation itself.

Of course, we cannot know precisely what Haydon said to Keats as they walked around the temporary building which had been erected to display the Marbles, but we do know exactly what Haydon thought of them, so we can fairly reconstruct what he would have wanted to emphasise to a young poet with an interest in classical civilisation, one who had already translated *The Aeneid* and memorised large sections of *Lemprière's Classical Dictionary*. He might have begun by explaining to Keats how the Marbles, after 2,200 years decorating one of the most iconic buildings on Earth, the Parthenon on the Acropolis in Athens, had come to be in London, deposited in a ramshackle shed in the garden of a house in Piccadilly. Haydon had heard the story directly from Lord Elgin himself.[137]

Lord Elgin had recounted to Haydon that back in 1802 he had been appointed ambassador to the Ottoman Empire, which included Greece, and had set sail for Constantinople. Before leaving for his new post, a conversation with an architect had produced the idea of taking moulds of the 'fragments at Athens' (the Parthenon had been turned into a ruin in 1687 after being used as an explosives store by the Ottomans and taking a direct hit from a shell fired by the Venetians). These moulds would not only advance British academic knowledge of Greek classical architecture but would have the added benefit of providing inspiration for the decoration of his lordship's mansion in Scotland. The government having turned down his request for funds, Lord Elgin decided to fund the venture out of his own personal fortune (or, more accurately, his wife's fortune).

During a stopover in Palermo, Sicily, Elgin hired a landscape painter who then went off to Rome to employ a coterie of artists who would travel to Athens and subsequently spend three years drawing, moulding and measuring the Parthenon sculptures and friezes, all at Lord Elgin's expense. Eventually, Lord Elgin boarded a ship and sailed from Constantinople to Athens to see the Parthenon sculptures for himself. To his shock and dismay, he found 'several of the figures lying about, that had fallen from the building' and later discovered that a local man had ground some of the fragments down to dust because they 'made such excellent mortar to build his house with'. In the face of such barbarity, Haydon tells us, Lord Elgin 'thought himself fully justified in securing those that remained, for in all probability, were they to fall, they would share the same fate'.[138]

After obtaining permission in an edict known as a 'firman' from the Ottoman authorities (the 'permission', of course, remains controversial to this day), Lord Elgin employed a small army of local workers to help him save the Marbles. They erected wooden scaffolds and then hammered, chipped and prised dozens of the remaining sculptures free of the Parthenon. They lowered them on ropes, boxed them up and sent them to England by sea. A storm and a shipwreck almost caused the Marbles to be lost for ever (they were 'in the deep bosom of the Ocean buried' wrote Haydon, eagerly quoting from the opening of Shakespeare's *Richard III*), but Lord Elgin paid for a salvage operation. Finally arriving in London, the

Marbles were deposited in a shed at the back of Lord Elgin's house in Piccadilly, the place where Haydon had first seem them in 1808. In 1816, just a few months before Haydon took Keats to view them at Montague House, the Marbles were purchased for the nation, but at less than half Lord Elgin's total outlay (calculated to have been around £74,000). Lord Elgin was by now divorced, financially ruined and facially disfigured, possibly by a skin cancer on his nose, although it was rumoured at the time that he had contracted syphilis.

The Elgin Marbles consist of 17 statues from the west pediments of the Parthenon, 15 metope panels (rectangular carved depictions of the battle between the centaurs – part human, part horse – and the lapiths, the Greek mythological warriors) and 247 feet of the Parthenon frieze. Many of the sculptures were originally painted in bright colours. We can recall from Chapter 3 that when Haydon first saw them he was completely captivated by their anatomical accuracy; it was clear to him that the Greeks had perfected their art by observing nature itself, not by studying the paintings and statues of any previous civilization. As he walked around the Marbles with Keats, pointing to this and commenting upon that, we can be sure that he would have emphasised their truth to nature and that Keats would have understood his meaning because he was a classicist who had been trained in anatomy. Haydon later wrote:

> I shall never forget the horses' heads – the feet in the metopes! I felt as if a divine truth had blazed inwardly upon my mind and I knew they would at last rouse the art of Europe from its slumber in the darkness.[139]

In talking about a 'divine truth', Haydon was in fact talking in scientific terms. He seems to have believed that the Greeks had managed to mould the bodies of men and animals while they were actually in motion:

> I have no doubt of the Ancients catching all the markings of instant exertion, by dashing something on that took the impression, then casting it, and making their own use of it, it is the only plan to attain certainty as you then have a momentary action set for ever, and can draw it at leisure...[140]

and

> Like the momentary beauties of a star – if, supposing [the artist's] mind was thoroughly versed in anatomy, he would not be able to give the shape by mere knowledge, if it remained in action so short a time, what method can be surer than moulding it instantly, casting it, and at leisure studying it?[141]

Haydon had filled pages of his diary with long and detailed anatomical descriptions of the Elgin Marbles. He had spent years amassing a collection of drawings and casts and had stated again and again that this muscle or that tendon was depicted exactly as it would have appeared if the moving man or galloping horse had been instantly captured, as if frozen in time. It was incumbent upon the modern artist to study the Marbles and become familiar with the perfection of Greek sculptural anatomy before he attempted to convey his own imaginative conceptions, his own 'fancies':

> This standard once fixed, and once seated in every man's mind, he will be able without error and without stumbling to vary it, according [to]

his own fancies, feelings or visionary conceptions – This I think was the principle of the Greeks…'[142]

Among dozens of remarks about the Marbles throughout Haydon's diaries and essays, these two comments – written many years apart – sum up his feelings about them. The first is from his autobiography:

> I foretold that they would prove themselves the finest things on earth, that they would overturn the false beau-ideal, where nature was nothing, and would establish the true beau-ideal, of which nature alone is the basis…[143]

and from his diary of 1813, written several years before he took Keats to see the Marbles:

> **Beauty of form** is but the vehicle of conveying Ideas, **but truth of conveyance** is the first object.[144] [My emphasis]

From the moment he first saw the Marbles, with David Wilkie in Piccadilly, this amalgamation of beauty and truth became central to Haydon's philosophy of art and stayed so for the rest of his life. Keats, too, was captivated by this idea. We have seen that he had a talent for *poetical* emulation which amounted to genius (writing wholly convincingly in the style of Spenser or Wordsworth) but the question now was whether he could empathise not just with a poem but with an *idea*, an intellectual concept, with the same degree of imaginative brilliance. For the time being, he was certain that the task was beyond his abilities. We know this because (as we are now coming to expect) Keats expressed his innermost thoughts and feelings in a poem. When he was back at his lodgings in Cheapside, he wrote a poem called *To B.R. Haydon, with a Sonnet Written on Seeing the Elgin Marbles*. It began:

> Haydon! forgive me that I cannot speak
> Definitively on these mighty things.
> Forgive me that I have not eagle's wings,
> That what I want I know not where to seek…

At the end of the poem, he acknowledged Haydon as the leading expert on the Elgin Marbles, the man who had proved all of the Marbles' detractors wrong (including Richard Payne Knight, who had publicly stated that they were Roman, not Greek), even comparing him with one of the Magi who followed the Star of Bethlehem to the cradle of the newborn Jesus:

> For when men stared at what was most divine
> With browless idiotism, o'erwise phlegm,
> Thou hadst beheld the Hesperian shine
> Of their star in the East, and gone to worship them.

Aware that the poem was weak and that he had not even started to explain the difficulties he was facing (as though he lacked 'eagle's wings'), Keats immediately began to think of a second poem. In this, he laments his lack of the 'godlike' powers he would need to articulate his feelings about the Elgin Marbles (powers akin to keeping the 'cloudy winds' fresh before dawn). Even thinking about such powers, such 'dim-conceivèd glories of the brain', brings him some emotional turmoil. (It may be worth pointing out here that a grave accent è adds a syllable in accordance with a rhyme scheme, thus 'conceivèd' is pronounced conceive-*ed*.) His ideas about the age of the Marbles, their immortality and immutability, are in fact so complex that they bring about a 'dizzy pain' as his imagination compares them, or 'mingles' them, with their antitheses, objects that are moving or fleeting and ephemeral. He uses as examples a ship's sail as it billows in the wind, the sun as it rises and sets each day and a shadow circling a large object. This second poem, a Petrarchan sonnet, is called, simply, *On seeing the Elgin Marbles*:

> My spirit is too weak – mortality
> Weighs heavily on me like unwilling sleep,
> And each imagined pinnacle and steep
> Of godlike hardship, tells me I must die
> Like a sick eagle looking at the sky.
> Yet 'tis a gentle luxury to weep
> That I have not the cloudy winds to keep
> Fresh for the opening of the morning's eye.
> Such dim-conceivèd glories of the brain
> Bring round the heart an indescribable feud;
> So do these wonders a most dizzy pain,
> That mingles Grecian grandeur with the rude
> Wasting of old Time, with a billowy main,
> A sun, a shadow of a magnitude.

Keats sent both poems to Haydon with copies to Hunt and Reynolds, and they were duly published in both the *Examiner* and the *Champion* the following Sunday. Aware that many people across London would be reading these two new poems, Haydon replied with a letter:

My Dear Keats,

Many thanks, my dear fellow, for your two noble sonnets. I know not a finer image than the comparison of a poet unable to express his high feelings to a sick eagle looking at the sky...I feel deeply the high and enthusiastic praise with which you have spoken of me in the first sonnet. Be assured you shall never repent it. The time shall come, if God spare my life, when you shall remember it with delight.

God bless you!

B.R. Haydon[145]

The truth was that after failing to secure a commission from the Grand Duke Nicholas, Haydon needed all the publicity and exposure he could get. His painting, *Christ's Entry into Jerusalem*, which it will be remembered was not actually a commission from anybody, just a speculative venture on Haydon's part, was taking an age to complete. It was very large, it depicted a crowd, and it was painted in such anatomical detail that after three years of work it was still only half completed. Haydon was now in desperate financial difficulties.

***

Debt in Regency England was a serious business. Thousands were incarcerated in dark, filthy, louse-infested debtors' prisons and, not having any means of paying their creditors, an unfortunate few were never released. Haydon knew that any of his creditors could at any time call in their debt and put him seriously at risk of a long spell in the King's Bench prison, a huge, high-walled edifice standing between the New Bridewell and Horsemonger Lane prisons in

Southwark. Around the time of the visit of the Grand Duke Nicholas, Haydon had approached Sir George Beaumont for 'pecuniary assistance'. Sir George, mindful of the runaway success of *Solomon* as well as Haydon's new-found reputation as a writer, considered that his financial distress must be a temporary affair and easily resolved, and so he had provided Haydon with some financial help and advice:

> Pray excuse me if I again take the opportunity of recommending some profitable mode of practice. I know you object to portraits… [but] the greatest artists have not considered the practice as beneath their notice… Indeed, my dear sir, you must attend to this necessary concern, or circumstances more mortifying than what I recommend cannot fail to attend you…[146]

Haydon, of course, refused to lower his sights from the grand ideal of High Art to paint family portraits for wealthy merchants or the petty nobility, even if his beloved Raphael had done so to the great advancement of his reputation and career. In any case, it was too late for Haydon to accept Sir George's caution that 'circumstances more mortifying' than portrait painting would attend him if he did not engage with this seemingly simple means of making money. Haydon was already in debt to the moneylenders, and he would be in their clutches for the rest of his life.

It was back in 1815, Haydon recounts, that he had first crossed the threshold of a moneylender's house. A friend of his who was already acquainted with the murky and secretive rituals of the moneylender had set up an appointment for Haydon with a man who, it was said, had amassed a fortune of £100,000. The first thing that Haydon noticed when he was standing outside the man's house was that there was an outer as well as an inner door, a facility which the visitor – 'the thief, the profligate, the murderer, the pickpocket, the seducer, the necessitous and the ruined' valued as shelter from notice. Haydon was well aware of his degradation. After many years of hard and devoted study and the attainment of great fame, he was now standing at the door of a moneylender 'like a culprit, poor [and] sinking fast to ruin'. He takes up the story:

> A head at this moment peeped through the glass… the door was cautiously opened, and a mean, skinny, malicious face said, 'Walk in…'. I went in and found his wife, who seemed quite accustomed to receive people in want. The wretch came in, surveying me under his little eyelids, which were red, inflamed, without lashes and pendent. 'Well, Mr Haydon, you want to borrow [a] hundred pounds.' 'I do.' He hummed and said he had respect for my talents but that he feared he could not do it. This was the usual artifice. He saw my anxiety, and with the wary practice of a villain hung back to raise the terms. I left him with a curse.[147]

Haydon's experienced friend intervened and the painter found himself back at the moneylender's house the next day. Haydon has embellished the story to make the man seem more despicable than he really was, to seem quite literally reptilian ('his little skinny lips drew back and smiled'). He was in fact a wine merchant as well as a moneylender and his house was 'respectable'. To keep within the usury laws (which since 1714 had limited the interest rate on a loan to

The Pursuit of Beauty and Truth

5%, with the punishment for transgression being severe), he did not charge excessive interest. The way in which he exploited his 'customers' and had amassed his fortune was by offering to sell some piece of domestic debris to the unfortunate and invariably desperate person to whom he was lending money ('I don't like dealing with gentlemen,' he said). The items he offered were bits of clothing, hats, books, paintings and the general paraphernalia that he had wrought from those who had been unable to make a repayment on time. He had a room full of these items and would ask 20 or 30 guineas for a book or a picture 'worth ten pence', add it to the loan and then charge a reasonable rate of interest on the whole amount. (A guinea was worth 21 shillings and a pound 20 shillings.) Haydon chose to 'buy' for 20 guineas a poor copy of a painting by Rubens, suspecting that the moneylender had placed it in a prominent position in order to catch his eye. So, for an advance of £100 and a 'ten pence' painting, Haydon now owed £121 at 5% interest with the 'loan' being due for repayment in three months' time.

Knowing he would not be able to repay the loan, Haydon quickly perfected the art of borrowing from one moneylender to pay another. The second moneylender he visited lived very close by, in Poland Street:

> I got him to the light; his eyes shrank; his face was the meanest I ever saw; the feeble mouth and little nose, brassy eyes, blotched skin, low forehead, and foetid smell, all announced a reptile.[148]

Now, two years after having suffered the humiliation of these first encounters with the moneylenders, and even without the burden of having to pay for rent and dinners, he was in even deeper trouble. He was still spending large amounts of money hiring the models he needed for the crowd scene in his picture (the faces of Wordsworth, Hazlitt and Keats were now in the picture as members of the crowd watching Jesus ride into Jerusalem, but the crowd was comprised of dozens of people), and he needed a regular flow of funds to pay Charles Smith in Piccadilly for the large orders of mineral pigments, solvents and oils that the painting was consuming. He was still buying books, and he was still buying prints. All the while he was keeping up the appearance of a stylish, sophisticated and generous host who moved in the highest circles of London society. In fact, he became so well known to the moneylenders, so reliable a source of income, that they eventually began to compete for his business, offering him a better rate of interest than their rivals.

After receiving the assistance and (unwanted) advice from Sir George Beaumont, he decided that he needed to move to a new studio, one large and airy enough to dissipate the solvent fumes that everyone who visited him found sickening. 'My room was so small,' he said, 'the air so confined, the effluvium of paint so overpowering, that many people of fashion advised me to move if I wished to save my life.' This was no idle rhetoric. Haydon's health was beginning to fail him again, just as it had when he was trying to complete *Solomon*. He had to stop work to spare his eyes, and he was 'shaking like an aspen leaf'.

***

John Hamilton Reynolds had read many of Keats' poems, including the *Chapman's Homer*, long before they appeared in print and by early March 1817 he had spent a lot of time in Keats' company, both at Hunt's house and Haydon's studio. Living in the heart of London, Reynolds, Keats and Haydon would have enjoyed an active social life, dining together in the many taverns around Cheapside and Oxford Street and watching performances in the theatres of Drury Lane and Covent Garden. (Haydon had always been an avid theatre-goer, and Reynolds reviewed performances for the *Champion*). Having thus got to know Keats as a poet and friend, Reynolds, the writer of *Safie*, *The Eden of the Imagination* and *The Naiad* made no secret of the fact that he thought Keats a better poet than himself. In fact, despite Keats having produced just a handful of youthful poems, Reynolds considered him to be a genius who would outshine most, if not all, of his contemporaries. The day after Keats and Haydon had been to see the Elgin Marbles, Haydon invited Reynolds, Keats and Charles Cowden Clarke to his studio in order to celebrate the publication of Keats' *Poems 1817*. (Hunt, to whom Keats' book was dedicated, was not invited because Haydon had not yet forgiven him for his behaviour at Horace Smith's dinner party; in any case, Keats had already celebrated the occasion with Hunt, and Hunt was now courting the Shelleys at their new house in Marlow.)

Despite Haydon's ill health and penurious state (and doubtless contributing to the latter), he was always unsparing with his wine and hospitality. Even when he made tea he was so generous that his friends would say, 'Let's go to Haydon's and drink tea in the Grand

Style.' It was probably there in Haydon's painting studio, beneath the towering painting of *Christ's Entry into Jerusalem* and amid Haydon's plaster casts, drawings and beautiful, leather-bound volumes, that Keats gave Reynolds an early presentation copy of his book (complete with an extra, hand-written poem). Reynolds treasured the book and ordered a second copy from the Olliers to be sent to a family friend, a man called Benjamin Bailey who was studying theology at Oxford University. Keats himself sent a presentation copy to Wordsworth at Rydal Mount in the Lake District 'with the Author's sincere Reverence'. Would this wider audience be as effusive in its praise as had been Hunt and his friends? It was a question that was worrying Keats. Haydon recorded in his dairy, about a fortnight later,

> Keats has published his first Poems, and great things indeed they promise. He is a sound young man, and will be a great one. There are parts in his 'Sleep and Poetry' equal to anything in English Poetry… Keats is really & truly the man after my own heart. We saw through each other at once, and I hope in God are friends forever.[149]

But even this genuine and heartfelt compliment was mild in comparison with Reynolds' review of *Poems 1817* in the *Champion* on Sunday 9 March, 1817. It appeared in the Literature section under the heading, 'Poems by John Keats, Price 6s, London, Ollier, Welbeck Street. 1817'. Reynolds wrote it anonymously:

> Here is a little volume, filled throughout with very graceful and genuine poetry… At a time when nothing is talked of but the power and passion of Lord Byron, and the playful and elegant fancy of

[Thomas] Moore, and the correctness of [Samuel] Rogers, and the sublimity and pathos of [Thomas] Campbell... a young man starts suddenly before us, with a genius that is likely to eclipse them all... Mr Keats is faced, or 'we have no judgement in an honest face,' to look at natural objects with his mind, as Shakespeare and Chaucer did, and not merely with his eye as nearly all modern poets do; to clothe his poetry with a grand intellectual light, and to lay his name in the lap of immortality...[150]

The article went on to quote large sections of Keats' poetry, from the *Imitation of Spenser*, *To Charles Cowden Clarke*, *To My Brother George*, *Sleep and Poetry* and *Chapman's Homer*, the latter being quoted in full. It is true that there were some minor criticisms; Reynolds noted some technical defects, and he wasn't particularly enamoured of some of the earlier poems – *To Hope* and *On Receiving a Curious Shell* being among them. But all in all, Reynolds' article was praise indeed. Keats was somewhat startled by the review. He was astute enough to know that it was extremely subjective, written by a new friend who was also young and ambitious. He wrote Reynolds a slightly guarded letter of thanks:

My dear Reynolds,

Your kindness affects me so sensibly that I can merely put down a few mono- sentences – your criticism only makes me extremely anxious that I should not deceive you.

It's the finest thing by God – as Hazlitt would say. However, I hope I may not deceive you...[151]

Haydon was not pleased with the review. He considered Keats to be his own protégé, if not his own discovery, and with Hunt now focusing his attention on Shelley he was becoming jealous of the attention that Keats was receiving from Reynolds. He wrote Keats a most extraordinary letter, one that confirms in abundance Haydon's loneliness, his desperate desire for success, his need for understanding and his desire for a sympathetic companion. He was in ill health at this time and even more worried about money than usual, so we can only assume he wrote this rather morbid letter when he was particularly tired, distracted or anxious:

My dear Keats,

Consider this letter a sacred secret – Often have I sat by my fire after a day's effort, as the dusk approached, and a gauzey veil seemed dimming all things – and mused on what I had done and with a burning glow on what I would do till filled with fury I have seen the faces of the almighty dead crowd into my room, and I have sunk down and prayed the great Spirit that I might be worthy to accompany these immortal beings in their immortal glories… My dear Keats, the Friends who surrounded me were sensible to what talent I had – but no one reflected my enthusiasm with that burning ripeness of soul, my heart yearned for sympathy – believe me from my soul in you I have found one – you add fire, when I am exhausted & excite fury afresh – I offer my heart and intellect and experience… I have read your Sleep and Poetry – it is a flash of lightening that will round men from their occupations, and keep them trembling for the crash of thunder that will follow –

God bless you and let our hearts be buried in each other.

B.R. Haydon

I'll be at Reynolds' tonight but latish

March 1817 –

I confide these feelings to your honour.[152]

The crash of thunder never came. By early April 1817, just a few weeks after its publication, it was clear that Keats' book was not selling. His younger brother George, who it will be remembered worked in Abbey's counting house as a clerk and who was more accustomed to moving in London society than was Keats, took it upon himself to write to the Olliers. Whether he complained too much (perhaps blaming the Olliers for the lack of sales) or was just impolite we cannot tell, but when James Ollier (Charles Ollier's younger brother and business partner) wrote back, the reply came as a shock:

3, Welbeck Street, 29th April, 1817

Sir, we regret that your brother ever requested us to publish his book, or that our opinion of its talent should have led us to acquiesce in undertaking it. We are, however, much obliged to you for relieving us from the unpleasant necessity of declining any further connexion with it, which we must have done, as we think the curiosity is satisfied, and the sale has dropped. By far the greater number of persons who have purchased it from us have found fault with it in such plain terms, that we have in many cases offered to take the book back rather than be annoyed with the ridicule which has, time after time, been showered upon it. In fact, it was only on Saturday last that we were under the mortification of having our own opinion of its merits flatly contradicted by a gentleman, who told us he considered it 'no better than a take in'. These are unpleasant imputations for any one in business to labour under, but we should have borne them and concealed their existence from you had not the style of your note shewn us that such delicacy would be quite thrown away. We shall take means without delay for ascertaining the number of copies on hand, and you shall be informed accordingly.

Your most, &c.

C & J. Ollier[153]

Once Keats had recovered from the initial surprise, he turned to his friends for help and advice. James Ollier stated that Keats had 'requested' that the Olliers publish his book, and ended his letter by saying that George Keats would be informed of the number copies 'on hand' (the inference being that he could collect them), and this strongly suggests that Keats had indeed paid for the publication and printing himself. What was he to do now? Unlike Shelley, he could not afford to lose a substantial sum of money on a failed publishing venture. His only source of income was what remained of a meagre inheritance administered by someone – Richard Abbey – who had disapproved of his decision to give up medicine in the first place. Abbey was clearly not going to be any more sympathetic to Keats' predicament now.

Fortunately, Keats had not been idle. Having anticipated a rather less dramatic and costly dénouement for his first book, he had been planning an ambitious new poem. It would be called *Endymion* and was to be an attempt to emulate Shelley's achievement in writing

Alastor, or the Spirit of Solitude, an epic poem of 720 lines. Keats knew from *Lemprière's Classical Dictionary* and other sources that Endymion was the youth that the moon goddess Cynthia saw asleep on Mount Latmos; she was so struck by his physical beauty that she came down from heaven every night to join him on the hillside. Keats thought the story had great potential; his poem was going to contain no fewer than 4000 lines.

Reynolds quietly stepped in and brought Keats to the attention of his own publisher, John Taylor, who with his business partner James Hessey duly offered to publish Keats' new poem under the Taylor & Hessey imprint, and even gave him a little bit of financial assistance. Keats was understandably relieved and forever grateful to Reynolds. He now turned his attention to *Endymion*, a poem whose 4000 lines are little read today, but whose first line, *A thing of beauty is a joy forever*, is so famous that it is known by almost everyone. John Taylor later wrote that 'Keats will be the brightest Ornament of this Age.'[154]

Chapter 8

The love of fame is a species of emulation.
William Hazlitt: *On Posthumous Fame*

Even before George Keats wrote to the Olliers, Haydon had advised Keats to take himself away from London for a while. The young poet needed time to reflect, said Haydon, time to think, time to improve himself. For Haydon, 'self improvement' meant transforming oneself into a true scholar, memorising whole tracts of great literature, perhaps learning a new language. Keats agreed that he needed to leave London, and he almost immediately began to emulate Haydon in his scholarship; he even began to build a modest library.

Haydon had always placed Shakespeare alongside Phidias and Homer as being one of those rare men of genius who capture the very *truth* of nature in their art. Many years later his son was to say that Haydon put Shakespeare 'next to Holy Scripture itself'. We have already seen that he constantly referred to Shakespeare, and frequently quoted him in his diary and later in his autobiography:

> Phidias, Homer and Shakespeare were the most learned of all men in nature. All other learning ought to be a means to adorn and improve the learning of nature. Every fault will be excused if that learning be true, whilst no acquirement will interest if that be deficient.[155]

Keats had already come face to face with Phidias, so to speak, at the British Museum and as we have seen, he was so overwhelmed by the Elgin Marbles that he was unable to adequately express himself in words. He was already familiar with Homer, too, after having discovered Chapman's translation. He now began to think about Shakespeare in a much more serious and intensive manner. Hitherto, Keats had enjoyed 'spouting Shakespeare' with Haydon, because he had read Shakespeare as he had read Spenser, Virgil and Tasso, with an eye for the beauty of the verse and the 'felicity and power' of the epithets. Haydon's influence now raised him to a higher level of Shakespearean scholarship. In March 1813, Haydon had read *Othello* all through in one sitting and then written several pages of analysis in his diary:

> My heart beat, my frame perspired, I wept for Desdemona, cursed Iago, pitied Othello, **with all the acuteness of reality**. I do not remember ever to have been so touched, so completely knocked up with agitation.[156] [My emphasis.]

It is worth noting that Haydon wrote this comment about a year and a half before Hazlitt wrote the following in a review of Mr Kean's *Macbeth* in The Champion:

> If to *invent according to Nature* be the true definition of genius, Shakespeare had more of this quality than any other writer. He might

be said to have been a joint-worker with Nature, and to have created an imaginary world of his own, which has all the appearance and truth of reality.[157]

Keats now bought a compact, seven-volume edition of Shakespeare from a bookshop in London. It was printed in 1814 by the innovative Charles Whittingham at his printing shop in Chiswick (Whittingham began the trend of printing cheap, illustrated editions of popular authors) and sold at various booksellers in the city, including Gale, Curtis and Fenner at 23 Paternoster Row which was just a short walk down Cheapside from Keats' lodgings. Each of the seven volumes was a sturdy little book and deliberately made to be 'pocket size'; there were four or five plays in each one, with a preface by Dr Johnson in volume 1.

Keats wrote his name 'John Keats' and the date '1817' on the title pages of volumes 1 and 2, and began reading. The first play in volume 1 was *The Tempest*, Shakespeare's story of the magician Prospero and his beautiful daughter Miranda who share an enchanted island with the spirit Ariel and monster Caliban. Any description, line or passage which he found interesting, Keats would mark with a pen; and thus began a habit he was to continue for the rest of his life. Before long, the play had completely captured his imagination, and the book was full of markings.

Wondering where he should go for his period of solitude and reflection, Keats decided to visit an island that at the time still had a largely unspoilt and evocative landscape of castles and woods, rivers and beaches. He went along to the General Post Office in Lombard Street and booked a passage on a mail coach to the Isle of Wight.

***

The Southampton mail coach picked up its passengers at the Bell and Crown, a prominent coaching inn right next door to the magnificent neoclassical facade of the Furnivals Inn at Holborn. Like the White Horse Cellars in Piccadilly, it was a busy, bustling place full of porters and passengers carrying luggage to and from the many coaches departing for the south-west of England. Keats climbed aboard the coach on Monday, 14 April 1817. In his luggage, along with his clothes, were the seven-volume set of Whittingham's Shakespeare, a book of Spenser's poetry, some pens and ink and a picture drawn by Haydon. Unlike the regular passenger or stage coaches, the mail coach's primary purpose was to deliver letters and parcels in a timely fashion, which meant that passenger comfort was always a secondary consideration. The mail coaches differed from the stage coaches in that their livery was the same throughout the kingdom; the doors and lower panels were maroon, the upper panels black and the wheels red. On the front was the insignia of the reigning monarch and at the rear was the number of the coach – 41 in the case of the Southampton coach. A guard stood outside at the back, above the mailbox. He had a blunderbuss with pistols and ammunition. Absolutely nobody, not even a troop of soldiers, was allowed to get in the way of the mail coach once it was on the road. Pulled by four horses – these were regularly changed at the coaching inns – it was fast, efficient and virtually unstoppable. The main dangers it faced were the roads themselves, little more than unpaved dirt tracks full of ruts and potholes. Coaching accidents were common, and sometimes fatal.

Keats climbed up and sat on top of the coach. Once underway, the coaches swayed and rocked so much that the topside passengers had to hang on for their lives. Southampton was 85 miles away and the journey would take all night; after travelling south-west out of London the coach (lit with oil lamps during the hours of darkness) went through the towns of Brentford, Staines, Bagshot, Farnham, Alton and Alfresford before rattling through the city of Winchester and, an hour after sunrise, pulling into Southampton. Before reaching Winchester, Keats gave in to the cold and paid the extra few shillings required to climb inside for a little bit of sleep.

He disembarked in Southampton's High Street and went for breakfast at one of the city's many inns. After breakfast he took a walk around the town in the early morning light. The bottom of Southampton's High Street led on to the Town Quay just as it does today, although the huge area of docks we find there now did not yet exist. Adjacent to the Town Quay was a custom house (smugglers kept the authorities very busy) and it was probably here that Keats enquired about the next ferry to the Isle of Wight. He then returned to the inn and wrote a letter to be taken back to his brothers in London by a returning mail coach:

> I am safe at Southampton – after having ridden three stages outside and the rest in for it began to be very cold. I did not know the Names of any of the Towns I passed through – all I can tell you is that

sometimes I saw dusty hedges – sometimes ponds… I felt rather lonely this morning so I went and unbox'd a Shakespeare – 'There's my Comfort'. I went immediately after Breakfast to Southampton Water where I enquired for the Boat to the Isle of Wight… it will go at 3, so shall I after having taken a Chop…[158]

'*Here's* my Comfort' is a phrase uttered by a character, Stephano, in *The Tempest*. He enters the scene with a bottle of drink in his hand, singing a song:

> I shall no more to sea, to sea,
> Here shall I die ashore.
> This is a very scurvy tune to sing at a man's funeral.
> Well, here's my comfort. [Drinks]

After his dinner, or 'chop', Keats caught the 3 o'clock ferry, probably a wherry, an attractive wooden boat with both oars and sail which was very common around the Channel ports at the time. He was already coming to love the sea. We can recall how even as a schoolboy he had enjoyed the imagery of the 'sea-shouldering whales' of Spenser, and how Charles Cowden Clarke had written particularly about his love of the image of Ulysses in Homer, 'the sea had soak'd his heart through'. At Margate, he had written of the sea's

> …vastness, its blue green,
> Its ships, its rocks, its caves, its hopes, its fears,
> Its voice mysterious, which whoso hears
> Must think on what will be, and what has been.

Now he was sailing to a beautiful, largely unspoilt island with a copy of *The Tempest* in his pocket.

Some parts of the island were industrialised. Cowes in 1817 was a bustling port and naval dockyard. On the approach, Keats would have seen the town's houses and shops seeming to rise above the harbour, with wooded hills beyond. After disembarking from the ferry he shared a coach from Cowes to Newport, about five miles up river, with another traveller but he was disappointed to find that a large military barracks, the Albany Barracks, had been built on the approach road. He arrived in Newport and took lodgings, but soon decided to move to a different part of the island. Newport was a river port with a series of wharves and mills so it was too busy and noisy for a young man who was seeking the peace and solitude he needed to study and write. He decided to spend just one night in Newport before exploring the island in search of new lodgings the next day.

***

On Monday 7 April, exactly a week before Keats left London for Southampton, Haydon had written in his diary:

> An old Lady… told [Keats'] Brother George, when she asked what John was doing, and on his replying that he had determined to become a poet – that this was very odd, because when he could just speak, instead of answering questions put to him, he would always make a rhyme of the last word people said, and then laugh…[159]

The task that Keats had set himself with *Endymion* was to 'make a rhyme of the last word' in 4000 lines of heroic couplets, a verse meter of rhyming pairs in iambic pentameter (the five syllable 'foot', or rhythm of words which was favoured by Shakespeare). Here are the first few lines of *Endymion* – as we noted earlier, he had already begun the poem before he left London for Southampton:

> A thing of beauty is a joy for ever:
> Its loveliness increases, it will never
> Pass into nothingness; but still will keep
> A bower quiet for us, and a sleep
> Full of sweet dreams, and health, and quiet breathing.
> Therefore, on every morrow, we are wreathing
> A flowery band to bind us to the earth,
> Spite of despondence, of the inhuman dearth
> Of noble natures…

The task before him was to continue the rhyming couplets ending, *ever, never; keep, sleep; breathing, wreathing; earth, dearth* and so on 2000 times. It was an immense undertaking, a 'test of invention' as Keats called it. He planned to write the poem in four books of roughly 1000 lines each and he knew it would take him months rather than weeks to complete. The book (at 4000 lines, it would be a whole book) was to be finished, as Keats himself said, by the autumn, '…with universal tinge of sober gold… all about me.' It is likely that he didn't sleep very well during that first night in Newport; he was exhausted from the journey and later said that he was rather 'narvus'.

***

Back in London, Haydon was having recurring problems with his health and was, as always, worrying about his debts. His eyes were failing him again so he spent a lot of time just sitting in his rooms, musing on such subjects as Voltaire's views on religion, Shakespeare's

Last Will & Testament and the failure of the British Government to encourage the commissioning of historical paintings. He was missing Keats' company but Reynolds and William Hazlitt were regular companions in his studio. The three men had plenty to talk about: Reynolds' *Naiad* had recently been published and was dedicated: *To Benjamin Robert Haydon, Esq., this tale is inscribed by one who admires his genius and values his friendship.*

Hazlitt's new book of essays, *The Round Table*, had been out for just a few weeks, and his penultimate theatrical review for *The Examiner*, called *Mr Booth's Iago*, had been published six weeks earlier. (Hazlitt suspected that the actor Junius Brutus Booth, who was then playing Iago at the Drury Lane Theatre, had merely been imitating the greatest actor of the day, Edmund Kean, and thus had 'the chameleon quality of reflecting… all objects that come in contact with him'. Keats had been delighted by this imagery, as we shall see.)

Haydon had other friends, of course, and had recently been reconciled with Leigh Hunt because a few weeks earlier Hunt had called on him unexpectedly and found him reading a copy of Hunt's latest poem, *Rimini*. Haydon was actually pleased that Hunt had made a show of appeasement:

> Old associations crowded on us and we soon forgot our 'irritations' and talked instead of Raphael and Shakespeare. There is no resisting him, I got as delighted as ever by his wit, his poetry, his taste, his good humour… Peace to him. I would never have called again if he had not called on me. I'll now go and see him as usual.[160]

Hunt can't have told him that he and his family were about to move out of Hampstead to Marlow, to live with Shelley and his family.

***

Keats woke up in his Newport lodgings and decided to explore the island, to find somewhere to settle. From Newport he took a coach down to the little village of Shanklin on the southern coast. Shanklin was a village of perhaps 150 residents and the surrounding landscape was noted for its natural beauty, particularly the 'Shanklin Chine' a cleft in a 300-foot cliff which led down past an old oak tree, a cottage and some fisherman's huts to the sea. When Keats walked down it, one side was covered in primroses all the way to the water.

Many artists and writers in Keats' day took notebooks with them on their travels. Shelley's numerous vellum-bound notebooks still exist and are full of ideas and drawings (Shelley had a penchant for sketching trees and sailboats); these notebooks are now kept in the Bodleian Library in Oxford and the New York Public Library. Keats, however, just scribbled his thoughts on scraps of paper and in the margins of his books. In fact, in his writing he was surprisingly messy and disorganised – we noted earlier that he underlined and marked whole passages of *The Tempest* in his brand new volume of Shakespeare, and his markings were anything but neat. They were wavy, scratchy and blotchy because the underlinings were drawn without any sort of rule. Pens were, at the time, mere goose feathers cut with a 'pen knife' so they wore out quickly and a writer would require several feathers in the course of a day's work. Each of them was liable to leave globs of ink on paper and fingers. The ink, though, faded over time; it was known as iron gall ink and had for centuries been made of tannin from the gall of oak and nut trees. (Keats' former friend from his days as a student apothecary, Henry Stephens, was destined to invent a new, more indelible type of ink). Keats later complained of a fastidious friend who

> ...affronts my indolence and luxury by pulling out of his knapsack, first his paper; secondly his pens; and last, his ink. Now I would not care if he would change a little. I say now, why not take his pens first sometimes? But I might as well tell a hen to hold up her head before she drinks, instead of afterwards.[161]

Once he had descended the Shanklin Chine, Keats put his thoughts about *Endymion* to one side and composed a Petrarchan sonnet called *On the Sea*. As well as studying *The Tempest* in volume 1 of his Shakespeare, he had been reading *King Lear* in volume 7 and he later said that the line of Edgar to the recently blinded Duke of Gloucester, when Gloucester *thought* they were approaching a cliff at Dover, 'Hark, do you hear the sea?' (*King Lear*, Act IV, Scene VI) had haunted him intensely. The point, of course, was that there was no sea to hear; the Duke of Gloucester wanted to be brought to a cliff in order to throw himself off and his (disguised) son, Edgar, wanted him to believe he was nearing it. Now here was Keats, actually standing in front of the sea as it moved across the sand and shingle below the cliffs at Shanklin. And he listened to it intently.

On the Sea is a beautiful and technically brilliant evocation of this single experience. Keats used the technique of alliteration (as we have seen, the repetitive use of a letter or sound) and onomatopoeia (words which when spoken imitate the sound of the thing being described) throughout the whole of the octave to replicate the hissing of the waves across sand and shingle, as, for example:

> It keeps eternal **whis**perings around
> Desolate **sh**ores…

The octave describes the immense bulk and power of the sea but notes that the twice-daily tides are controlled by the moon goddess, Hecate, who (as Tooke's *Pantheon* had informed Keats) keeps 'all the ghosts and spirits in subjection'. Sometimes the sea is very gentle and stays so for days until the wind heaves it up again. In the sestet, he implores people who are 'vexed' and have 'tired eyes' to enjoy the palliative effect of looking at the sea, and those who have been subjected to too much noise (the implication being people who are trapped in towns and cities, as Keats had been himself for almost the whole of his life) to sit near a cavern and simply listen to it. You will be lost to yourself, as Keats had been. You will 'brood', as he had brooded. When, finally, some intervening thought brings you back to yourself, you will be aware of the 'music' of the sea (the verb 'quired' in the last line is an archaic form of 'choired'). Here is the final version of Keats' *On the Sea*, with its 'whispering' octave:

> It keeps eternal whisperings around
> Desolate shores, and with its mighty swell
> Gluts twice ten thousand caverns, till the spell
> Of Hecate leaves them their old shadowy sound.
> Often 'tis in such gentle temper found
> That scarcely will the very smallest shell

> Be moved for days from where it sometime fell,
> When last the winds of heaven were unbound.
> O ye! who have your eye-balls vexed and tired,
> Feast them on the wideness of the sea;
> O ye! whose ears are dinned with uproar rude,
> Or fed too much with cloying melody,
> Sit ye near some old cavern's mouth and brood
> Until ye start, as if the sea-nymphs quired!

There are references to sea nymphs and magical spells in Shakespeare's *Tempest* and, as we noted earlier, Keats himself says that a phrase about *hearing* the sea had 'haunted' him. But it is possible that a starting point for *On the Sea* was a piece of music *about* the sea, the beautiful terzettino, *Soave sia il vento* [May the wind be gentle] from Mozart's opera, *Cosi fan tutte*. Keats would certainly have been familiar with it. Italian opera was staged at the King's Theatre in the Haymarket throughout the 1810s, and Leigh Hunt had reviewed *Cosi fan tutte* for the *Examiner*. A seat in the gallery cost just five shillings and the price remained the same for decades. Opera was also performed at Covent Garden; on 11 April 1812, Haydon wrote in his diary: 'At the Opera in the evening. The most delightful ballet I ever saw.' From 1813 onwards, concerts, including selections from *Cosi fan tutte*, were performed by The Philharmonic Society of London at the Argyll Rooms on the corner of King Street, just around the corner from Haydon's studio in Great Marlborough Street.[162] Finally, it will be remembered that Keats' school friend Edward Holmes was Mozart's first English biographer, and Keats still met him occasionally at the house of a mutual friend, the musician Vincent Novello, where Mozart was played.

Keats loved Mozart's music. He called Mozart 'divine' and once said that the beauty of a woman had kept him awake one night 'as a tune of Mozart's might do'. *Soave sia il vento* is an aria that a lover of Mozart could hardly fail to recall if he had escaped from the city and was standing on the shore watching the movement and contemplating the 'temper' and the 'music' of the sea:

Soave sia il vento [May the wind be gentle]
Tranquilla sia l'onda [May the waves be calm]
Ed ogni elemento [And may every one of the elements]
Benigno risponda [Answer warmly]
Ai nostri desir [To our desires]

Whether Keats wrote *On the Sea* while standing on the shore at Shanklin as scratchy scribblings on a scrap of paper, or composed it more carefully back in his lodgings at Newport, we will never know, but it was included in a letter to Reynolds the next day. By that time, however, he had packed up his meagre belongings and moved to new lodgings, about 15 minutes walk from the centre of Newport, on the road to Carisbrooke.

***

Keats was worried about Reynolds, and with good reason. Reynolds had by now given up his job at the Amicable Assurance Company to work full time for the *Champion*; this was a risk which was mitigated by the fact that Leigh Hunt's wealthy friend, the stockbroker Horace Smith, had bought a part share in the newspaper. Reynolds remained by far the major contributor and supplied a constant stream of theatrical reviews from Drury Lane and Covent Garden (he had an almost encyclopaedic knowledge of Jacobean and Elizabethan drama, and, like Haydon, almost worshipped Shakespeare), as well as book reviews, essays and poems. But for all his hard work and dedication, Reynolds knew that a successful journalist could never be as famous and wealthy as a successful poet. Partly because of his early precocity and promise, partly because of the expectations of those who knew and respected him (Leigh Hunt especially), but mostly because he was by now in love with a young woman and wanted to earn enough money to provide for her, Reynolds was becoming increasingly desperate to attain fame as a poet. Popular poems sold in huge quantities at this time – William Cowper's 6000-line poem, *The Task*, was published in 1785 and was still selling 30 years later, while *Childe Harolde's Pilgrimage* had made Lord Byron famous almost literally overnight.

However, the sheer quantity of Reynolds' output affected its quality so that it rarely rose above the level of competent literary reportage – he emulated Hazlitt in his theatrical reviews, for example and his review of Keats' *Poems* shows us that he sometimes lacked balance in his judgement. To make things worse, there was an increasing amount of competition in the market place. The introduction of the swift and powerful Stanhope Iron Printing Press in the first decade of the nineteenth century, with a selling price of around 70 guineas, had made newspaper publishing accessible to anybody with a political agenda and a modest sum to invest. There were at least 50 newspapers and magazines printed in London at the time that Reynolds worked for *The Champion*, many of them with offices clustered around the Strand and Catherine Street and, even with Reynolds' prolific output, *The Champion* couldn't attract a large enough readership to make it viable. In 1816, Horace Smith and the newspaper's other shareholder, the writer, publisher and editor, John Scott, sold *The Champion* to a Mr Jennyns, and though Scott and Reynolds continued to work on the paper, sometime around August 1816 Scott went to live in Paris, leaving Reynolds with an even greater burden of work.

By the time Keats left for the Isle of Wight, Reynolds was afflicted with ill health, probably brought on by over-work (he suffered from regular bouts of ill health throughout his life). We noted earlier that Reynolds had recently published a book, *The Naiad and Other Poems*, and he was now trying to write another, *The Romance of Youth*, but had done little or nothing with it in recent weeks because he had taken to his bed. Not long after writing to thank him for his (rather over-enthusiastic) review of his own *Poems*, Keats had written to Reynolds again, imploring him to look after his health but also to follow his – Keats' – example and settle down without distractions to the work in hand:

> …You must soon bring all your present troubles to a close, and so must I, but we must, like the Fox, prepare for a fresh swarm of flies. Banish money – Banish sofas – Banish Wine – Banish Music; but right

> Jack Health, honest Jack Health, true Jack Health – Banish Health and banish all the world...[163]

Reynolds would have recognised and appreciated Keats' parody of Falstaff's speech to Prince Henry in Act II, Scene IV of Shakespeare's *Henry IV, Part 1*:

> ...banish Peto, banish Bardolph... but for sweet Jack Falstaff, kind Jack Falstaff... banish plump Jack, and banish all the world.

It was only a week or two since Haydon had advised Keats to leave London and 'improve' himself, but in that short space of time Keats had written two letters and each had contained Shakespearean allusions – a quotation from *The Tempest* ('There's my comfort') in the letter to his brothers, and a parody of *Henry IV, Part 1* in the letter to Reynolds. (Reynolds himself regularly quoted Shakespeare in his own letters – three of his letters to Haydon survive from late 1816 and two of them contain allusions to Shakespeare.) Keats' next letter would also be written to Reynolds; it was to be the first of a series of outwardly playful but increasingly thoughtful letters which show just how deeply Keats was reading Shakespeare, how desperately he was missing his friends – especially Reynolds – and how bravely he was facing the challenge he had set himself.

***

Having nursed his eyes for a fortnight, Haydon had recovered sufficiently that he could return to his work on *Christ's Entry into Jerusalem*. It is astonishing to think that, even taking its huge size into account, Haydon had been working on this single painting for three years and it would take him another three years to complete. Of course, he did not know that at the time; he actually felt he was making good progress. Many of the central characters (the centurion, the Samaritan woman, Jairus and his daughter, St Peter, St John, etc.) were now complete. All were as anatomically correct as Haydon could make them and all were dressed in historically accurate clothing. Their cloaks of red, black, gold and white, their head dresses, jewellery and even the straps on their sandals were all, thought Haydon, exactly as they would have been worn at the time that Jesus entered Jerusalem. The various characters had been harmoniously arranged around the central figure of Jesus riding an ass. When Haydon wanted to paint an ass, or a horse, it was brought to his studio (or, at least, to the ground floor) so that he could study it and measure it and sketch it, this despite his having sketched and dissected many animals (and several humans) in the preceding years. He had always been, and still was, painstakingly thorough in his research.

Around the time Keats was preparing to leave for the Isle of Wight, Haydon was distracted by an argument between Hazlitt and Wordsworth. The lofty poet Wordsworth and the brilliant critic Hazlitt had once been firm friends, but Hazlitt now considered Wordsworth to be a political turncoat and often said so publicly, especially when reviewing Wordsworth's poetry in the newspapers. For his part, Wordsworth considered Hazlitt to be beneath him both socially and intellectually. It was an affront to Wordsworth's genius that Hazlitt even considered himself capable of understanding, let alone criticising, Wordsworth's poetry. (Hazlitt, of course, was more than capable.)

Haydon, as a friend of both men, always found himself in the middle of their quarrels. It is not to his credit that he invariably sided with the man to whom he was currently writing or speaking, whilst always maintaining a friendship with the other. Here's an extract from a letter that Wordsworth wrote to Haydon on Monday, 7 April 1817 from his study at Rydal Mount, his home in the Lake District:

> … Where is Scott [of the *Champion*], and is he well? … I have ceased to be a reader of the 'Champion' for several months, supposing that he had discontinued writing in it, and not approving the tone of its politics. The miscreant, Hazlitt, continues, I have heard, his abuse of… myself, in the 'Examiner'. I hope that you do not associate with the fellow; he is not a proper person to be admitted into respectable society, being the most perverse and malevolent creature that ill-luck has ever thrown in my way. Avoid him, he is a ------ [word missing] and this I understand is the general opinion where he is known in London.[164]

Haydon replied on 15 April. He reminded Wordsworth of a scandalous, historical incident widely known to Hazlitt's friends. Back in 1803, during a visit to the Lake District, Hazlitt had been involved in a fracas with a village girl and been run out of the village by the locals. Over the years, the story had been retold and embellished with petty sexual intonations such that it was now understood that Hazlitt had deserved all that he had got from the affronted villagers, and Wordsworth (or Coleridge, if Coleridge was telling the tale) had become known as the hero of the hour, saving Hazlitt from his pursuers. Here is an extract from Haydon's reply – it will be remembered that this incident in Wordsworth's 'neighbourhood' had occurred 14 years earlier:

> With respect to Hazlitt, I think his motives are easily enough discernible. Had you condescended to visit him when he praised your 'Excursion' [Wordsworth's latest poem], just before you came to town, his vanity would have been soothed and his virulence softened. He was conscious of what an emergency you had helped him from; he was conscious of his conduct while in your neighbourhood, and then your taking no notice of his praise added to his acrid feelings. I see him scarcely ever, and then not at my own house… My turn will come with Hazlitt, for he has the malignant morbidity of early failure in the same pursuit [i.e. painting]… In the 'Edinburgh Encyclopaedia' speaking of English Art, he mentioned every living painter now eminent, but me! By leaving me out, the blockhead, he made people remark it, and so he has, in fact, done me good…[165]

Exactly three weeks later, on 6 May, we find this entry in Haydon's diary:

> Hazlitt sat to me for a head. I never had so pleasant [a] sitter. He amused me beyond all description…[166]

This new but growing inconsistency in Haydon's behaviour towards his friends has the same source as the 'sacred secret' letter that he wrote to Keats. The fact was that Haydon's unshakeable confidence in his intellectual and artistic abilities was beginning to show signs of weakening. He had never doubted that he was a genius and that he was destined to create a new Renaissance in English art, but he was now beginning to worry that his friends were starting to lose faith in him and were beginning to avoid him. It will be remembered from Chapter 7 that he had written to Keats:

> My dear Keats, the Friends who surrounded me were sensible to what talent I had – but no one reflected my enthusiasm with that burning ripeness of soul, my heart yearned for sympathy…

By May 1817, his health was almost broken by over-work, and the sheer weight of his debts was beginning to overwhelm him. He knew that he had no hope whatsoever of paying his creditors (and avoiding prison) unless he completed *Christ's Entry into Jerusalem* and then sold it for a very large sum. During a conversation with Horace Smith, possibly at one of Haydon's Sunday gatherings, it was suggested that he try to raise a large loan and move to a new studio. 'If you stay here you cannot live,' said Smith, referring to the stench of paint and solvent fumes. 'Many people say they become faint after a few minutes.' Haydon agreed that moving to a new studio would be seen as an investment; he could regain his health and his energy and complete his painting more quickly. It seems, however, that by now he had exhausted his credit even with the moneylenders.

Haydon wrote a letter requesting a loan to an M.P. called George Watson, a man who had recently come into a very large fortune. He never received a reply but later found out that Watson had considered his request a liberty. Horace Smith suggested he approach Jeremiah Harman, the head of a company of merchant traders, Harman & Co. They had interests in warehouses and wharves, and had offices right in the heart of the City, at Adam's Court in Old Broad Street, just off Threadneedle Street. Jeremiah Harman was a governor of the Bank of England and, of interest to Haydon, an important art collector. Haydon was only faintly acquainted with this wealthy and influential member of London's financial elite (he said he met him 'by accident' so Harman may have met Haydon through Horace Smith whose office was just across the street from Harman's office), but he decided to approach him for help anyway.

Harman initially rebuffed him by pointing out that he had more claims on his generosity than he could possibly meet, but he left his door open by saying that Haydon was welcome to visit him at his office in Adam's Court if he felt it would make any difference. Haydon duly went along and laid out his case. *Solomon* sold for a handsome sum, and his latest masterpiece (there is no doubt that Haydon considered *Christ's Entry* to be a masterpiece) was progressing well but Haydon was in very ill health due to the unsuitability of his current lodgings. If Mr Harman would lend him the money required to move to more suitable lodgings, he would insure the painting in Harman's name, and give him the policy. Harman was clearly persuaded because he arranged a loan of £300, the amount Haydon had calculated he would need to move into and furnish a new studio. With the money in hand, Haydon returned with renewed energy to his painting of *Christ's Entry into Jerusalem* but he was not quite as confident as he had always been that he was going to make Sir Joshua Reynolds' dream of a new Renaissance a reality.

With his isolation growing, his debts mounting and his health failing, he was now working for his own salvation.

Chapter 9

Most friendship is feigning...
Shakespeare: *As You Like It*

On the western outskirts of Newport there is a fork in the main road where the busy Carisbrooke Road meets the Castle Road. The area was called New Village at the time Keats was visiting the Isle of Wight, and a near-contemporary map shows that it was very much a rural location with no fewer than three water mills on the nearby Lukeley stream. A lady called Mrs Cook had a guest house in New Village, and Keats rented one of her rooms. He moved in the day after he wrote *On the Sea*.

Mrs Cook, 'an old lady' according to Keats, had a picture of Shakespeare hanging in the hallway. When she learned that her young guest was a poet who had come to the Isle of Wight to find the peace and inspiration he needed to write a book, she allowed him to take the picture and hang it in his room. After unpacking his clothes and books, and putting up the portrait of Shakespeare, Keats went out to explore the area.

Walking around the ruins of Carisbrooke Castle, with its walls covered in smooth green ivy and its colony of jackdaws, Keats discovered what was to become a favourite place where he could sit and read his books. It was a far cry from the slums of Southwark and the noisy thoroughfares of Cheapside; this was a rural idyll. Once back in his room at Mrs Cook's he settled down to write a letter to Reynolds, to describe his visit to Shanklin Chine the day before:

> Shanklin is a most beautiful place; sloping wood and meadow ground reach round the Chine, which is a cleft between the cliffs of the depth of nearly 300 feet at least. This cleft is filled with trees and bushes in the narrow part, and as it widens becomes bare, if it were not for primroses on one side, which spread to the very verge of the Sea, and some fisherman's huts on the other, perched midway in the Balustrades of beautiful green Hedges along their steps down to the sands. But the sea, Jack, the sea – the little waterfall – then the white cliff – then St Catherine's Hill…[167]

He went on to describe Carisbrooke Castle:

> I dare say I have seen many a descendant of some old cawer who peeped through the bars at Charles the First when he was in confinement there.[168]

Admitting that he was already lonely and missing his closest friends and brothers, he said that he would like Haydon to make a sketch of Reynolds with George and Tom, and send it to him. He admitted that he had been nervous from want of regular rest, and then he copied *On the Sea* into his letter and dated it, knowing that Reynolds would in turn copy it and thus help to preserve it for posterity.

(Reynolds truly believed that both Keats and Haydon were destined for historical fame. He once asked Haydon to write to him with his current thoughts about art and literature, saying that 'Children of the 20th Century shall lisp [Haydon's name] in a National Gallery'.)[169]

Keats was thinking of closing his letter when he decided to continue writing, to tell Reynolds about his growing passion for Shakespeare and the awe with which he was reading *The Tempest*. Whether sitting in his room at Mrs Cook's, or in his favourite place near Carisbrooke Castle, he was poring over the text, analysing it line by line, thinking about every word, teasing out the meaning and context. He was absorbing the play just as Haydon might have done, using his imagination to see and feel what was being depicted, as if in 'actuality'. For example, when the monster Caliban first enters the play, he insults both the magician Prospero and his beautiful daughter Miranda, wishing a curse upon them both. For this, says Prospero,

> ... be sure, tonight thou shall have cramps,
> Side-stitches, that shall pen thy breath up; **urchins**
> **Shall, for that vast of night that they may work,**
> **All exercise on thee**...

Keats underlined the passage in his little pocket Shakespeare (which still exists; it is in the Houghton Library at Harvard University) and quoted the part in bold in his letter to Reynolds, saying that it had never struck him 'so forcibly as at present'. In this scene, Caliban is sleeping on the beach or in his cave at night. The 'vast of night' is the sky overhead as it would appear from an island in the middle of the sea, that's to say, with myriad stars shining from horizon to horizon.

The 'urchins' – sea urchins, spiky creatures like hedgehogs – come out of the sea and *work* upon him, crawling all over him, nipping and pinching him. They are *exercising* – as well as *exercising their art* – upon him. It is a powerful and vivid image.

In his letter, Keats also drew Reynolds' attention to the phrase that Prospero uses when he asks his daughter Miranda about her memories, *In the dark, backward and abysm of time*. In Prospero's question, memory itself is represented visually because the magician asks his daughter what she sees ('what *seest* thou in the dark backward…'). When memories fade, *backward* time becomes opaque and then impenetrable; it becomes *dark*. Eventually, it is impossible to cross the *abyss*, the metaphorical chasm that has formed between the past and the present. Keats delighted in this sort of complex wordplay and became almost obsessive in his reading of it.

> I find I cannot exist without Poetry – without eternal Poetry – half the day will not do. I began with a little, but habit has made me a Leviathan. I had become all in a Tremble from not having written anything of late – the Sonnet overleaf [*On the Sea*] did me good. I slept the better for it last night.[170]

As well as Shakespeare, he had Spenser's *The Faerie Queene* with him. This was still a major source of inspiration. 'Just now I opened Spenser,' he told Reynolds, 'and the first Lines I saw were these –

> The noble heart that harbours virtuous thought,
> And is with child of glorious great intent,
> Can never rest until it forth have brought
> Th' eternal brood of glory excellent…'[171]

We saw in Chapter 3 that Haydon had written these very same lines in his diary more than three years earlier, towards the end of 1813. Keats may have read them in Haydon's diary (we can recall that Haydon allowed his friends to read his diary) but it is more likely that the sentiment alone reminded him of Haydon because in the next line of his letter to Reynolds he said,

> Let me know particularly about Haydon, ask him to write to me about Hunt, if it be only ten lines – I hope all is well.[172]

Despite the beauty of his new surroundings, his freedom to study and write and his new-found passion for Shakespeare, all was not well with Keats himself. He was struggling a great deal with the loneliness he felt on the Isle of Wight and, despite trying to write every day, he felt he had made little progress with *Endymion*. He was neither sleeping nor eating properly, and became 'not over capable in my upper stories'.[173] Around the end of April he left the island and his landlady, Mrs Cook, insisted that he take the picture of Shakespeare with him, a generous gesture that Keats considered a good omen. In leaving the island he was by no means disregarding Haydon's advice that he should live away from London for a while. From Southampton he travelled some 150 miles to Margate with renewed determination to make progress with his book. Once again, his youngest brother, Tom, joined him.

***

By the beginning of May, with Mr Harman's money in hand, Haydon was forging ahead with his painting. On 10 May he wrote in his diary that the week had been 'a week of glorious labour. I have advanced my picture and worked with my old and accustomed energy.' And on 18 May he wrote, 'Worked on the whole week.' Clearly fired up with his energy and enthusiasm, he was also beginning to socialise a little and enjoy himself again. On 7 May he heard Johann Spurzheim talking about skulls. Spurzheim was a German physician and phrenologist who gave public lectures in which he dissected human brains in front of audiences of anatomists. Haydon wrote in his diary that, according to Spurzheim, French skulls were remarkable for their organ of individuality, or *facts*. Haydon agreed. The language shows it, he said, 'and God knows their art does'.

On 18 May he went for a stroll through the suburb of St John's Wood, on the road out to Hampstead. The former proprietor of the John o'Groats Tavern in Rupert Street, John Seabrook, had retired and moved to a cottage there and when Haydon passed the cottage he was called over and invited in for tea. It will be remembered that John Seabrook had provided Haydon with free dinners throughout the years when he was painting *Solomon* and Haydon came to consider this generous man to have behaved 'like a father' to him. Of course, *Solomon* had been a great success, so Haydon was delighted when he entered the cottage and was 'overwhelmed with congratulations' from Seabrook and his family. Seabrook told him that he had retired from business, and Haydon later wrote that he found the old tavern keeper to be contented and lighthearted, talking about his garden, for example, and the sweetness of the air away from the smog-filled streets of the city. Haydon, however, felt that his own presence in the cottage 'excited old associations', so much so that Seabrook would become nostalgic and soon be thinking again about commerce and business. He added a footnote to his diary that John Seabrook later took an inn at Stanmore.

Haydon's diary is full of such anecdotes and observations. He habitually studied the people with whom he socialised, noting their conversations, characteristics and peculiarities. Around this time he recorded that a young man 'of rank and fashion' was looking over Haydon's drawings of a dissected lion. As Haydon was enthusiastically explaining the movement of the animal's muscles he placed his finger and thumb on each side of the young man's arm, and held them for a moment. The young man was startled, but he quickly regained his composure and continued talking and laughing. Haydon found the incident fascinating. This young man, he wrote, clearly thought that being touched on his arm was a *liberty*. About a day or two afterwards they were at a dinner together and the young man, while talking of something, said, 'It is just like this,' and put his finger and thumb on Haydon's arm in precisely the same way. 'He did it without looking at me,' said Haydon.

With a wide circle of friends and acquaintances, Haydon had many opportunities to observe the behaviour and mannerisms of those around him, but few would be as fruitful as the farewell dinner for the actor John Kemble at the Freemasons' Tavern, Great Queen Street, on Friday 27 June. Kemble had just retired from the stage so the cream of London's theatrical, artistic and literary circles were gathered together in the Grand Banqueting Saloon of the tavern to present him with a gift, a vase 'of rich and beautiful work' (or a drawing of it, at least, because it wasn't ready yet). We know a lot about this dinner because a book, *An Authentic Narrative of Mr Kemble's Retirement from the Stage...* was written about it afterwards. The banquet was presided over by Lord Holland, the head of a prominent London family of whig politicians, scholars and socialites. Among the hundreds of guests were Haydon's former patrons Sir George Beaumont and Lord Mulgrave (now the 1st Earl of Mulgrave), along with Benjamin West, Thomas Campbell, a Scottish poet who had inherited a fortune and Thomas Moore, an Irish poet and songwriter. During a speech, John Kemble referred to the collected assembly before him as composed of 'men admired for their genius, honoured for their rank, and valued for learning and talents of every kind'. A band played the music of Handel during the dinner, and there were numerous speeches afterwards, including one about the friendly rivalry between the Covent Garden and Drury Lane theatres.

Somewhere in the audience was Edmund Kean, the energetic 'new man' of the stage, the man who had been called 'low company' at a dinner party attended by Keats and the man whom Hazlitt (and many others) thought a greater actor than Kemble himself, indeed the greatest actor of the day. Here's how Haydon wrote about the event in his diary the next day:

> Dined at Kemble's dinner. A more complete farce there never was acted. Many, I daresay, regretted his leaving us, but the affectations of all parties disgusted me. The Drury Lane actors flattering the Covent

Garden ones, the Covent Garden flattering in turn the Drury Lane. Lord Holland flattered Kemble, Kemble flattered Lord Holland. Then Campbell, the poet, flattered Moore (whom I knew he hated), but Tom Moore, like an honest, sensible genius, as he is, said not a word, drank his wine and flattered no one… The dinner to Kemble, under the affectation of honouring him, was in reality a masked attack on Kean & his genius…[174]

After analysing the motives of those who had gathered to honour Kemble ('a struggle to put a little oil in the socket of an expiring lamp'), and affirming Hazlitt's view that Kean was the better actor, he said,

I never in my life felt a contempt for human nature till last night, and last night I really retired disgusted. I knew the real feelings of half the visitors, and saw them bowing, flattering, cringing & lying… An English public dinner is after all the greatest farce on the face of the Earth.[175]

***

Haydon's thoughts turned back to Keats, and around 11 May 1817, at the end of his 'week of glorious labour', he wrote to him. He was aware that Keats was having difficulties and had moved from the Isle of Wight to Margate, but he clearly did not know that Tom had joined him:

I have been intending to write to you every hour this week, but have been so interrupted that the postman rang his bell every night in vain… I think you did quite right to leave the Isle of Wight if you felt no relief; and being quite alone, after study you can now devote your eight hours a day with just as much seclusion as ever…[176]

Keats had written a letter in reply to one from Leigh Hunt in which he had told Hunt that he had been feeling despondent and had moved to Margate:

> I vow that I have been down in the mouth lately at this work. These last two days, however, I have felt more confident – I have asked myself so often why I should be a poet more than other men, seeing how great a thing it is – how great things are to be gained by it, what a thing to be in the mouth of Fame, that the idea has grown so monstrously beyond my seeming power of attainment, that the other day I nearly consented with myself to drop into a Phaeton…[177]

A phaeton was a horse-drawn carriage, but Phaeton himself was a character from the Greek myths who almost set the earth on fire while attempting to drive the chariot of the sun. He was killed in the attempt and his epitaph read: 'Greatly he failed, but greatly he dared'. Keats was mindful of the connection:

> Yet, 'tis a disgrace to fail even in a huge attempt; at this moment I drive the thought from me. I began my poem about a fortnight since, and have done some every day, except travelling ones… I see nothing but continual uphill journeying. Now is there any thing more unpleasant… than to be so journeying and to miss the goal at last? But I intend to whistle all these cogitations into the sea, where I hope they will breed storms violent enough to block up all exit from Russia…[178]

This very interesting letter shows just how desperately Keats wanted to succeed as a poet, and just how much his confidence was being eroded by his inability to make progress with his new poem. The sentence about whistling all of his cogitations into the sea where 'they will breed storms' is a fine example of his ability to conjure up powerfully visual or 'poetical' images almost at will. In his letter dated 11 May, Haydon, perhaps having talked to Leigh Hunt, responded to the musings of a clearly depressed Keats:

> Do not give way to any forebodings. They are nothing more than the over-eager anxieties of a great spirit stretched beyond its strength, then relapsing for a time to languid inefficiency. Every man of great views is, at times, thus tormented, but begin again where you left off without hesitation or fear…

After assuring Keats that he was now one of the 'great spirits', he urged him to turn to God for support during his time of forebodings:

> Trust in God with all your might, my dear Keats. This dependence, with your own energy, will give you strength, and hope, and comfort.

Haydon then alluded to his own worries about money, his 'troubles, and wants, and distresses' and says, in a startlingly melodramatic fashion, that he finds help and consolation from prayer:

> From my soul I declare to you I never applied for help, or for consolation, or for strength, but I found it. I always rose up from my knees with a refreshed fury, an iron-clenched firmness, a crystal piety of feeling that sent me streaming on with a repulsive power against the struggles of life.

Keats, of course, had written about his disgust of such 'vulgar superstition' in an earlier poem, and in his reply to this letter, he made it clear that he had no intention of emulating Haydon by dropping to his knees and praying to God for help. He would, however, look to the spirit of Shakespeare as a presider over his efforts:

> I do begin arduously where I leave off, notwithstanding occasional depressions; and I hope for the support of a High Power while I climb this little eminence... I remember your saying that you had notions of a good Genius presiding over you. I have of late had the same thought... Is it too daring to fancy Shakespeare this presider?[179]

It was this mutual striving after fame and distinction, this High Calling, that had always bound Keats and Haydon together because each recognised something of himself in the other. Haydon, however, was becoming ever more aware that his youthful and energetic days as an artist were behind him; that he was, for the time being at least, in a struggle for survival in the face of his creditors. He suspected that Keats, too, was starting to be overwhelmed by the difficulties he was facing. Whether consciously or not, but with a degree of unintended irony, Haydon ended his letter by urging Keats not to despair, but to emulate Haydon himself in his pursuit of fame:

> God bless you, my dear Keats! do not despair; collect incident, study character, read Shakespeare, and trust in Providence, and you will do, you must...

Keep a diary or journal ('collect incident'), study people, read Shakespeare and trust in God; these were the habits which underpinned Haydon's life as an artist.

Keats' response to this letter showed that the axis of influence was slowly beginning to turn in the relationship between the painter and the poet. Keats was maturing rapidly, both emotionally and intellectually, and he now began to understand the depth of Haydon's difficulties. His response was twofold. First, he tried to encourage Haydon not to give up his own striving for fame, and to assure him that he empathised with his difficulties. In a rousing homily, he began by quoting (actually, slightly misquoting) the opening lines of Shakespeare's *Love's Labour Lost*. The original letter is written in Keats' neater style of handwriting, as if he took care over it. My dear Haydon, he wrote,

> Let Fame, that all pant after in their lives,
> Live register'd upon our brazen tombs,
> And so grace us in the disgrace of death;
> When spite of cormorant devouring time
> The endeavour of this present breath may buy
> That Honour which shall bate his Scythe's keen edge
> And make us heirs of all eternity.
>
> To think that I have no right to couple myself with you in this speech would be death to me, so I have e'en written it – and I pray God that our 'brazen tombs' be nigh neighbours.[180]

Haydon added a note against this last comment, 'I wonder if they will be. B R Haydon.' Keats continued:

> …the endeavour of this present breath will soon be over, and yet it is as well to breathe freely during our sojourn [our sojourn; reminding us once again of the great spirits… sojourning] – it is as well as if you

have not been teased with that Money affair, that bill pestilence. However, I must think that difficulties nerve the Spirit of a Man – they make our prime objects a refuge as well as a passion. The Trumpet of Fame is as a tower of Strength, the ambitious bloweth it and is safe.

To reinforce this message, Keats told Haydon of his own difficulties with *Endymion*:

– truth is I have been in such a state of Mind as to read over my lines and hate them. I am one that 'gathers Samphire dreadful trade' – the Cliff of Poesy Towers above me…

This image of the samphire-gatherer was bound to please a Shakespearean scholar such as Haydon, but it also shows how the passage in *King Lear* we noted earlier (*King Lear*, IV, 6 iv) had gripped Keats' imagination. We noted that Edgar had said to the recently blinded Duke of Gloucester, when Gloucester *thought* they were approaching a cliff at Dover, 'Hark, do you hear the sea?', the point being that there was no sea to hear. To reinforce the deception, Edgar had described a scene at the (imaginary) cliff edge, that of a samphire-gatherer half way down the cliff (samphire, a culinary delicacy, was collected in this way during Shakespeare's lifetime):

Come on, sir, here's the place. Stand still. How fearful
And dizzy 'tis to cast one's eyes so low!
The crows and choughs that wing the midway air
Show scarce so gross as beetles. Halfway down
Hangs one that gathers samphire, dreadful trade!
Methinks he seems no bigger than his head.

> The fishermen that walk upon the beach
> Appear like mice…

This complete absorption in Shakespeare was now having a real and dramatic effect upon Keats' thoughts, and Haydon understood and appreciated this as much as if not more than, anybody else in Keats' circle of friends.

***

The town of Marlow in Buckinghamshire grew up around a wooden bridge across the river Thames. It was 35 miles west of London and in 1817 the daily coach from the capital took around three hours to reach it. Marlow could hardly have been more different from London; it was set among a landscape of chalk hills covered in beech woodlands above extensive river meadows. The townspeople were generally poor and many of them worked in the local watermills. England was on the cusp of the Industrial Revolution in 1817 and a gazetteer from 1815 states that the Temple Mills near Marlow contained copper and brass works with a separate mill for making thimbles. Another mill pressed oil from rape and linseed. On the edge of the town were some paper mills, paper at that time being made from rags which were pulped with water-powered hammers.[181]

Other employment within the town centred around the brewing industry – there was a large brewery, Wethereds, just off the High Street, as well as several malthouses, wagon-yards, a bakehouse and some corn lofts. The town was also renowned for the quality of its lace which many of the women made in their houses, while along the riverbanks the men could often be seen fishing with nets. Being a town built around a major river crossing between Reading and High Wycombe, Marlow boasted a coaching inn and many taverns.

The main road out of the town towards Henley was called West Street and it was here that a house by the name of Albion House was built next to a grammar school. The house was a long, low building featuring distinctive Gothic-style windows (with peculiar pointed arches) and large, generally dark, sometimes damp rooms. The house had a garden to the rear that looked out over fields to the north. Shelley and his wife Mary took out a lease on Albion House and moved in during March 1817, furnishing it expensively (on credit) from English & Becks in Bath. The largest room, which overlooked the garden, was converted into a library, and statues of Venus and Apollo were brought out from London and installed there. The atmosphere in the house was intensely intellectual; many years later, in the *Shelley Memorials* edited by Mary Shelley, a list of the books that she and Shelley read together that spring and summer at Marlow was published. They enjoyed their books, 'At home or travelling, before breakfast or while waiting for the midday meal... one read while the other listened'. The list included Plato (always a favourite with Shelley), Aeschylus, Sophocles, Homer, several volumes of Gibbon, *Political Justice* by William Godwin (Mary's father), the plays of Beaumont and Fletcher, Davis's *Travels in America*, Spenser's *Faerie Queene*, 'besides many novels... etc.'.[182]

Leigh Hunt and his family left Hampstead and moved to Shelley's new house in April and thus it was that, for a short period in the spring and summer of 1817, West Street in Marlow became a hive of literary activity. Apart from the Shelleys and the Hunts, the sometime novelist and poet Thomas Love Peacock, a friend of Shelley, lived along the street and was in the process of writing a novel set in a medieval castle (called *Melincourt*) soon to be followed by *Nightmare Abbey*, a satirical novel in which many of the characters are based on members of the Shelley circle at Albion House. The character of Scythrop is based on Shelley himself. Thomas Love Peacock was aware of Shelley's penchant for self-publishing political pamphlets (his pamphlet, *A Proposal for Putting Reform to the Vote*, was now in circulation) and in *Nightmare Abbey* he wrote a delightful caricature of Shelley as Scythrop:

> To get a clear view of his own ideas, and to feel the pulse of wisdom and genius of his age, [Scythrop] wrote and published a treatise, in which his meanings were carefully wrapt up in the monk's hood of transcendental technology, but filled with matter deep and dangerous, which he thought would set the whole nation in a ferment; and he awaited the result in awful expectation, as a miner who has fired a train awaits the explosion of a rock. However, he listened and heard nothing; for the explosion, if any ensued, was not sufficiently loud to shake a single leaf of the ivy on the towers of Nightmare Abbey; and some months afterwards he received a letter from his bookseller, informing him that only seven copies had been sold, and concluding with a polite request for the balance.

With his family installed in its new home, Shelley was working on a poem called *Laon and Cynthia* that would eventually surpass Keats' *Endymion* in length, at 4,818 lines. He was not writing it within the confines of the house, however, presumably because Albion House was a crowded, raucous place. The Shelleys had a son called William, and there was also another child, Alba, who was the illegitimate offspring of an affair between Mary's stepsister and Lord Byron. Hunt and his wife Marian had brought along their own four young children as well as Marian's sister, Bess. And then there was the gardener, the cook and the housemaid. Each morning Shelley and Mary would get up early and, with the children running around the garden and the servants doing the domestic chores, Mary would settle down to put the final touches to her novel *Frankenstein* while Shelley escaped to the river and the woods, notebook and pens in hand. (Hunt generally got up much later, dubbing this regime 'country hours'.)

The river Thames was a short stroll across the water meadows from Albion House, and Shelley kept a boat moored there. He liked to lie down in the boat with his face upwards towards the sun, and think, and write his poem. He would often cross the river and walk up into the nearby Bisham Woods, again with his notebook and pens. An extant notebook containing a draft of *Laon and Cynthia* is written in a scrawl and is covered in crossings-out, blots and drawings of trees. Hunt's sister-in-law, Bessie, later wrote about Shelley in the preface to her very learned little book, *Flora Domestica*:

> Of a strong and powerful intellect, his manners were gentle… his tastes were pure and simple: it was his delight to ramble out into the fields and woods where he would take his book, or sometimes his

pen… and would return home with his hat wreathed in briony, or wild convolvulus…[183]

The second stanza of *Laon and Cynthia*, later published as *The Revolt of Islam* (the poem written in Spenserian stanzas and is about a pair of lovers who initiate a revolution against the Sultan of the Ottoman Empire), was addressed to Mary Shelley. It is an apology for the hours Shelley spent away from her, lying in his boat on the Thames, and walking in the surrounding woods:

> The toil which stole from thee so many an hour,
> Is ended, and the fruit is at thy feet!
> No longer where the woods to frame a bower
> With interlaced branches mix and meet,
> Or where with sound like many voices sweet,
> Waterfalls leap among wild islands green,
> Which framed for my lone boat a lone retreat
> Of moss green trees and weeds, shall I be seen,
> But beside thee, where still my heart has ever been.

Leigh Hunt stayed in the house when Shelley wandered down to the river and woods because he was writing a poem of his own, *The Nymphs*, later to be published as the first poem in a collection called *Foliage*. Unlike Shelley, Hunt had to earn a living, which meant frequent trips to London and the *Examiner*, and often staying up later than the rest of the household to write his articles and reviews. He tended to work in the garden, seemingly not too distracted by the children. Compared to his cottage at Hampstead, Albion House must have seemed large and luxurious.

The preface to Hunt's *Foliage* includes some 'cursory observations on poetry and cheerfulness', in which the author reveals that the object of his book is to 'cultivate a love of nature outdoors, and of sociality within', exactly the atmosphere at Albion House. He deprecates Alexander Pope and the 'French School' of poetry, there having been, he says, a recent re-awakening of the 'poetical faculty' in England (referring to Wordsworth, but also to his own discoveries, Shelley, Keats and Reynolds). The real properties of poetry, says Hunt, are a 'sensitiveness to the beauty of the external world… and above all, imagination, or the power to see, with verisimilitude, what others do not.'[184] We are, said Hunt, 'creatures made to enjoy more than to know… to put our own shoulders to the wheel and get out of the mud upon the green sward again'.[185] He then gave his reasons for writing:

> I write to enjoy myself; but I have learnt in the course of it to write for others also… The main features of the book are a love of sociality, of the country, and the fine imagination of the Greeks.[186]

When Hunt did venture down to the river to look at the landscape along the banks of the Thames near Marlow, his imagination saw 'what others do not'. He filled this imaginary landscape with figures from Greek mythology, some as originally portrayed by the Greeks, some inventions of his own:

> Close by, from bank to bank,
> A little bridge there is, a one railed plank;
> And all is woody, mossy and watery.
> Sometimes a poet from that bridge may see

> A Nymph reach downwards, holding by a bough
> With tresses o'er her brow,
> And with her white back scoop
> In a green gourd cup, shining sunnily…

This is exactly what Keats was doing with *Endymion*, creating an imaginary landscape, sometimes drawn from his surroundings on the Isle of Wight and Margate, and filling it with figures from Greek mythology. But of course his aim was very different from that of Hunt because Keats was pursuing a philosophical view of poetry. He had no interest in a 'poetry of cheerfulness', though he admitted that he sometimes suffered from depression ('notwithstanding occasional depressions… I hope for the support of a High Power'), or a 'horrid morbidity of temperament'. It was just this state of mind that Hunt was arguing should be fought against.

Haydon had a completely different view; he thought that Hunt's 'philosophy of cheerfulness' was merely that of a morbid character trying to hide its true nature in a *false* outward cheerfulness. Back in January, after his argument with Hunt over Christianity, he wrote:

> …my picture seems to have brought up all Hunt's bile and morbidity, boiling with froth into his acrid and gloomy imagination, for Hunt's imagination is naturally and inherently gloomy, and all his leafy bowers and clipsome waists & balmy bosoms proceed not from a lovely fancy… but are the product of a painful, hypochondriac Soul that struggles by dwelling on the reverse of its own real thoughts, perpetually to illuminate its natural and forlorn dinginess… hence his wish to be surrounded by inferior intellects and being delighted to

suck in their honey praise… and hence his horror of being left alone for even an hour![187]

Haydon had a point, but it was totally misplaced. He knew, but had conveniently forgotten (or deliberately overlooked) the fact that Hunt had spent two years in Horsemonger Gaol defending the right to free speech of newspaper editors and writers who published articles and poems in newspapers and magazines – people like Shelley, Keats, Reynolds, Hazlitt and, of course, Haydon himself. Hunt had been almost destroyed by the experience. In his *Autobiography*, written in later life, he said:

> It was for a good while after leaving prison that I was unable to return the visits of the friends who saw me there. Two years confinement, and illness in combination, had acted so injuriously upon a sensitive temperament, that for many months I could not leave home without a morbid wish to return, and a fear of being seized with some fit or other in the streets, perhaps with sudden death; and this was one of the periods when my hypochondria came back. In company, however, or at the sight of a friend, animal spirits would struggle even with that; and few people, whatever ill-health I showed in my face, had the slightest idea of what I had suffered.[188]

Haydon's outburst is not particularly surprising or unusual; he had a history of attacking those with whom he disagreed, or disliked. What is much more perplexing is Keats' response to Haydon's admonition that he beware of Hunt's 'delusions and sophistications'. In his reply to a letter from Haydon, Keats agreed that Hunt was delusional and, in addition, castigated him for considering himself a 'great poet'. It is wholly uncharacteristic of Keats and is revealing of how loyal he was to Haydon at this time:

> I wrote to Hunt yesterday – scarcely know what I said in it. I could not talk about Poetry in the way I should have liked because I was not in humour with either his or mine. His self delusions are very lamentable – they have inticed [sic] him into a Situation which I should be less eager after than that of a galley slave.... What you observe thereon is very true... Perhaps it is a self delusion to say so, but I think I could not be deceived in the manner that Hunt is – may I die tomorrow if I am to be. There is no greater Sin after the seven deadly than to flatter oneself into an idea of being a great Poet...

Earlier in this same letter, Keats had responded to Haydon's comment about money troubles, his 'troubles & wants & distresses', with information about a pending financial crisis of his own. He had received a letter from his brother George with news of financial difficulties which, said Keats,

> are not like Envy and detraction stimulants to further exertion... but rather like a nettle leaf or two in your bed. So now I revoke my Promise of finishing my poem by the Autumn... I cannot write while my spirit is fevered in a contrary direction... You tell me never to despair – I wish it was as easy for me to observe the saying – truth is I have a horrid Morbidity of Temperament...

Keats then told Haydon just how close he was to him, how much he empathised with him and how important was their mutual endeavour to gain fame and distinction:

> I am very sure that you do love me as your own Brother [a greater love was not yet known to Keats; as we saw earlier, he said that his love for his brothers had grown into an affection 'passing the Love of Women'] – I have seen it in your continual anxiety for me – and I assure you that your wellfare [sic] and fame is and will be a chief pleasure to me all my life. I know no one but you who can be fully sensible of the turmoil and anxiety, the sacrifice of all what is called comfort… the looking upon the Sun the Moon the Stars, the Earth and its contents as materials to form greater things – that is to say ethereal things – but here I am talking like a Madman greater things that our Creator himself made!![189]

After assuring Haydon that he is reading Shakespeare ('indeed, I shall I think never read any other Book much… I am very near Agreeing with Hazlitt that Shakespeare is enough for us') and then commenting upon a letter that Haydon had sent to the *Examiner*, Keats asked Haydon to give his respects to Wordsworth, *John* Hunt (Leigh's brother) and Reynolds. 'So now in the name of Shakespeare, Raphael and all our Saints,' he concludes, 'I commend you to the care of heaven!' He signed the letter, 'Your everlasting friend, John Keats'.

Keats was never so much under the influence of Haydon in matters of art, friendship and ambition as he was in the spring and early summer of 1817. But Reynolds was about to introduce Keats to his Oxford friend, the man to whom Reynolds had sent Keats' book of poems soon after it was published. He was called Benjamin Bailey and he would provide Keats with a new awareness of what it means to be a poet, and what it means to value somebody for their character and qualities as a friend.

Benjamin Bailey was studying for the Church and was steeped in what Keats had called 'vulgar superstition'. Despite this, Keats was destined, for a while at least, to consider him one of the most noble, upright and admirable men he had ever met. Haydon tried to impose his authority and influence upon this friendship, too, but this time there were unintended consequences.

Chapter 10

The tide of blood in me
Hath proudly flowed in vanity till now...
Shakespeare: *King Henry IV, Part II*

Having some of Mr Harman's money left, and feeling that he had made some progress with his painting, Haydon decided to escape from the confines of London for an extended holiday. This involved travelling to study the art of a great country house ('making my pleasures subservient to my art'), and in the middle of July 1817, when Parliament was in recess and many Londoners took their holidays, he chose the greatest country house of them all: Blenheim Palace, near Oxford. Haydon may have borrowed or hired a carriage for this journey because he records in his diary that he 'drove about the park' at Blenheim. The park was expansive and impressive, but Haydon was much more interested in the palace and its valuable collection of paintings. A national art gallery was still in the future, but a painter such as Haydon – or Hazlitt when he was at Winterslow – would not have had too much difficulty in gaining access to the private art collection of a grand country house. And there were plenty to choose from, with at least three situated within a short ride of Blenheim (Ditchley House, Heythrop Park and Cornbury House, each with its own art collection).

As an historical painter who had grown up near the navy base at Plymouth, Haydon took a special interest in the military; this was one reason that his first patron, the soldier and statesman Lord Mulgrave, had found him such stimulating company. When he was walking around Blenheim Palace, perhaps the only palace in England truly fit for a king at the time (Buckingham Palace was as yet the relatively modest Buckingham House), he mused upon the character of Blenheim's first owner – John Churchill, 1st Duke of Marlborough – a brilliant soldier in the employ of several English monarchs around the turn of the eighteenth century. A grateful Queen Anne had rewarded Churchill for his prowess in the War of the Spanish Succession, particularly his victory at the Battle of Blenheim, by building this magnificent tribute at a cost to the country of almost a quarter of a million pounds. It was widely regarded as one of the finest and most opulent buildings in Europe (it is now a World Heritage Site).

As he contemplated the grandeur of the building, Haydon wondered why the country rewarded its greatest military men with tremendous wealth, but not its finest artists. Why hadn't Shakespeare, for example, been given a country house? Because, wrote Haydon, in order to gain the rewards of the monarch and parliament,

> ...their comforts must be threatened, their existence [must be] at stake, their daughters ravished and their houses burnt, and then if

some great and politic, keen & cunning man takes advantage of the state of their minds... no reward is adequate to express their feelings for their rescue, and this is the secret of such rewards as Blenheim.[190]

A near-contemporary Blenheim Guide gives us some idea of the splendour of the palace and its art collection at the time Haydon visited it in 1817:

> The apartments of this Palace are furnished with princely magnificence... The [paintings]... are nearly unrivalled for their beauty and value; and... unquestionably form the finest collection in this kingdom.[191]

And these were no exaggerations: the ceiling in the Grand Hall was 67 feet high, the library held 17,000 books (to a bibliophile such as Haydon, this must have been astonishing), and the art collection included paintings by Raphael, Tintoretto, Leonardo da Vinci, van Dyck, Correggio and Rubens (there was an 'unrivalled assemblage' of Rubens at Blenheim) among many others. There was a whole room devoted to the paintings of Titian, while portraits of the Churchill family by Sir Joshua Reynolds were scattered throughout the apartments. Haydon was so impressed that when he saw the 'glories of Rubens' upon entering the palace, all thoughts of the Duke of Marlborough and his battles vanished from his mind. In fact, what came into his mind was the question: 'Would he, Haydon, prefer to be known as a great painter or a great soldier?'

> Some little demon whispered, 'which would you rather be, Rubens or Marlborough?' 'Rubens, a million times over, & Raphael ten million

times – but I should have no objection to… a palace and a park added.'[192]

Haydon consoled himself for his own lack of wealth with the notion that 'poets and painters… identify themselves with all ages', meaning they will enjoy eternal fame, even if neglected during their lifetimes. He often consoled himself in this manner; he would try to convince himself that a great painter – a painter such as himself – was among the most noble and worthy of human beings. Uncharacteristically for Haydon, however, his thinking on the matter was muddled. He felt mortified, he said, that Rubens should be made subservient 'like the upholsterer' to adorn the breakfast rooms and dining rooms of a general. He then found some solace in the idea that a great general such as the Duke of Marlborough could only be rewarded by presenting him with great paintings, such as those of Rubens.[193]

He had thoughts along similar lines when he left Blenheim and travelled the eight miles to Oxford, booking himself into one of its many inns:

> I spent a most delightful week at Oxford. Every thing was new and fresh. I knew nothing of colleges and their habits, & felt mortified that I had not been educated there & was thus deprived [of] the power of presenting at a future time my portrait when worthy to be thought an honour.[194]

Before the arrival of the motor industry, early nineteenth century Oxford was one of the most beautiful cities in Europe. Nestled between the rivers Thames and Cherwell (the Thames is known as the Isis in Oxford), and surrounded in summer by golden cornfields and green meadows, its medieval streets and ornately decorated colleges seemed timeless and unchanging. J.M.W. Turner visited Oxford many times in the first decades of the nineteenth century and has left us several images of the city and its people. Around the Gothic spires, sunlight falls on the pale, soft, honey-coloured limestone that had been extracted for centuries from the local quarries and carved into the ornate Gothic tracery, statues and gargoyles that decorate many of the buildings. In the muddy streets below, dogs run around and children fly kites while gowned scholars walk in pairs. The city's women all seem to be carrying bundles as if they are washerwomen, or returning from a market. Everywhere, it seems, stonemasons are repairing the buildings.

Rather surprisingly, considering the importance he placed on scholarship, Haydon wrote very little in his diary about his stay in Oxford. He must, however, have mingled with either the scholars or the dons, perhaps both, for he does say:

> It was interesting to see the effect of habit at Oxford of meeting Classical people. Every body shewed you Latin & Greek books to explain any question, as if it had been English. It seemed never to enter their conception that there were people in the World who knew nothing of one or the other.[195]

The first Oxford School of Art was not founded until 1865, and the first Slade Professor of Art was not appointed until 1871 (when John Ruskin took the post), so there were no art professors or students for Haydon to converse with. He may have had access to the art collection in the Bodleian Library, a collection Hazlitt considered mediocre. We do know that Haydon visited the chapel of Magdalen College and viewed its altarpiece. This was (and still is) a painting of Christ carrying the Cross which Haydon attributed to the sixteenth-century Spanish artist, Luis de Morales, but which is now thought to be the work of the seventeenth-century Spanish artist Juan de Valdés Leal. There, amid the 'indiscriminate and barbarous' style of the chapel interior (as a local guide of 1839 described its former condition before its restoration and refurbishment in 1833), Haydon watched a young man copying the painting. This young man was called Charles Cripps, and he would come to have a prominent place in the story of Haydon and Keats, as we shall see.

Haydon never mentioned any of this in his diary at the time. Instead, he ruminated on the foibles of the waiter who served him breakfast:

> I was at an Inn where the Waiter's great ambition was to convince me they never brought the same thing twice, so every morning I had different cloths, cups, saucers & tea pots, & milk jugs... So many shapes does human vanity take, in truth. Passions, propensity, or innate dispositions of any kind use the materials whatever they be of the situation into which birth or accident has thrown them, with the same views.[196]

It is difficult to disentangle Haydon's thoughts and emotions when he wrote this rather abstruse entry. But it is characteristic of him that in this summer of 1817, when he was surrounded by the splendours of Oxford, even when he was conversing with scholars who were showing him Latin and Greek books or watching a young man copy a great painting, the thing that struck him most forcefully was the vanity of his waiter.

***

Dawson Turner lived in a large, red-brick Georgian house in the coastal town of Great Yarmouth. It was called Bank House and overlooked the Haven Bridge. Turner was a partner in a bank, and a brewer. He was also an academic botanist who enjoyed rummaging around on the seashore. He had published a serious scholarly work on a type of seaweed, *A Synopsis of The British Fuci* and its introductory sentence was cleverly devised to capture the interest of the reader:

> Before I enter upon the talk of describing the several species of Fuci, it cannot be amiss to offer some slight remarks upon the peculiarities connected with the physiology of these curious vegetables.[197]

His writings were copiously illustrated by his talented wife and daughters and in 1815 one of these daughters, Maria Dawson Turner, married a botanical artist named William Jackson Hooker, later *Sir* William Hooker, Professor of Botany at Glasgow University and the first Director of the Royal Botanic Gardens at Kew. Hooker had already published a very entertaining account of a sailing trip to Iceland, *Journal of a Tour in Iceland in The Summer of 1809*. He faithfully recorded in a journal that the ship, and all of his botanical specimens, went up in flames at the end of the tour.

When William Hooker married Turner's daughter he was working on the drawings for a book about a group of liverworts, *British*

Jungermanniae, and his new father-in-law soon employed him to create many of the splendid drawings in his own book, *A Synopsis of The British Fuci*. And so it was that William Hooker became a member of the clever and industrious Turner family of artists, scientists and collectors at Bank House. Dawson Turner was an art connoisseur, a serious collector with a discerning eye for quality; during his lifetime he owned paintings by Rubens, Canaletto and Holbein. He also amassed a huge and valuable collection of books, manuscripts, letters and illustrations, eventually owning 8,000 books. On his death, the sale of his collection of letters and manuscripts (many bound in fine leather) took five days and 719 lots to complete.[198] In fact, having a magpie mind, seemingly endless resources, and an obsession for order and classification, Dawson Turner collected almost anything that could be bound together in volumes. He even collected railway tickets, advertisements and shop bills, all handed over to the Yarmouth bookbinders to be bound in fine quality leather.

Dawson Turner's mother, Elizabeth (*née* Cotman), was a relative of the painter John Sell Cotman, yet another talented artist who lived and worked in Yarmouth. Cotman earned some of his income as the Turner family's drawing master. He had studied in London and was a personal friend of Haydon's former patron, Sir George Beaumont. Dawson Turner himself had many London connections; he knew, for example, Haydon's old friend David Wilkie (he had bought two of Wilkie's paintings and later went on a tour of France and Italy with him). It was probably through one or more of these mutual friends and connections that Dawson Turner became a personal friend and patron of Haydon and lent him, or gave him, significant amounts of money.

Upon his return to London from Oxford, Haydon was feeling unwell; his spirits were low, perhaps because the trip had left him financially destitute again. Many of his friends were absent from town or occupied in their own affairs: Reynolds was busy at the *Champion*, which had a new editor, and he was also writing a poem, called simply *Devon*; Keats had returned to London from Margate and a short trip to Canterbury, and was now working hard on the second book of *Endymion*; and Hazlitt had just published his *Characters of Shakespeare's Plays* and left London for a short break. So when Haydon received an invitation to stay at Bank House with Dawson Turner and his family, it was gratefully accepted.

Yarmouth was around 120 miles from London by coach from the White Horse in Fetter Lane, or the Saracen's Head in Aldgate. It was, said a near-contemporary guide:

> ...from its traffic and maritime intercourse... more independent of the company that go [to] Brighton, Margate or Ramsgate; not a new-fangled place, built by greedy and insatiable swallows for a season, who live on the giddy summer-flies from London and its vicinity... provisions of every kind are to be had at a much cheaper rate...[199]

The town quays at Yarmouth were very close to Bank House and they were bustling with merchant brigs lifting the bulky sacks of malt and corn that were brought in from the surrounding countryside, and unloading coal and timber from the Baltic. The town, said a Gazetteer of 1815, has 'one of the most beautiful quays in Europe...

the markets on Wednesday and Saturday have abundant supplies... and the place affords every convenience for health and pleasure.'[200] However, upon his arrival at Yarmouth, Haydon took to his room, because he felt ill and unable to dine with the rest of the family. At two o'clock, 'my usual hour', as he called it, a little dinner of chops was brought to him (chops apparently being all he could eat). Being thus indulged in his 'old habits', he soon recovered and was able to eat in the family dining room. Haydon's diary shows us that Bank House was run like a school for the Turner children; they were never allowed to be idle. After breakfast, at eight o'clock, Turner went off to work at his bank while the children occupied themselves in drawing, French grammar and spelling. Turner, although undoubtedly a kind and loving father, seems to have ruled his family with a strict code of self-improvement. He was a man of many facts, like the headmaster Mr Gradgrind that Dickens would later create in his novel *Hard Times*. Here is Haydon's description of his host:

> Turner himself is a banker & a most extraordinary man of his kind. He is a celebrated botanist, published 'The Fuci or sea weeds', for which he has been honoured by Foreign Societies... In travelling he had too much [the] habits of the Botanists, pushing from one thing to another with a searching quickness and excessive restlessness that kept his mind ever on the look out, but never on the look in. His life was one incessant scene of fact collecting. At a Collection of Pictures, he never stopped to consider the beauties of any thing, but noted down who it was by, what I thought of it, and then turning instantly to another, would ask, 'what d'ye think of this?' Then he would have the whole

collection by heart, and could tell every Master & Picture in the House if you asked him the next day. He was an immense, living Index.[201]

Haydon spent three weeks with the Turners at Yarmouth but it seems it was not a completely harmonious stay. According to Haydon, Turner became angry or rude towards him 'once or twice' because he felt his guest was monopolising the family's conversations and attracting too much attention from the host's artistic wife and daughters. (In Haydon's view, Turner was 'jealous of attentions'.) There are at least two pages torn from Haydon's diary at the time of this visit, so we will probably never know what he really said or did to attract Turner's displeasure. However, the two men eventually parted on friendly terms and Haydon was grateful for his three-week stay at Bank House. It seems to have turned his head somewhat because on his return to London he decided, once and for all, that he must move out of his cramped, smelly lodgings in Great Marlborough Street.

Haydon had recently received some money from a Mr Phillips for a commission (the details of which weren't specified), and more money from his wealthy friend, Horace Smith. These funds, plus what (if anything) was left of Mr Harman's loan, would be wholly used up in moving expenses because there would be rent to pay in advance, furniture and crockery to buy, and a servant to employ. His painting of *Christ's Entry into Jerusalem* wasn't going to supply any of the necessary funds because its 195-square foot of canvas was propped up against the wall in Great Marlborough Street, still being painted with exactitude, inch by inch. Haydon would therefore require another loan to help him survive the first few months after the move, especially for the Christmas period. For this, he turned to one of the wealthiest and most generous bankers in London, Mr Thomas Coutts.

***

Benjamin Bailey was regarded by his friends as a rather serious young man, even if he liked to flirt with Reynolds' sisters and write humorous verse. He had briefly met Keats at Reynolds' house earlier in the year, and when Keats returned from his recent trip to Margate, Bailey met him again. Like Haydon, Keats was in rather depressed spirits. *Endymion* was not going well (he had just finished Book II which meant he had written some 2000 lines, but he had recently learned that Shelley's even longer poem, *Laon and Cynthia*, was almost complete), and he was short of money. As if that were not enough, he and his two brothers had moved out of Cheapside and into new lodgings, a few rooms in a postman's house in Well Walk, Hampstead. Unfortunately, these lodgings were proving wholly unsuitable – they were cramped, noisy and smelly. (Keats complained of the smell of the worsted stockings worn by his landlord's children.)

We saw earlier that Reynolds had sent Bailey a copy of Keats' *Poems of 1817*. Bailey had been surprised that Keats, a young man with no formal university education and no structured knowledge of philosophy or literature, could show himself to be 'a Poet of rare and original genius'. Knowing that Keats was struggling to make progress with his new book and that most Oxford scholars had left town at the end of the Trinity (or Act) term, Bailey invited Keats to spend a few weeks with him in the peaceful surroundings of Oxford. Desperate to make progress with *Endymion*, Keats accepted the invitation and thus was to begin a friendship based on genuine, heartfelt admiration, each man for the other, each having his own particular reason.

Unlike Reynolds' other friends, the majority of whom were self-educated, Bailey was a true scholar, actually studying at a university. He had matriculated the year before at the age of 25 and was now studying Holy Orders at Magdalen Hall (later incorporated into Hertford College) in Oxford. The son of a wealthy landowner, Bailey could afford a certain degree of luxury. There was a sofa in his rooms, a collection of books, snuff and cigars (or *segars* as Keats called them). Outside of his formal studies he liked to read poetry and philosophy, but as a student of the Old and New Testaments he was being trained as a linguist, a necessary qualification for a scholar of the Bible. In 1817, there was a Professor of Divinity at Oxford as well as Regius Professors of Hebrew and Greek, the primary languages of the Old and New Testaments. (In 1853, the Reverend E.B. Pusey, for 24 years a professor at Oxford, wrote to a Royal Commission about the teaching of theology to those taking Holy Orders at the university: 'When I first became a professor, I had… a class of 50 to learn the elements of Hebrew.') The Principal of Bailey's own college, Magdalen Hall, was a specialist in Arabic called John David MacBride. In later life, Benjamin Bailey would become an expert in the language of Malay.

After marrying a Bishop's daughter and taking various ecclesiastical posts in England, Bailey eventually moved abroad and settled in Ceylon. For several decades he was assumed to have died young. It was only when a first biography of Keats came out in 1848 and a copy found its way to Bailey (he was by then the Archdeacon of Colombo) that the literary world learned that Bailey was not only very much alive, but that he had an interesting story to tell about those few weeks he spent with Keats in Oxford in 1817. He wrote a letter to Keats' first biographer, Richard Monkton Milnes, dated 15 October 1848, informing him that, 'I am that "Mr Bailey" of whom at p. 62 of your first Volume, you say... Mr Bailey died soon after Keats.'[202]

This was the first of a series of letters that Bailey would write about Keats and they constitute an important account of him at the time he was writing *Endymion*. The first thing that Bailey wanted to emphasise was Keats' lack of an education:

> The errors of Keats's character – and they were as transparent as a weed in a pure and lucent stream of water – resulted from his education; rather from his want of education. But like the Thames Waters, when taken out to sea, he had the rare quality of purifying himself...[203]

By the 'rare quality of purifying himself' Bailey meant that Keats made up for his lack of a formal education by studying hard and learning quickly. Socially, he was,

> ...the most loveable creature, in the proper sense of that word as distinguished from amiable, I think I ever knew as a man. And he had

abundantly more of the poetical character, a hundred times told, than I ever knew in any individual.[204]

After telling Milnes a little about his own situation, that his wife had died many years previously and that he was recovering from an illness, he stated his intention to write more about Keats in the future. He didn't write again until May 1849, from Ratnapoora in Ceylon, but this second letter was much longer and full of his reminiscences of Keats:

> It was, I think, about the end of 1816, or the beginning of 1817, that my friend, Mr Reynolds, wrote to me at Oxford respecting Keats... He conveyed to me the same impressions, which the poet made upon the minds of almost all persons who had the happiness of knowing him, & subsequently upon myself. Early in 1817 his first volume of Poems was published by Ollier, which was sent to me. I required no more to satisfy me that he indeed was a Poet of rare and original genius.[205]

Bailey said that he had been delighted with the 'naturalness and simplicity' of Keats' character, and went on to describe his appearance. For this, he referred Milnes back to a description of Keats in a letter that had already been published. It was from the wife of a former friend of Keats who wrote,

> I never saw him but twice but the countenance lives in my mind as one of singular beauty and brightness – It has an expression as if he had been looking upon some glorious sight. His eyes were large... and his hair Auburn, he wore it divided down the centre of his head and it fell in rich masses on each side of his face...[206]

Bailey added his own recollection:

> His hair was beautiful – a fine brown, rather than auburn, I think; & if you placed your hand upon his head, the silken curls felt like the rich plumage of a bird… The eye was full & fine, & softened into tenderness, or beamed with a fiery brightness, according to the current of his thoughts and conversation…[207]

He then described their time together in Oxford when Keats was writing Book 3 of *Endymion*. Bailey was not overly impressed with the opening of this part of the poem, thinking it too much of 'the cockney school', a derogatory remark used by the critics of Leigh Hunt and his friends, but he did think the poem 'full of beauty, both of thought and diction, & rich beyond any poem of the same length in the English language'.

***

Bailey and Keats left London together on the 3 September 1817 on a coach called The Defiance which travelled from London to Oxford via a coaching Inn at Henley on Thames. The coach stopped outside the Mitre Inn on Oxford's High Street, just a short walk from Bailey's rooms in Magdalen Hall, an ancient edifice originally built in the 1480s as a grammar school. The building was located next to a tree-lined path alongside Magdalen College and close to the banks of the river Thames. As well as the student lodgings, there was a library 'with many valuable books', a refectory (with a portrait of William Tyndall), a common room and a chapel. Even before a fire destroyed much of the building in 1820, the main hall had been, said an Oxford guide book of 1822, 'in a very precarious and tottering state'.

Bailey had returned to Oxford between terms in order to catch up on some reading, and Keats settled in alongside him to work on his poem. The scholarly ambience was unlike anything Keats had experienced before – it could hardly have been more different from Margate or the Isle of Wight. In those places he had walked on beautiful beaches and stared at the sea, but he had felt aimless and isolated, unsure of how to go about his work and overwhelmed by the difficulties he faced. Now, with Bailey in Magdalen Hall, he found peace and quiet among libraries of books. Most importantly, in Bailey, he had an erudite companion, a scholar of poetry and philosophy who was genuinely interested in what he, John Keats, was trying to achieve. Keats wrote while Bailey studied, sometimes at the same table and sometimes at separate desks. They worked like this from 'breakfast [until] two or three o'clock.'[208]

Within days of arriving in Oxford, Keats began writing to his friends. It is clear from these letters that Bailey was discussing with Keats his own work on the Old Testament and stressing the importance of studying languages. Here are some examples of Bailey's influence, often made comical by a happy and playful Keats:

To Jane and Mariane Reynolds on 5 September:

> … But you are by the sea side… [and finding out] resemblances between… Dolphins and Madonas – which word, by the way, I must acquaint you was derived from the Syriac… when that Tamer Kewthon sold a certain camel called Peter to the overseer of the Babel Sky works, he thus spake… My dear Ten-story-up-in-the-air! This here

Beast... not only has the power of subsisting 40 days and 40 nights without fire and candle but he can sing...[209]

To his sister Fanny on 10 September:

...While I was speaking about France it occurred to me to speak a few Words on their language – it is perhaps the poorest one ever spoken since the jabbering in the Tower of Babel... I wish the Italian would supersede French in every school throughout the Country, for that is full of real poetry and romance...[210]

To Jane Reynolds on 14 September:

This is an age for typical Curiosities; and I would advise you, as a good speculation, to study Hebrew, and astonish the world with a figurative version in our own tongue... the Earth is our throne and the Sea a mighty minstrel playing before it – able, like David's harp, to make such a one as you forget almost the tempest cares of life... Tell Dilke [Charles Dilke, a family friend of the Reynolds] ...to rein in if Possible all the Nimrod of his disposition, he being a mighty hunter before the Lord – of the Manor...Give my sincerest respects to Mrs Dilke... had I remained in Hampstead I would have made precious havoc... and astonished [Charles Brown, a friend of Dilke]; whose letter to her... I would rather see than the original Copy of the Book of Genesis.[211]

And finally, to Reynolds on 21 September:

...These devils are a set of women, who having taken a snack or Luncheon of literary scraps, set themselves up for towers of Babel in languages...[212]

Many writers find it useful to set a target of so many lines or words a day, and Keats was no exception. When he was not penning these playful letters he was aiming to write 50 lines a day of the third book of *Endymion* and most days he achieved his target. At the end of the day he would read his lines out to Bailey and then the two men would go for a walk around the colleges or along the riverbanks of Oxford.[213] When they were not working, they read Shakespeare together, and Hazlitt. 'How is Hazlitt?' wrote Keats to Reynolds. 'We were reading his Table last night [*Table Talk*, Hazlitt's recently published book of essays]. I know he thinks himself not estimated by ten people in the world – I wish he knew he is.'[214]

There is a clue in one of the letters that Bailey and Keats read together Hazlitt's *Principles of Human Action*, (Hazlitt's first book, mentioned earlier), which has the supplementary title *Being an Argument in Favour of the Natural Disinterestedness of the Human Mind*. Keats later owned a copy of this book and its main argument in favour of 'disinterestedness' was to become profoundly important to him, as we shall see. The clue that he learned of it while at Oxford with Bailey is in the letter we noted above, when Keats wrote to Jane Reynolds on 14 September. Keats said that he would be forever grateful that the Reynolds family had introduced him to 'so real a fellow as Bailey. He delights me in the selfish and (please God) the disinterested part of my disposition,' adding that if the 'old poets' (primarily Shakespeare, who came to epitomise the principle of disinterestedness) have any pleasure in looking down at the enjoyers of their works, 'their eyes must bend with double satisfaction upon him. I sit as at a feast when he is over them'.

During their walks around Oxford, Bailey listened intently as Keats talked about his poetry. He revealed his thoughts about the construction of verse and Bailey, a linguist, remembered this discussion 30 years later. We have already seen how carefully Keats crafted his poems, from the early adoption of a Shakespearean device and the effective use of colour in the *Imitation of Spenser*, through the careful construction of the rhyme scheme in *Chapman's Homer*, to the exceptionally effective use of alliteration and onomatopoeia in the beautiful sonnet, *On the Sea*. Many years later in a letter to Richard Monkton Milnes, Keats' first biographer, Bailey wrote,

> One of his favourite topics of discourse was the principle of melody in Verse, upon which he had his own notions, particularly in the management of open and close vowels. I think I have seen a somewhat similar theory attributed to Mr Wordsworth. But I do not remember his laying it down in writing. Be that as it may, Keats' theory was worked out by himself. He was himself… a master of melody, which may be illustrated by almost numberless passages in his poems… You mention Keats' taste for painting and music [viz., in Milnes' biography]. Of the first I remember no more than his general love of the art, & his admiration for Haydon. But I well remember his telling me that, had he studied music, he had some notions of the combinations of the sounds, by which he thought he could have done something as original as his poetry.[215]

Such was the tone of the conversation. As we have seen, Keats was keeping Reynolds and his sisters apprised of his comings and goings and also of his discussions with Bailey but, as far as we can tell, he never wrote to Haydon, at least not until Haydon wrote to *him* on 17

September. (Keats mentioned that he had received this letter when he wrote to Reynolds on 21 September.) Once again, Haydon was jealous of the attention that Keats was receiving from others, so he fired off a letter that may be construed as an attempt to assert his artistic and intellectual authority over Keats, or at least to remind the poet that he, Haydon, was expecting to hear from him. Despite Haydon having taken no particular interest in the young painter Charles Cripps when he was in Oxford himself – not even writing about him in his diary – he now stressed that he was 'anxious to know about him' and asked Keats to contact Cripps and make an assessment of his work:

> ...Will you oblige me by going to Magdalen College and inquiring of the porter there about a young man who, when I was lately at Oxford, was copying the altar-piece at Magdalen by Morales. I am anxious to know about that young man – the copy promised something. Will you, if you can, see the young man and ascertain what his wishes in Art are? if he has ambition and seems to possess power? all of which you can soon discover. In these cases should any friend be disposed to assist him up to London and to support him for a year, I will train him in the Art with no further remuneration than the pleasure of seeing him advance...[216]

Keats, having now been Bailey's guest for three weeks, could not have known anything about Cripps so may have misunderstood the apparent urgency. 'Do oblige me,' said Haydon. 'Exert yourself by obliging me.' And for good measure: 'Perhaps Mr Bailey may also feel interest.' Keats did indeed seek out Charles Cripps and show him

Haydon's letter. Bailey, following Haydon's invitation, likewise took an interest in the young painter, the result being that Haydon got more than he bargained for when Keats replied on 28 September:

> I read your last to the young Man, whose name is Crip[p]s. He seemed more than ever anxious to avail himself of your offer... He does not possess the Philosopher's stone... but at Bailey's suggestion, whom I assure you is a very capital fellow, we have stummed up a kind of contrivance whereby he will be enabled to do himself the benefits you will have laid in his Path... If he can get ready in time to return to town with me, which will be in a few days – I will bring him to you...[217]

After hearing that Cripps might appear on his doorstep within the next few days, Haydon was told about Keats' progress with his poem:

> You will be glad to hear that within these last three weeks I have written 1000 lines – which are the third Book of my Poem. My Ideas with respect to it I assure you are very low... I am tired of it... and all the good I expect from my employment this summer is the fruit of Experience which I hope to gather in my next Poem...[218]

Keats had profited immensely from his stay with his erudite new friend and from now on he was to consider himself more of a scholar than he ever had before. But *Endymion* was depressing him and the thought of returning to London to finish it in the cramped lodgings in Hampstead was dampening his spirits. The journey was going to be long and uncomfortable and, to make matters worse, he was feeling unwell.

***

John Charles Felix Rossi was a sculptor whose father had originally come from Siena in Italy but had emigrated to England where he became a medical practitioner (unlike Keats, it seems he was not medically qualified.) The young John Rossi did not perhaps have an intellectual flair because he did not follow his father into medicine, he was apprenticed to a sculptor in London called John Baptist Locatelli. After completing his apprenticeship, Rossi entered the Royal Academy schools and, in 1785, won a travelling scholarship, a lucrative prize that took him to Rome for three years. He became a member of the Royal Academy in 1802 and in later life worked on some prestigious projects, including the stoneworks of Buckingham Palace and Somerset House, and some monumental work in St Paul's Cathedral. His career also included a spell at Coade's of Lambeth, an industrial manufacturer of durable 'artificial stone' from which decorative sculptures were cast. He specialised in making figures and reliefs in terracotta.

By 1817, John Rossi was about 55 years old with a very large family and a comfortable house in a new development called Lisson Grove. This was just to the south of St John's Wood, close to Lord's Cricket Ground and the new Regent's Canal. Rossi enjoyed improving his property so he rented out some rooms to supplement his income and one of these rooms came to the attention of Haydon. Compared to his painting room in Great Marlborough Street it was large – 30 feet long, 20 feet wide and 15 feet high – and well lit, a perfect studio for an artist. There were additional rooms – a separate bedroom and a servant's bedroom and a room which Haydon was later to refer to as 'the painting room', presumably a store room for his casts, unsold paintings and materials – although it is not clear whether these were adjacent to the main room or perhaps in a separate wing (the house still stands and is enclosed by several structures on different levels).

The rooms were let unfurnished and the rent was £30 a quarter. Haydon, back from his trip to Dawson Turner's in Yarmouth, paid Rossi two quarters' rent in advance. He moved all of his worldly goods, including his valuable collection of books and the painting of *Christ's Entry into Jerusalem*, the two miles or so from Great Marlborough Street to Lisson Grove on Saturday, 27 September 1817. At some point, he found the time to go shopping and he enjoyed his purchases in a happy, almost childlike, manner for the next day he wrote in his diary that he had breakfasted for the first time in his life 'on my own tea cup and saucers. I took up my own knife. I sat on my own chair. It was a new sensation!'[219] He went on to say that on his first night in his new bed he had been terribly tempted to steal into his servant's bedroom:

> I heard her step softly to her room. I heard her gown rustle. I sat up, my heart beat so violently. I listened! The bed creaked. She was in and near me! Was it manly to let a nice girl sleep so near one and at least without making an attempt?[220]

Fortunately for the girl, he remembered that her father had expressed his 'great comfort' that his favourite daughter was under Haydon's care, and this deterred him from attempting any 'manly' act. He later thanked God for his resolution.

Once he was settled into his new lodgings, Haydon set up his picture (it was no longer propped against the wall, but raised off the ground on an easel) and paused to reflect. He thought about the amount of time it was taking him to paint this picture and, quite characteristically, compared himself with Titian and Michelangelo. Titian, he said, took years to complete a painting because he painted every individual thing, every plant and tree stump, every cloud, directly from nature, 'that the means of conveying his ideas might be as perfect as the conception'.[221] Michelangelo, on the other hand, painted very quickly – the Sistine Chapel in 20 months, said Haydon, because he 'was utterly regardless of [the] truth of imitation... and was satisfied if the mind could comprehend his intention by a hint.'[222] This shows that Haydon was still adhering to the tenet he had developed whilst studying the Elgin Marbles back in 1813: 'Beauty of form is but the vehicle of conveying ideas, but truth of conveyance is the first object.'

Haydon believed that the ideas expressed in any work of art were the primary consideration, but it was the *truth of their conveyance* that separated the Elgin Marbles or a painting by Titian or Raphael or Haydon from most other works. But in his own case the enormous effort of ensuring that every painted object was depicted exactly as it would appear naturally was taking years to achieve. His son later remembered that a student called Bewick had said that every nostril and every fingernail of *Christ's Entry* was 'a complete study'. (A later generation of painters adopted Haydon's ideas and created brilliantly coloured works of art based on the minute study of nature.

Considering Haydon's worship of Raphael, it is both interesting and ironic that they were known as the Pre-Raphaelites – they believed that European art had been formalised and ruined by the academies that sprang up in the wake of the Renaissance.)

In his new studio in Lisson Grove, as he studied his painting of *Christ's Entry*, Haydon believed that when it was finally completed and exhibited it would create a sensation and bring him even more fame and money than *Solomon* had. All he had to do was look after his health, especially his eyes, and continue to borrow the money he needed for food, rent and painting materials. He lost no time in inviting his friends and neighbours to visit him, to admire his spacious new lodgings and contemplate his beautifully detailed and colourful painting.

***

After vacating the cottage in Hampstead and spending much of the summer with the Shelleys at Marlow, Leigh Hunt and his family moved back to London, to 13 Lisson Grove where, purely by coincidence, they found themselves near neighbours of Haydon. Shelley was a regular visitor to Lisson Grove because he was using Hunt's new house as a base for his literary affairs and publishing schemes. He had found a publisher for Mary's recently completed *Frankenstein* (having negotiated a favourable deal) and had now finished his own poem *Laon and Cynthia* which, he believed, needed a different publisher. He wrote to one company from Hunt's house:

> …my wish… is first, to know whether you would purchase my interest in the copyright – an arrangement which, if there be any truth

in the opinions of my friends Lord Byron and Mr Leigh Hunt of my powers, cannot be disadvantageous to you...[223]

As Shelley went about his literary pursuits, Hunt travelled between his new home in Lisson Grove and the offices of the *Examiner* which had recently moved to Catherine Street, opposite Somerset House. On 10 September, Hunt went to the Theatre Royal, Drury Lane in order to write a theatrical review. The famously spacious and opulent theatre (it could seat over 3,000 people) had just re-opened after a refurbishment which had included new spiral staircases, pagodas with 'Chinese' decoration and the installation of gas lighting (which many who were used to the subtle and diffused light of the candelabra found too glaring).

Reynolds was at the same performance for the same reason. He was there to write a review for his own newspaper, the *Champion*, and the two old friends met in the rows of benches below the stage, known as the 'pit'. As they chatted, Keats came up in conversation. He was still working on *Endymion*, said Reynolds, and making good progress towards his objective of completing 4,000 lines. Hunt replied that if it hadn't been for *him*, for Hunt's own steadying influence, Keats would have written 7,000 lines, the implication being that Keats had a tendency to be diffuse and verbose in his poetry but that Hunt had cured him of this. In the next letter he had sent to Keats in Oxford, Reynolds had mentioned Hunt's comment which Keats seemed to shrug off when he wrote a letter in reply:

> ...I think I see you and Hunt meeting in the Pit... Failings I am always rather rejoiced to find in a man than sorry for; they bring us to a Level. He has them, but his makes-up are very good.[224]

We are reminded here of what Haydon said about Hunt when Hunt had called on him after their relationship had cooled:

> There is no resisting him. I got as delighted as ever by his wit, his poetry, his taste, his good humour... Peace to him. I would never have called again if he had not called on me. I'll now go and see him as usual.

Hunt did indeed have a great talent for friendship and he was exceptionally good at keeping hold of his friends, but his '7,000 lines' comment to Reynolds was to prove a major irritation to Keats, as we shall see.

***

Keats had returned to the Hampstead lodgings that he shared with his two brothers by way of two or three coaches from Oxford. He had completed 3,000 of the 4,000 lines he was trying to write, but as we saw in his letter to Haydon he was unhappy with the poem. The sheer effort of writing thousands of rhyming couplets within a meaningful narrative was beginning to wear him down. Bailey, in the letter we noted above, admitted that he did not like many of the 'forced rhymes' in *Endymion*. One small extract from Book 3, which Keats wrote when he was in Oxford with Bailey, will give an idea of what he meant. Endymion is walking on the bottom of the sea having fallen in love with Cynthia, the goddess of the moon:

> Far had he roamed,
> With nothing save the hollow vast that foamed
> Above, around and at his feet – save things
> More dead than Morpheus's imaginings:
> Old rusted helmets, anchors, breast-plates large
> Of gone sea warriors; brazen beaks and targe;
> Rudders that for a hundred years had lost
> The sway of human hand; gold vase embossed
> With long-forgotten story, and wherein
> No reveller had ever dipped a chin
> But those of Saturn's vintage; mouldering scrolls
> Writ in the tongue of heaven by those souls
> Who first were on the earth...

Keats was clearly desperate when he rhymed 'breast-plates large' with the old English word for a shield, 'targe', and also when he talked about a reveller dipping a 'chin' into a gold vase. What was much worse for Keats was knowing that he had another *thousand* lines to write.

After being reunited with his brothers in Hampstead Keats put the poem aside for a day or two and went to Lamb's Conduit Street in Bloomsbury to deliver a parcel from Bailey to Reynolds. Reynolds wasn't at home, so he walked or took a cab out to Lisson Grove to visit Hunt and Haydon, neither of whom he'd seen since before he left London for Oxford. Shelley was at Hunt's, as usual, and Keats later remarked that Hunt was still 'infatuated' with him. (Hunt was still in a minority. A few weeks later the diarist Henry Crabb Robinson met Shelley for the first time and described him as 'vehement and arrogant and intolerant'.) Horace Smith may have been visiting Hunt, too.

Keats and Hunt then walked along the street to visit Haydon. The artist's pride in his new home can readily be imagined, and the fact that his painting room was so much larger than before meant that he had more space to entertain his guests and show off his painting, even if it was still only half finished. We noted earlier that Haydon's picture contained dozens of portraits and that Haydon had used many of his friends – Hazlitt, Keats, Wordsworth and more – as models. With Keats looking on, and possibly Shelley and Horace Smith, too, Hunt now walked up and down Haydon's painting room, criticising the picture. Haydon's reaction in his diary was particularly vehement, even for him:

> There is not a more selfish being living than Leigh Hunt. He rides along the surface of the Earth on the skin of a little poney [sic] filled with the air of his own vanity and fancies it a blood charger, chattering of all things & ignorant of most things with sparkling delight holding a mirror in his hand to contemplate with infinite satisfaction his own feeble and foppish countenance, dreading to see Truth, who stands behind with a sigh, ready to blaze in his eyes if the looking glass could be but moved from his enchanted grasp. Thus he skims away, talking of music & Painting & Poetry & Morals… He is suffered to ride because no one cares to unhorse him… but the day of retribution will arrive. Someone enraged at his insufferable conceit & pricking from his needle stabs will drive a pen knife into his horse's side and let out the air, with a reeking puff, that now supports his arrogant rider…

Why I am nettled at Leigh Hunt so I cannot tell, but I really begin to despise him.[225]

All of a sudden, the sheer pettiness of these seemingly endless infatuations and squabbles – Hunt and Shelley baiting Haydon at Horace Smith's dinner; Haydon constantly warning Keats of Hunt's 'delusions'; Hunt claiming that he was a controlling influence over Keats' verbosity in poetry; and now Hunt's criticisms of Haydon's picture – they all tipped Keats over from a state of frustration to one bordering on disgust. When he was back in his lodgings, he wrote to Bailey with the latest news from London:

> ...every Body seems at Loggerheads. There's Hunt infatuated – there's Haydon's picture in statu quo – There's Hunt walks up and down his painting room criticising every head most unmercifully. There's Horace Smith tired of Hunt... I am quite disgusted with literary men and will never know another except Wordsworth... Haydon and Hunt have known each other many years – now they live, pour ainsi dire, jealous neighbours...[226]

Keats decided that, in order to find the peace and space he needed to finish the final 1,000 lines of *Endymion*, he would need to get away from London (and Hunt and Haydon) yet again. For his part, Haydon had started to think about a grand dinner party in his new lodgings, one to which he would invite some of his most trusted friends – Keats and Wordsworth among them, but Hunt definitely not. First, though, Haydon would need to borrow more money. He either didn't realise, or didn't care, that while his relationship with Leigh Hunt was deteriorating daily another issue was fermenting that would have a detrimental effect upon his relationship with Keats. It was that of Charles Cripps. Despite the continuing efforts of both Keats and Bailey to help the young Oxford artist raise the finances he would need to move to London, it was becoming clear that Haydon had made this offer whilst 'filled with the air of his own vanity'.

Chapter 11

'...are we to be bullied into a certain Philosophy engendered in the whims of an Egotist?'

John Keats: *Letter to John Hamilton Reynolds* (February 1818)

In his large and airy studio at 22 Lisson Grove, Haydon was trying to make a fresh start with his painting and to resume his habit of deep thinking (or 'conjuring' as his servant called it). On Saturday 8 November 1817, he had seen in London a cast of Michelangelo's *Moses*, the magnificent marble statue commissioned for the tomb of Pope Julius II and installed at San Pietro in Vincoli, Rome. As with the Elgin Marbles, Michelangelo's *Moses* had inspired Haydon to write several pages of thoughts and observations in his diary. This time, however, he was not enamoured of the statue.

For Haydon, Michelangelo had committed the cardinal sin of making a man – Moses in this case – look unnatural. The statue was 'awkwardly composed' and 'vulgar in its limbs'. The famous surgeon John Bell had said much the same after viewing the original in Rome; he was of the opinion that several of the greatest artists of the Renaissance had ruined their work by exaggerating the muscular anatomy of their statues. (As we saw in Chapter 3, John Bell was Charles Bell's brother and the author of *The Anatomy of the Human Body* with its flayed corpses hanging by ropes.) At the very end of his life, John Bell wrote a book called *Observations on Italy* in which he said of Michelangelo's *Moses*:

> Because the moderns...found that the human body was composed of bones, muscles, tendons, and ligaments, is the statuary called upon to perpetually remind us of [this]? ...even the great Michael Angelo himself was not exempt from... producing coarseness... The right arm full, muscular, and nervous, is fine, especially in the anatomy, and well proportioned to the size of the figure, but seems too large, contrasted with the left... [and] the largeness of the limbs and length of the body hardly correspond with the size of the head...[227]

Haydon thought that Michelangelo's greatness was due to the power of his imagination, but 'the mode of conveying his idea was false & mannered'. The result was that when Michelangelo turned away from nature's design in order to create his own, asymmetrical and exaggerated version of human musculature, he created a *style*. Continuing to muse about this, he granted that on rare occasions an artist may deviate from nature when an idea is so beautiful that 'the errors or inadequacy of the means of representation may be forgiven'. He added, however, that if an artist wants to emulate the perfection of the ancients, 'there must be nothing to forgive'. He summarised these thoughts as follows:

> The Greeks always considered the intentions of Nature in whatever objects they represented, and their ideal beauty in their finest time

> never proceeded beyond restoring the represented object to the essential qualities which nature had bestowed on it…

He also applied these ideas to the art of poetry, it being one of the arts

> whose mode of conveying intellectual associations is per se capable of exciting beauty of feeling…

and which

> ought surely to have its intellectual feelings engaged in all the truth & purity of which its language is capable; our Brothers the Poets are not born if their grammar is bad or the language obscure.[228]

Haydon committed these thoughts to his diary between Saturday 8 November and Monday 17 November 1817, just before Keats left London again in a further attempt to find the peace and quiet he needed to complete *Endymion*.

We know that Keats was feeling unwell during this period, and avoided walking outdoors in the winter weather. He was still writing letters to Haydon because he wanted to discuss the progress that he (Keats) and Bailey were making in their continuing efforts to bring Charles Cripps down to London from Oxford, but Haydon was not replying. It must have been apparent to Keats that Haydon was procrastinating over taking Cripps into his household and 'training him in the Art'. This was puzzling because by now Haydon had taken on some pupils. They lived in lodgings and came to the Lisson Grove studio for instruction though Haydon appears not to have charged them anything. One of them, William Bewick, genuinely admired

Haydon, calling him a 'great man' and regarding him almost as a father. We cannot doubt that Haydon was an excellent and conscientious teacher – he clearly saw himself as a beacon of light to the next generation and was convinced that his pupils would carry forward his ideas. Perhaps he hoped the Royal Academicians would one day regret their failure to admit him to their ranks.

Haydon's arrangement with Bewick was informal, so quite why he had earlier decided that Cripps should be officially 'bound' to him is a mystery. The motive cannot have been financial; it is true that Cripps would have had to pay Haydon a substantial sum of money, but in return Haydon would have been legally bound to provide Cripps with food and lodging. When Haydon did finally respond to Keats, his letter indicated that he took it for granted that Keats (and presumably Bailey) would continue to do their utmost to raise a subscription for Cripps in order to pay his fee. (The arrangement would have been similar to the one that had tied Keats to the Enfield doctor, Thomas Hammond.)

Now, for some reason, Haydon seems to have changed his mind and decided he didn't want Cripps as a pupil after all. When Bailey wrote to him about the matter he received a reply (unfortunately now lost) which clearly offended Bailey. The Oxford scholar complained to Keats who had just moved to the Fox and Hounds at Burford Bridge, a coaching inn between Leatherhead and Dorking in Surrey, in order to work on his book. Keats replied to Bailey on Saturday 22 November:

> To a Man of your nature, such a Letter as Haydon's must have been extremely cutting... As soon as I had known Haydon three days, I got enough of his Character not to have been surprised at such a Letter as he has hurt you with.[229]

Keats wrote to Reynolds on the same day and mentioned to him, too, the problems that he and Bailey were having with Haydon over the issue of Cripps. However, despite these distractions and frustrations, Keats' opinion of Haydon's artistic and intellectual gifts never wavered. He told Bailey that Haydon was a man of genius whose failings had to be allowed for:

> I wish you knew all that I think about Genius and the Heart...Men of Genius are great as certain ethereal Chemicals operating on the Mass of neutral intellect – but they have not any individuality, any determined Character...[230]

Keats truly believed that Haydon's stature as an artist and as a man of letters was akin to that of the great Renaissance artists. (Despite Haydon's recent misgivings and doubts, he still put on the airs of a Renaissance Master. He continued to wear his hair unfashionably long, for example, like Raphael's, even if it was by now receding at the front.) In his letter to Bailey Keats gave the following advice: '...don't because you have suddenly discovered a Coldness in Haydon, suffer yourself to be teased.'

Keats had in fact been moving towards this position, that Bailey would suffer if he worried too much about Haydon's deficiencies, in an earlier letter of Monday 3 November:

> I hope you will receive an answer from Haydon soon – if not, Pride! Pride! Pride!... If I did not know how impossible it is, I should say – 'do not at this time of disappointment, disturb yourself about others.'[231]

It was while writing this latest letter in defence of Haydon that an extraordinary train of thoughts came tumbling from Keats' mind:

> I am certain of nothing but the Holiness of the heart's affections, and the truth of Imagination. What the Imagination seizes as Beauty must be Truth whether it existed before or not, for I have the same idea of all our passions as of Love: they are all, in their sublime, creative of essential Beauty.[232]

This last sentence goes well beyond the commonplace notion that we tend to idealise the object of our love, that 'beauty is in the eye of the beholder'. Keats was saying that our passions can create *essential* beauty, that is to say beauty that is pure in the highest degree, by imaginative means. This was written just days after Haydon had said in his diary that poetry is an art 'whose mode of conveying intellectual associations is *per se* capable of exciting beauty of feeling.' Later, when Keats was comparing his own mode of writing with that of the much more famous and successful Lord Byron, he wrote,

> There is this great difference between us. He describes what he sees – I describe what I imagine – Mine is the hardest task.[233]

These ideas appear to draw heavily on Plato, the ancient Greek philosopher who taught that all beauty is just an imperfect reflection (or a shadow) of an ideal, sublime or perfect beauty in a celestial domain, and that earthly goodness and justice, etc., are similarly imperfect reflections (as discussed in the famous *Allegory of the Cave* in Book VII, 514a-520a, of Plato's *Republic*). We can recall from Chapter 3 that when Haydon studied the Elgin Marbles he was conscious that he was 'contemplating what Socrates looked at and Plato saw'. We know that Bailey read Plato at Oxford, and Keats was soon to use an expression from Plato's discourse on poetry in a letter to Reynolds. We shall explore the connection with Plato in more detail later.

For now, despite all this philosophising, Keats still believed that Bailey should not think too much about Haydon. Living a life of sensations, feeling life 'on the pulse' (to use another of Keats' expressions) was preferable to a life of thought, because a life of sensations is a *real* life, here and now. As we saw earlier, the idea that people should enjoy their lives here in the present moment was the sentiment expressed in Wordsworth's *Prefatory Sonnet*, a poem that Keats had admired and emulated:

> Nuns fret not at their Convent's narrow room;
> And Hermits are contented with their Cells;
> And Students with their pensive Citadels:
> Maids at the Wheel, the Weaver at his Loom,
> Sit blithe and happy; Bees that soar for bloom,
> High as the highest peak of Furness Fells,
> Will murmur by the hour in Foxglove bells…

From his lodgings at Burford Bridge, Keats now wrote a little poem about a tree that had been frozen on a December night. Like the nuns, the students and the bees in Wordsworth's sonnet, the frozen tree is 'happy' just to exist in the present moment. Its branches do not hark back to the warm summer when they were full of foliage because they 'know' that neither the cold north wind nor the freezing winter temperatures can stop them from budding again next year:

> In drear-nighted December,
> Too happy, happy tree,
> Thy branches ne'er remember
> Their green felicity.
> The north cannot undo them
> With a sleety whistle through them
> Nor frozen thawings glue them
> From budding at the prime.

Bailey was, of course, a Christian, so he did not believe that the 'here and now' was all there was to life; he believed that he (or his soul) would survive death and experience an afterlife. In his letter to Bailey, Keats acknowledged the latter's Christianity by modifying his message. He said that living a life of sensations 'here and now' would be a *precursor* to a spiritual life:

> O for a life of Sensations rather than Thoughts! It is 'a Vision in the form of Youth', a shadow of reality to come, and this consideration has further convinced me... that we shall enjoy ourselves hereafter by having what we call happiness on Earth repeated in a finer tone. And yet such a fate can only befall those who delight in Sensation rather than hunger as you do after Truth. Adam's dream will do here, and seems to be a Conviction that Imagination and its empyreal reflexion is the same as human life and its spiritual repetition.[234]

The Pursuit of Beauty and Truth

***

In early December, 1817, Haydon became so desperate for money that he approached one of the wealthiest men in London for a loan, hoping that his slight acquaintance with the man's wife might be of significance. She had been an actress called Harriet Mellon and Haydon had got to know her through his acquaintance with another actress, Maria Foote. The latter was the daughter of the manager of a Plymouth theatre and had been playing leading roles on her father's stage since she was twelve years old. By 1814, she was firmly established in London, and a great success at Covent Garden. Her best performance (according to a contemporary magazine, the *Ladies Monthly Museum*) was as Prospero's daughter, Miranda, in *The Tempest*.

Maria Foote's parents had been friends of the Haydon family, so it had been natural for Haydon to ask her to sit for him as a model. She came to his studio one day in November 1815:

> Dear Maria sat again today and tormented me while I painted, with her lovely archness & wicked, fascinating fun. After sitting for some time she insisted she could paint the hair better than mine, & taking the brushes out of my hand… she dabbled a lock over the forehead, & then laughed with a rich thrilling at her own lovely awkwardness… I could have eat her bit by bit…[235]

She sat for three hours that day, sometimes singing, sometimes mimicking ballad singers, and sometimes asking Haydon's opinion 'on different things'. After the sitting, she went shopping in the fashionable Bond Street.

It was Harriet Mellon, however, who now became the focus of Haydon's attention. She was the daughter of parents who had worked in a travelling theatre company back in the late 1780s. Harriet's mother, Mrs Entwistle, was a violent woman with a short temper who had both worshipped and terrorised her little girl; her stepfather was a musician who drank too much. Harriet herself took to the stage when still a teenager, and her first real break came in 1794 when the playwright and theatre impresario Richard Brinsley Sheridan saw her perform in a provincial play. He was the owner and manager of the Drury Lane theatre in London and after speaking with Harriet he promised to consider her for a part in one of his productions. As a result of Sheridan's interest, the family moved to London and rented rooms in a house near Southwark. The rent was minimal, around ten pounds a year, on account of the house being located in 'a dismal swamp [with] mounds of earth and stagnant pools'. However, according to Harriet's first biographer, the young actress did not find it miserable at all because it was the first house in which the family had been able to install its own furniture. To her it seemed to have 'a very high degree of respectability'.[236]

Sheridan kept his promise and the teenage Harriet Mellon duly appeared on the stage at Drury Lane. She became so successful that it wasn't long before the family could afford to move across the Thames into London proper. They took new lodgings at 17 Little Russell Street, directly opposite the Drury Lane theatre. Harriet was well liked by almost everyone at Drury Lane because of her talent and her willingness to play the parts that other actresses did not want to play. She also had a great sense of fun and was a brilliant mimic. With her career at Drury Lane progressing and her reputation growing, she became well acquainted with the greatest actors and actresses of the day, including the doyenne of Drury Lane, the great Mrs Siddons.

It soon became apparent that Harriet was financially astute, too, because she began to invest her earnings in property. She occasionally played at the theatre in Cheltenham, a fashionable spa town in Gloucestershire, and believing this to be a sound investment, bought her parents a music shop and post office in the town. It was in 1805 that the now 28-year-old actress got her second lucky break. She was appearing at the theatre in Cheltenham and during a morning walk she was seen and admired by a man who was rumoured to be the wealthiest person in London, the near 70-year-old banker, Thomas Coutts ('a man whose name was a proverb of wealth even in country towns').[237] Coutts was in Cheltenham to recover from a bout of ill health brought on by the stress of looking after his demented wife. Even though he was an 'old, pallid, sickly, thin gentleman in a shabby coat and brown scratch wig', Mrs Entwistle lost no time in inviting him to one of her daughter's performances and it didn't take long for the old man to become rather besotted with Harriet.

A family friendship was established in Cheltenham and kept up in London where Coutts became a regular visitor at Harriet's lodgings in Little Russell Street. Soon afterwards it was rumoured that Harriet had won a £5000 lottery ticket; she bought the house in Little Russell Street and also a spacious two-storey Georgian house called Holly Lodge at Highgate. It had its own extensive gardens where Harriet held regular parties for her numerous friends. This is where Haydon met her, when he went along to one of these parties with Maria Foote. Haydon said there was a 'fun room' at Holly Lodge for dancing and that there was nothing in Harriet Mellon but 'a girlish, romping, full-hearted' woman who wished to see everybody as happy as she herself was.[238] When old Elizabeth Coutts died in 1815, Thomas Coutts proposed to Harriet and must have been delighted when she accepted. When she moved into the family mansion in Stratton Street, Mayfair, all of fashionable London was aware that the former child actress now circulated in the very highest social circles.

In December 1817, Haydon was told by his old friend Fuseli that Mr Coutts had acted 'in a princely way' when he purchased one of Fuseli's paintings. Haydon decided to ask Mr Coutts for a loan, but having had no direct connection with him, he wrote to the new *Mrs* Coutts and asked her to intercede on his behalf. The reply did not come from Harriet, but from her husband, from his office on the Strand:

> Sir,
>
> I have considered with attention your letter and I confess tho' my feelings tell me I ought not to consent to the request it contains... I feel an inclination to put the sum of Four Hundred pounds in your powers, and to indulge the flattery of seeing by that means your Picture finished, & your fortune established in the manner you have pictured...[239]

A day was duly appointed for Haydon to visit the Coutts family home in Stratton Street. Haydon, of course, was used to socialising with persons of consequence but he desperately needed this loan and so did his best to make a good impression. Thomas Coutts approached Haydon with the new Mrs Coutts on his arm. Would the former Miss Mellon be her 'girlish, romping, full-hearted' self?

> A look from her at once told me all was altered. No more 'fun rooms'. I bowed with stately gravity, and he welcomed me and shook my hand… All went on with gravity and decorum till we came to a bust of Mr Coutts by Nollekens [the sculptor, known as 'Nolly']… Harriet Mellon's love of humour made her forget Mrs Coutts' sense of dignity. She went off like a rocket and mimicked Nolly's manner to perfection. But times were altered; she was the great banker's wife… Mr Coutts gave her a look which iced her. In a minute or two she curtsied low to me, and swept out of the room; but she could not help turning that eye of hers as she went out. A glance was enough to convince me she was Harriet Mellon still.[240]

We can easily imagine Mrs Coutts giving Haydon 'a glance' to show that she was still her old fun-loving self, and this was exactly the sort of thing that Haydon noticed and delighted in recording in his diary. With the business of the day complete (Coutts had advanced him the £400), Haydon left the house to find a 'poor negro beggar' standing on the steps asking for help. Haydon wondered who was the greatest beggar, he who had asked for £400 and was received in the drawing room, or he who had asked for a bit of bread and was spurned from the door.

***

On the afternoon of Sunday 28 December 1817, several visitors turned up at Haydon's studio in Lisson Grove. Keats, back from his trip to Burford Bridge, had come from his Hampstead lodgings; Wordsworth had come from lodgings in Mortimer Street, about a mile away, and Wordsworth's brother in law Thomas Monkhouse had made the short trip from his home in nearby Queen Ann Street. Charles Lamb, the friend of Leigh Hunt whom we met briefly earlier, a man who was very close to both Wordsworth and Hazlitt, had arrived from Little Russell Street where he and his sister had recently taken a house two doors down from Harriet Mellon's old lodgings.

Keats, Wordsworth, Monkhouse and Lamb enjoyed dinner in Haydon's painting room on a table laid with silverware (presumably bought with Mr Coutts' loan). The servants for the occasion included the tall and muscular corporal Sammons, a retired soldier whom Haydon had used for years as a model but who now fulfilled the role of general servant or handyman. Dominating the room, illuminated by candlelight, was the huge, half-finished but richly coloured painting of *Christ's Entry into Jerusalem*. This was an impressive scene, and a far cry from the cramped conditions in Great Marlborough Street.

Leigh Hunt, who, we will recall, lived just a few doors away, had not been invited on account of his recent criticism of Haydon's picture, nor had Haydon's friend William Hazlitt because of his rift with Wordsworth. But Reynolds had been invited. When all the coats and hats had been taken and dinner was ready to be served, Haydon became annoyed that Reynolds had neither turned up nor sent any excuse for his absence. Reynolds was in fact going through a turbulent time in his life; he was still living with his parents and he was now in love with a young woman called Eliza Drewe. A marriage proposal was out of the question because he lacked any sort of financial security. Having agonised over his predicament, he had recently decided to give up his long-cherished literary ambitions and after giving notice of his intention to resign his post at the *Champion*, he accepted a friend's offer of a post in a solicitor's office (Keats wrote to Bailey on 3 November that Reynolds was to be articled that day). Just as he was making these momentous decisions, Reynolds heard (most likely from Bailey in Oxford) that Haydon was causing no end of problems due to his seeming indifference about Cripps and the offensive letter he had sent to Bailey.[241]

Reynolds was, of course, a close friend of both Haydon and Bailey. After deciding that Bailey was in the right, he temporarily put his own problems aside and wrote Haydon a letter of remonstrance. Haydon responded with a letter that turned out to be just as offensive as the one he had sent to Bailey, and then another which was intended to be palliative, but actually caused even more offence. Reynolds didn't receive these letters (or reply to them) until early January 1818, but when he did reply it was with a cutting letter which deeply upset Haydon.[242] At the time of Haydon's dinner party, the friendship between Haydon and Reynolds was effectively over.

The dinner went ahead and Haydon later considered it to have been such an enjoyable evening that he called it The Immortal Dinner. He has left us an excellent and famous description of the evening that is worth quoting at length. It reads like a theatrical farce, but is apparently a true record of an exchange that occurred after the meal was over and everyone had retired to another room. Despite being a well-known poet, Wordsworth had to supplement his income by working in the Lake District as a regional comptroller of stamps (an auditor of the district postal service). A man called John Kingston, who was a comptroller in London and technically Wordsworth's superior in the postal service, had decided to call at Lisson Grove and beg an introduction to the poet. He duly turned up on the doorstep after dinner, by which time Charles Lamb was rather drunk. Haydon recorded the ensuing conversation between Kingston and Wordsworth in his diary and worked it up many years later into a vivid and entertaining account. It is a delightful insight into the manners of gentlemen at this time:

> When we retired to tea we found the comptroller. In introducing him to Wordsworth I forgot to say who he was. After a little time the comptroller looked down, looked up, and said to Wordsworth: 'Don't you think, sir, Milton was a great genius?' Keats looked at me, Wordsworth looked at the comptroller. Lamb, who was dozing by the fire turned round and said: 'Pray, sir, did you say Milton was a great genius?' 'No, sir; I asked Mr Wordsworth if he were not.' 'Oh,' said Lamb, 'then you are a silly fellow.' 'Charles! My dear Charles!' said Wordsworth... After an awful pause, the comptroller said: 'Don't you think Newton a great genius?' I could not stand it any longer. Keats put his head into my books... Wordsworth seemed asking himself: 'Who is this?' Lamb got up, and taking a candle, said: 'Sir, will you allow me to look at your phrenological development?'...

The [comptroller], finding Wordsworth did not know who he was, said in a spasmodic and half-chuckling anticipation of assured victory: 'I have had the honour of some correspondence with you, Mr Wordsworth.' 'With me, sir?' said Wordsworth, 'not that I remember.' 'Don't you, sir? I am a comptroller of stamps.' There was a dead silence, the comptroller evidently thinking that was enough. While we were waiting for Wordsworth's reply, Lamb sung out:

'Hey diddle diddle,

The cat and the fiddle.'

'My dear Charles!' said Wordsworth.

'Diddle diddle dumpling, my son John,'

chaunted Lamb, and then rising, exclaimed: 'Do let me have another look at that gentleman's organs.'... Keats and I hurried Lamb into the painting-room, shut the door, and gave way to inextinguishable laughter. Monkhouse followed and tried to get Lamb away. We went back, but the comptroller was irreconcilable. We soothed and smiled, and asked him to supper. He stayed, though his dignity was sorely affected... All the while... we could hear Lamb struggling in the painting-room and calling at intervals: 'Who is that fellow? Allow me to see his organs once more.'[243]

***

Keats' circle of friends was now widening considerably. He had recently been introduced to Charles Wentworth Dilke, a friend of the Reynolds family. Dilke, who was 28 years old and liberal in his politics, had followed his father into the Navy Pay Office, an administrative department which was housed in Somerset House along with the Royal Academy of Arts and the Royal Society. (This may seem strange company for a group of naval clerks, but after years of sea battles against the French the navy was considered essential to the defence of the realm and its offices were quite magnificent. As the Thames waters lapped against the south side of Somerset House, the navy officers could be seen travelling by boat to and from the warehouses and shipyards at Deptford and Woolwich.)

Charles Wentworth Dilke was a loving family man who doted on his young son. His wife was a friendly and compassionate woman who seems to have taken pity on the Keats orphans – John, George, Tom and Fanny – and made them feel particularly welcome in her Hampstead home. She once described Keats as 'a very odd young man, but good tempered, and good hearted, and very clever indeed'[244]. Though he worked in the navy office, Dilke was a scholar who had recently edited a six-volume edition of *Old English Plays*. Like many of Keats' other friends – Haydon, Hazlitt, Hunt – he had never been to a university, but loved books and scholarship. Here is what he wrote to his son when the boy was around 16 years old and staying in Italy with a relative:

> I like your purchases, and envy you the pleasure of reading *The Letters of the Younger Pliny*. You seem to have something of your father and your grandfather in you, and to love books; but do not mistake buying them for reading them, a very common error with half the world... Once feel the pleasure of learning, or rather of knowledge, and I cannot conceive a man ever forsaking it.[245]

Such a man was bound to admire Keats, the young poet who even as a schoolboy had learned Lemprière almost by heart and translated Virgil in his spare time. For his part, Keats knew that Dilke had a certain disdain for literary fads and fashions – he had actually said so in his introduction to the *Old English Plays*:

> There are few things that would tend more immediately to repress our vanity…than an attentive examination of the fluctuation of opinion, in regard to the respective literary rank of authors. To contemplate the feverish elevation that superficial and obtrusive ignorance has sometimes risen to, as opposed to the cold and bitter neglect that has more frequently chilled the labours of retiring genius: to see the same man, perhaps,
>
> Who have sometime, like young Phaëton
> Rid in the burnished chariot of the Sun,
> Outliving his popularity, and in his own time forgotten…[246]

This would have been music Keats' ears, a man whose first book of poems had been almost completely ignored and who was about to publish a second, *Endymion*, a much more ambitious book.

We shall see that Dilke encouraged Keats to discuss his ideas about poetry, beauty and the imagination, and that they had a particularly interesting conversation during the weekend of 21 and 22 December, 1817. Leading up to this, on Monday 15 December, Keats had been to Drury Lane to see Edmund Kean as the Duke of Gloucester in Shakespeare's *Richard III*. He had written a review of Kean's performance for the next edition of the *Champion* (on 21 December) as a favour to Reynolds who had left London for a

Christmas break in Devon. In his review, entitled, simply, *Mr Kean*, Keats describes Kean as a romantic figure who would always make a dramatic appearance on the stage – 'who always seems just arrived from the camp of Charlemagne' as he put it. He draws the reader's attention to Kean's 'music of elocution':

> A melodious passage in poetry is full of pleasures both sensual and spiritual… The sensual life of verse springs warm from the lips of Kean, and to one learned in Shakespearean hieroglyphics – learned in the spiritual portion of those lines to which Kean adds a sensual grandeur, his tongue must seem to have robbed the Hybla bees, and left them honeyless…[247]

As a young and relatively unknown writer with a second book approaching completion, this was a golden opportunity for Keats to display his knowledge of classical literature to a relatively wide audience. The introduction of the 'Hybla bees' into a review of Kean's acting may at first have surprised his readers, but was in fact rather apt. In ancient times, Hybla was a town on the southern slope of Mount Etna in Sicily and was famous for its honey – it has an entry in Lemprière's *Classical Dictionary*. The Hybla bees are mentioned in both Virgil's *Eclogues* and in Shakespeare's *Julius Caesar* (V, 1, 31-34) where Cassius says to Antony:

> Antony,
> The posture of your blows are yet unknown;
> But for your words, they rob the Hybla bees,
> And leave them honeyless.

Keats also introduced a more perplexing reference into this short but accomplished review, and that was to Kean's *gusto* – another concept that was to become important to him as a thinker and a poet:

> There is an indescribable gusto in [Kean's] voice by which we feel that the utterer is thinking of the past and future, while speaking of the instant.

'Gusto' was a word adopted by Hazlitt for use in his vocabulary of art criticism. He devoted a whole essay to it in his book *The Round Table*, which we can recall Keats reading with Bailey in Oxford. Gusto, said Hazlitt, is 'power or passion defining any object' and he contradicted Haydon when he applied the concept to Michelangelo's style:

> His limbs convey an idea of muscular strength and moral grandeur, and even of intellectual dignity... This is what is meant by saying that his style is hard and masculine.[248]

When he talked of gusto in relation to 'Greek statues' Hazlitt echoed Plato when he said that the perfect form (real or imagined) is ideal, or spiritual. But Hazlitt went even further when he said that, by their beauty, the Greek statues themselves are *deified*:

> The gusto in the Greek statues is of a very singular kind. The sense of perfect form nearly occupies the whole mind, and hardly suffers it to dwell on any other feeling. It seems enough for them to be, without acting or suffering. Their forms are ideal, spiritual. Their beauty is power. By their beauty they are raised above the frailties of pain or passion; by their beauty they are deified.[249]

The Pursuit of Beauty and Truth

Keats would later use this idea as a starting point for his *Ode on a Grecian Urn*, one of the most famous poems in the English language. Though it owes a large debt to Hazlitt, it owes an even bigger one to Haydon, as we shall see.

***

On Friday 19 December, Keats went to see the Christmas pantomime at Drury Lane and travelled back to Hampstead with Charles Dilke. The next morning, Saturday 20 December, he went to the Royal Academy to see Benjamin West's painting, *Death on a Pale Horse*. He then spent the evenings of both Saturday 20 December and Sunday 21 December with Dilke. His review of Kean appeared in *The Champion* on the morning of Sunday 21 December. Keats wrote a letter to his brothers upon his return to Hampstead on the Sunday night. (His brothers, George and Tom, had taken a trip to Devonshire on account of Tom's poor health.) After telling them about his theatrical review, and discussing some political news from the *Examiner*, he went on to describe West's painting:

> It is a wonderful picture when West's age is considered [West was 79]; but there is nothing to be intense upon; no woman one feels mad to kiss; no face swelling into reality – the excellence of every Art is its intensity, capable of making all disagreeables evaporate, from their being in close relationship with Beauty and Truth... I dined with Haydon on the Sunday after you left, and had a very pleasant day...[250]

The excellence of every art is its *intensity*, said Keats, a measure of how far disagreeables 'evaporate' for being in close relationship with 'Beauty and Truth'. This idea is reminiscent of Haydon's comment (written, as we saw, just a few weeks earlier) that if a work of art is especially beautiful, then its errors or inadequacies may be forgiven. Keats continued this letter to his brothers with another new idea, certainly the most important idea in the context of Keats' astonishing rate of maturity as a thinker and a poet. It had struck him whilst talking to Charles Dilke:

> I had not a dispute but a disquisition with Dilke on various subjects; several things dovetailed in my mind and at once it struck me what quality went to form a man of achievement especially in literature and which Shakespeare possessed so enormously – I mean Negative Capability that is when a man is capable of being in uncertainties, Mysteries, doubts without any irritable reaching after fact and reason...[251]

'Negative Capability' is a new phrase, not previously found anywhere in Keats' letters nor in those of his friends. It is an expansion of the idea of the 'disinterested mind', the concept around which Hazlitt had constructed his now 12-year-old essay, *The Principles of Human Action*. We know neither what Dilke said to bring it so sharply to Keats' notice that weekend, nor how common the idea of 'disinterestedness' was in the conversations of those who knew Hazlitt, but we do know that back in October 1816 Haydon had written to Wilkie and expressed his admiration for Hunt's 'disinterestedness in public matters'.[252]

In *The Principles of Human Action*, Hazlitt states that our minds are as much interested in the welfare of others as they are in our own welfare. Our minds have knowledge of the past and the present, but can only *imagine* the future; therefore, we can only imagine our future needs and feelings and this is exactly the same mechanism by which we imagine the current needs and feelings of others. The very opposite of this condition is egotism, where a person is concerned only with themselves, and with their own thoughts and feelings. Hazlitt thought egotism was unnatural.

In the context of understanding the profound effect this idea had on Keats, we must focus on Hazlitt's comment that, 'The imagination *must carry me out of myself* and into the feelings of others' [my italics]. It was in Hazlitt's *Round Table* essay *On Posthumous Fame* that Keats would have found this idea applied to Shakespeare who, said Hazlitt:

> ... seemed scarcely to have an individual existence of his own, but to borrow that of others at will, and to pass successively through 'every variety of untried being' – to be now Hamlet, now Othello, now Lear, now Falstaff, now Ariel. In the mingled interests and feelings belonging to this wide range of imaginary reality... the author could not easily find time to think of himself.[253]

In his own imaginative world, Shakespeare could annihilate his self-consciousness – he could *negate his self* and thus take flight as Ariel; or contemplate suicide as Hamlet – because he no longer *was* Shakespeare, he was Ariel, Hamlet, etc. This observation from Hazlitt's essay resonated with Keats' own personality because he already knew that his imagination could carry him out of himself in exactly the same way. Charles Cowden Clarke had noted how Keats sat up, 'burly and dominant' when he first heard Spenser's description of 'sea-shouldering whales'. Several years later, listening to the sea on the Isle of Wight, Keats had become so lost in its 'music' that coming back to himself had made him 'start' ('...and brood until ye start as if the sea nymphs choired'). Back in November, when he was writing to Benjamin Bailey from Burford Bridge, he had said to Bailey:

> ...I scarcely remember counting on any Happiness – I look not for it if it be not in the present hour – nothing startles me beyond the moment. The setting Sun will always set me to rights – or if a Sparrow come before my Window I take part in its Existence and pick about the gravel.[254]

Keats explored and developed these new ideas for several months, not just in his poetry but also in the letters he wrote to his friends. Just at this time, Haydon again became jealous of Keats' other interests and attachments, so once again wrote declaring his everlasting admiration and friendship – he said that he would always be a 'devoted and affectionate brother' to him. Unfortunately, it was at this crucial moment in Keats' development that Haydon showed himself to be particularly self-absorbed and egotistical, and these were the very traits that Keats was coming to deplore. Keats wrote to Reynolds about Wordsworth, a man who, as we have seen, Keats truly admired as a poet, but whose imaginative world revolved around himself and his own thoughts:

> It may be said that we ought to read our contemporaries, that Wordsworth, etc., should have their dues from us. But, for the sake of a few fine or imaginative or domestic passages, are we to be bullied into a certain Philosophy engendered in the whims of an Egotist?

Every man has his speculations, but every man does not brood and peacock over them...[255]

Around the time that Keats was writing this letter, Haydon was doing two things. He was nursing a bruised ego after his squabbles with Leigh Hunt, and he was brooding over his speculations about his own genius, his *lack* of admiration for Chapman's Homer ('so completely unfeeling') and how one should paint the forehead of Christ.

Chapter 12

What is this soul then? Whence came it? It does not seem my own,
and I have no self-passion or identity.
John Keats: Endymion, Book IV

On New Year's Eve, 1817, Keats wrote to Haydon from his Hampstead lodgings to say that he had forgotten to discuss the matter of Cripps at the previous Sunday's dinner party (the 'Immortal Dinner') and had called at Haydon's house again on Monday, only to find him 'out in the sun'. He reneged on a promise to have dinner with Haydon on the following Sunday because he had just remembered that he was spending the day with some other friends in Hampstead.

Haydon, too, was writing a letter on that same New Year's Eve. He was writing to Leigh Hunt to tell him that their friendship was finally over. The fact that he was writing to a man who lived in the same street shows that he wanted to put his feelings 'on the record'. Keats explained to his brothers (in another letter)[256] that Haydon had lent Mrs Hunt his silverware but she had not been punctual in returning it, so Haydon had sent somebody round to collect it. Maybe the Hunts had dinner guests at the time – we don't know – but in any case Hunt had found this 'indelicate' and the incident had led to words.

Haydon's letter as we have it today is replete with scratchings out and corrections, as if he wrote it rather more quickly than carefully. First, he refuted a claim made by Hunt that he was 'not punctual' in money matters, supporting this by quoting from correspondence between himself and Hunt's brother, John, who had lent Haydon money in the past, apparently without any problems. Second, he claimed to have suffered seven years of sneering by Hunt's wife because he had once rejected her sister, Elizabeth Kent, as a potential wife. Third, he said that Hunt had been harassing him over a loan that he could not possibly expect Haydon to repay at this time because he was 'in the middle of a great work'. And so it went on… Hunt did not appreciate Haydon's personal gifts of sketches and prints, and never replied to his letters or returned his visits:

> You are a man totally absorbed in yourself… I was and am now so totally disgusted with your conduct [that] I now take my leave of you, for I have no longer pleasure in your presence.[257]

Hunt responded that Haydon was in the habit of making the most enormous gratuitous assertions and that he wouldn't have dared to say the things he had written in the letter to Hunt's face. Haydon's reply to *that* (on 6 January) was a long lament at the collapse of Hunt's character from one of the most pure and honourable beings to one of the most deluded, selfish people imaginable:

You tell me that I dare not tell you face to face what I have written, this is a shallow sophistication, at any rate I dare write it, why do you not answer it instead of filling your letter with unmanly insinuations... are you to act with the most outrageous want of common feeling and not be complained of?[258]

The sad fact is that Haydon had a habit of upsetting people (Hunt this time, Reynolds before him, Bailey before that) by demanding their attention and loyalty. Hunt's unpardonable offence was that he had neither appreciated Haydon's gifts of sketches nor replied to his letters; Reynolds' transgression was that he hadn't attended the 'Immortal Dinner'; while Bailey had supposedly put Cripps' interests before Haydon's. Watching all this was Keats, a man who wanted to remain friends with Hunt, who was very close to Reynolds and who admired Bailey enormously. But his friendship with Haydon left him in the position of constantly having to intervene and smooth over the waters. It was a thankless task.

During the Christmas holidays of 1817, Keats began to distance himself from Haydon. When he next wrote to him, on Saturday 10 January, it was to apologise once again for his not having visited, this time, he said, on account of his young sister wanting to spend time with him. I should spend time with you tonight, said Keats, but I am seeing other friends. I should see you tomorrow, he added, but I have 'an insuperable engagement'.[259] The message was clear: as things stand, I prefer the company of other people to yours. He also mentioned Cripps, saying that the young man had been to see him and had restated his desire to be bound to Haydon. It might perhaps be surprising that Keats said he would still help to raise Haydon's fee of between £150 and £200 but it is clear that even with his growing misgivings about Haydon as a friend, Keats still considered it almost a duty to assist and praise him as an artist. The final paragraph of the letter reiterates the value he placed on Haydon's paintings:

> Your friendship for me is now getting into its teens and I feel the past. Also, every day older I get, the greater is my idea of your achievements in Art: and I am convinced there are three things to rejoice at in this Age, [Wordsworth's poem] The Excursion, your pictures, and Hazlitt's depth of taste.[260]

Haydon must have read between the lines because he replied as follows:

> My dear Keats, I feel greatly delighted by your high opinion, allow me to add sincerely a fourth to be proud of – John Keats' genius! – this I speak from the heart… and now you know my peculiar feelings in wishing to have a notice when you cannot keep an engagement with me [a sideswipe at Reynolds]; there can never be as long as we live any ground of dispute between us – My friendship for you is beyond its teens, & beginning to ripen to maturity… you shall always find me a devoted and affectionate Brother…[261]

Haydon himself then addressed the matter of Cripps, the man who had unwittingly caused so much tension between Haydon on the one side, and Bailey and Keats on the other. He had finally met the young man and given him something to study:

> With respect to Cripps, I sincerely think it would now be to our mutual advantage to have him bound… do your utmost and so will

> I... with respect to our meeting the sooner, my dear Keats, the better – but accept this engagement as long as we live – every Sunday at three as long as you live and I live...[262]

Keats did go to Lisson Grove on Sunday 18 January, but he visited Hunt first. When he walked over to Haydon's for dinner, he found that Hazlitt was there, and Bewick. A day or two later he finished a letter to his brothers that he had begun about a week earlier; it contained an echo from his poem, *On the Sea*. When it came to his friends, said Keats, '...uproar's your only music...they are all dreadfully irritated against each other'.[263]

***

At his studio in Lisson Grove, having sent his final letter to Hunt, Haydon fell into despair. His eyes were beginning to fail him once again and, as was so often the case, he had almost run out of money. As if this were not enough, he was in agonies over his inability to paint a supernatural representation of Jesus into his picture of *Christ's Entry into Jerusalem*. His problem was *truth of conveyance*. What did Jesus look like? What would an *imaginary* Jesus look like? Wasn't it simply impossible to know? Haydon had long ago developed the habit of praying fervently and desperately when he was facing a particularly difficult trial, and he did so now as he recorded in his diary on Thursday, 8 January 1818:

> O God, shine inward on my brain with a great light, and in beaming effulgence let me see in all their ineffable divinity, sweetness, benevolence, compassion and Deity, the features & figures of the Saviour of Mankind! Grant me the most intense perception of them so

that I may express them clearly and convey to the World a new view of his lovely and benignant face.[264]

His failure to perceive a great inward light caused him to fall into a depression that was real and debilitating. He was 32 years old on 26 January, and he tormented himself with the idea that the best years of his life were over and that he would never fulfil his dreams as an artist: 'I have passed half the ordinary extent of [a] man's life. I must now decline imperceptibly to the grave...' and the next day, 'I'll shave my head and be cropped.'[265] In this mood he went down to Kensington, to 24 Phillimore Place, where his old friend David Wilkie lived in a large house. Haydon said that he and Wilkie 'condoled on our altered health – on the passed glories of our youth'. In fact, Wilkie was by now a respected academician and a relatively wealthy man. He travelled widely, was in good health and had many distinguished friends.

Haydon returned to Lisson Grove where the image of Jesus, or rather the lack of one, continued to haunt him; he distracted himself by going back to his beloved books, comparing the translation of Homer's *Odyssey* by Alexander Pope with that of George Chapman. Whenever he came to a difficult passage, he referred back to the original Greek and quoted it at length in his diary. Poring over a favourite pagan text seems to have brought enlightenment because on 6 February, he wrote:

> As I walked along the Strand today, I saw the Divine face for the first time – distinctly in my mind. My heart leaped. I'll now do it. I'm confident I shall...[266]

Though his eyes were still failing and his bank account was almost depleted, he had a renewed sense of mission. With his paints ground and his palette set, Haydon once again picked up his brush and set to work on *Christ's Entry into Jerusalem*.

***

We can recall that back in 1812 William Hazlitt had moved from Winterslow to London, and that soon after his arrival he had raised some money by giving a series of lectures on *The History of English Philosophy* at the Russell Institution in Bloomsbury. Hazlitt was now a public figure, a journalist, a theatre reviewer and the author of a popular book of essays, *The Round Table*, and the very successful *Characters of Shakespeare's Plays*. So when he approached a scientific and literary organization called the Surrey Institution and offered to deliver a series of eight weekly lectures on the English Poets, his offer was warmly welcomed. Hazlitt stood to gain around 200 guineas from the admission fees and the publication of the lectures, which was to him a small fortune at the time.

Haydon's student, William Bewick, befriended Hazlitt. He was a popular young man who made friends easily. When he wrote to his brother on Tuesday 11 February 1818 to say that he had taken lodgings at 15 Nassau Street ('rather expensive for me just now'), he also said that he had recently enjoyed 'two or three very intellectual dinners' with 'Horatio [Horace] Smith, Keats the poet, Hazlitt the critic, Haydon [and] Hunt the publisher...'[267] though we can be sure that Haydon and Hunt did not dine at the same table.

Hazlitt still lived at 19 York Street, the house where Haydon had endured the meal of slaty potatoes and a bony lump of beef (the site is now in Petty France, near Buckingham Palace). It was a large two storey house with gardens enclosed by high walls, and 160 years earlier it had been the home of one of England's greatest poets and staunchest republicans, John Milton. Hazlitt's study was almost bare – there was very little in the way of furniture, and it contained neither books nor pictures. According to Bewick, Hazlitt had covered one of the walls with scribblings – words, names, 'enigmatical exclamations', 'strange and queer sentences', quotations, snatches of rhyme, bits of arithmetical calculations and scraps of Latin.[268] Visitors to York Street would have been aware of Hazlitt's intellectual brilliance, but Bewick admitted that he could be rather difficult company. He would suddenly and without warning have terrible outbursts of rage, said Bewick, so that his companions could only

> gaze with wonder as at a frenzied being, amazed by the violence of the physical action which followed the phases of his mental excitement, at the expression of his features, and at his burning language.[269]

Hazlitt was doubtless temperamental, and we can remember Coleridge calling him 'brow hanging, shoe contemplating, strange', but Reynolds shows us the attractive side of his nature in a letter he wrote to a friend about nine months before Hazlitt's lectures at the Surrey Institution:

> On Thursday last Hazlitt was with me at home, and remained with us till 3 o'clock in the morning; – full of eloquence – warm, lofty & communicative on every thing Imaginative & Intelligent… Passing

from grand & comma[n]ding argument to the gaieties & graces of wit & humour, – and the elegant and higher beauties of Poetry. He is indeed great company and leaves a weight on the mind, which 'it can hardly bear'. He is full of what Dr Johnson terms 'good talk'. His countenance is also extremely fine: – a sunken & melancholy face, – a forehead lined with thought... – an eye dashed in its light with sorrow, but kindling and living at intellectual moments, – and a stream of coal black hair....[270]

Bewick sometimes accompanied Hazlitt on his walk over Westminster Bridge and along Great Surrey Street to the Surrey Institution, where lectures were delivered in an elegant circular room in the form of a Greek temple. When Hazlitt lectured on Shakespeare and Milton on Tuesday 27 January 1818 (the same day Haydon was at his most melancholy and writing in his diary about shaving his head), Keats was there in the audience, which, as the *Examiner* reported, 'was crowded to the very ceiling'. Once underway, Hazlitt reiterated his idea about Shakespeare's 'disinterestedness' (i.e. Keats' 'Negative Capability'):

> [Shakespeare] was just like any other man, but that he was like all other men. He was the least of an egotist that it was possible to be. He was nothing in himself; but he was all that others were, or that they could become.[271]

When Shakespeare was writing a scene, said Hazlitt:

> ...all the persons concerned must have been present in the poet's imagination, as at a kind of rehearsal... The poet may be said, for the time, to identify himself with the character he wishes to represent, and

to pass from one to another, like the same soul successively animating different bodies.[272]

Keats would have been listening intently, memorising Hazlitt's wonderful descriptions, but he would surely have been surprised when Hazlitt borrowed a phrase from Keats himself, from his review of Kean at Drury Lane back in December. He said that Shakespeare's language is *hieroglyphical*. 'It translates thoughts into visible images.'[273]

After moving on to Milton, and discussing Milton's desire to be remembered as a great poet, Hazlitt quoted the lines from Spenser that Haydon had written in his diary and Keats had subsequently quoted in a letter to Reynolds:

> The noble heart that harbours virtuous thought,
> And is with child of glorious great intent,
> Can never rest until it forth hath brought,
> The eternal brood of glory excellent.

Two weeks later, Bewick wrote to his brothers that Hazlitt's lectures

> are said to be the finest lectures that were ever delivered… He is the Shakespeare prose writer of our glorious country; he outdoes all in truth, style and originality.[274]

Despite this, and despite always being cheered on by his audiences, Hazlitt was in fact an extremely nervous lecturer. He was shy and still rather shabby in appearance (he was 'pallid as death', as Bewick put it), but his enthusiasm for his subject was infectious. Bewick tells a story of when he and Hazlitt met the dramatist Sheridan Knowles on a riverbank where Knowles had been doing a spot of fishing. This was a few years ahead, in 1824, when Hazlitt was even more famous:

> Knowles stopped to open his basket and show us the success of his sport. Hazlitt, drawing his breath, peeped timidly in, and was as nervous as if he were looking into a cradle containing dead infants. As Knowles took one of the fish in his hand, expatiating upon its merits when cooked, and on the table, etc., Hazlitt, sighing, exclaimed – 'How silvery! What rainbow hues and tints glisten and flit across its shining surface! How beautiful! Do you remember Waller?
>
> Beneath a shoal of silver fishes glides,
> And plays about the gilded barges sides,
> The ladies, angling in the crystal lake,
> Feast on the waters with the prey they take:
> At once victorious with their lines and eyes,
> They make the fishes and the men their prize.'

Hazlitt continued quoting whole passages of poetry about fish, said Bewick, until Knowles, caught up in the spirit of the thing, literally burst into song.[275]

Back at the Surrey Institution, Hazlitt was now expanding his ideas about Milton. He told his audience that Milton's mind was completely absorbed in whatever he was describing, that there is the same 'depth of impression' in Milton's descriptions of colours as there is in his descriptions of sounds or smells. In a quotation that was to prove particularly important to Keats, he said that in Milton, 'A sound arises "like a steam of rich distilled perfumes"'(from Milton's *Comus, A Mask*, lines 555-556: 'At last a soft and solemn-breathing sound / Rose like a steam of rich distill'd perfumes'). Keats later used this crossover of the senses, this literary synaesthesia, in one of his greatest poems, the *Ode to a Nightingale*:

> I cannot see what flowers are at my feet,
> Nor what soft incense hangs upon the boughs...

When Hazlitt finished this lecture on Shakespeare and Milton, Keats' education as a poet was almost complete. Hazlitt had reinforced the young poet's belief that 'disinterestedness' or 'Negative Capability' was an attribute of the greatest writers, and had introduced yet another concept for Keats to think about – 'depth of impression', the power of description of both colours and sounds, something very close to 'gusto' but positioned specifically in the context of poetry. With this store of knowledge, Keats was ready to embark on the path that would lead to his great works of 1819, but before he could start he had two major distractions. First, *Endymion* was about to be published, and he was worried about the reception it would get from the critics. Second, and much more worrying, his youngest brother, Tom, was showing the early signs of consumption, the disease that had so cruelly killed his mother.

***

The coastal climate of Devon was considered milder and healthier than that of London and Keats' brothers had by now been in lodgings there, at Teignmouth, for more than a month. Sadly, Tom's health was not improving. He was looking pale and had started spitting blood. Keats knew that he would soon have to travel to

Teignmouth himself because George needed to return to London, but he needed to stay in Hampstead just a little longer because he had not yet completed the fair copy of *Endymion* for his publishers. He wrote regularly to his brothers with news of their mutual friends, and to update them on the progress of his book.

Keats also wrote several letters to Reynolds because Reynolds was suffering from a painful and debilitating bout of rheumatic fever and was confined to his bed. All of these letters, and others to Bailey in Oxford, tell us much about Keats' thinking in the first few months of 1818. In one letter to his brothers, he said, 'I think a little change has taken place in my intellect lately. I cannot bear to be uninterested or unemployed, I who have so long been addicted to passiveness.'[276]

***

Around this time, the ancient Greek philosopher Plato was much in vogue among some of Keats' circle. Bailey had 'a patchwork collection of his works – Greek and English' at Oxford and ordered more of his writings ('I want his *Republic* very much') from Keats' new publishers, Taylor & Hessey,[277] while Shelley habitually studied Plato (we can recall him impressing Horace Smith with his knowledge of Plato during their walks on Hampstead Heath, and Mary Shelley saying that she and Shelley read Plato at Marlow). Shelley was to prove a translator of brilliance, producing a masterly version of Plato's treatise on love, *The Symposium*. Plato wrote a treatise on poetry and poets, *The Ion*, in the form of a dialogue between the philosopher Socrates and the poet or rhapsodist, Ion of Ephesus. An English translation of this had been available in London since at least

1759 (from an Oxford scholar by the name of Floyer Sydenham) and Shelley was later to translate it as well, but the most popular translation available in 1818 was that of Thomas Taylor, a Neo-Platonist scholar who devoted his life to studying ancient Greek texts. Bailey had at least four of Taylor's translations of Plato's dialogues at Oxford.[278]

As the *Ion* opens, its eponymous protagonist has just won first prize in a contest of rhapsodists, and Socrates is keen to find out what rhapsodic skills and knowledge he possesses. He establishes that the first requirement of a rhapsodist is a detailed knowledge of the works of the greatest poets, Homer in particular. Socrates, in his inimitable style, suggests that if Ion is competent to recite and interpret Homer, then he is an expert on poetry itself and thus should be able to recite and interpret Hesiod and the other great poets. Does an expert on painting judge the work of a single painter? Ion insists that he is an expert on Homer alone and that he could not be an expert on Hesiod in the same way. Socrates then establishes that Ion does not, in fact, have great knowledge of poetry, not even of Homer, but that he is *inspired* by Homer. Similarly, the poets themselves have no knowledge of the subjects they write about (a doctor knows more about medicine than does a poet, a charioteer knows more about chariots, and so on). No, says Socrates, the poets themselves are also inspired:

> For the souls of the poets have this peculiar ministration in the world. They tell us that these souls, flying like bees from flower to flower, and wandering over the gardens and the meadows, and the honey-

flowing fountains of the muses, return to us laden with the sweetness of melody; and arrayed as they are in the plumes of rapid imagination, they speak the truth. For a poet is indeed a thing ethereally light, winged, and sacred, nor can he compose anything worth calling poetry until he becomes inspired... or whilst any reason remains within him. For whilst a man retains any portion of the thing called reason, he is utterly incompetent to produce poetry...

> Plato, Ion, translated by Shelley (1821)[279]

Little by little, from the time he stayed with Bailey in Oxford, through the Hazlitt lectures, to the time he was preparing to stay with Tom in Teignmouth, echoes of Plato's philosophy of poetry – that a poet cannot have great knowledge of anything, that he cannot compose poetry 'whilst any reason remains within him', that he must use his imagination and be inspired to speak the truth – gradually began to appear in Keats' letters:

To Bailey, November 1817:

> I have never yet been able to conceive how anything can be known for truth by consecutive reasoning....[280]

To Bailey, January 1818:

> One saying of yours I will never forget... it being perhaps said when you were looking on the Surface and seeming of Humanity alone, without a thought of the past or the future – or the deeps of good and evil – you were at that moment estranged from speculation...[281]

To Taylor, his publisher, January 1818 (an amendment to *Endymion*):

> Wherein lies happiness? In that which becks
> Our ready minds to fellowship divine,
> A fellowship with Essence till we shine
> Full alchemised and free of space...[282]

To Reynolds, February 1818:

> It has been an old comparison for our urging on – the Beehive; however, it seems to me we should rather be the flower than the Bee... let us open our leaves like a flower and be passive and receptive – budding patiently under the eye of Apollo and taking hints from every noble insect that favours us with a visit.[283]

and again, to Bailey, March 1818:

> Now, my dear fellow, I must once for all tell you I have not one idea of the truth of any of my speculations – I shall never be a reasoner, because I care not to be in the right, when retired from bickering and in a proper philosophical temper.[284]

Keats wrote several unremarkable poems during this period but some aspects of his mature thought do come through in glimpses: he talks of growing 'high-rife with *old* philosophy' (my emphasis) in a poem called *On Seeing a Lock of Milton's Hair* (January 1818), and the following lines appear in an unrhymed sonnet called *O thou whose face hath felt the winter's wind* written in February 1818:

> Oh, fret not after knowledge – I have none,
> And yet my song comes native with the warmth.
> Oh, fret not after knowledge – I have none,
> And yet the evening listens. He who saddens

> At thought of idleness cannot be idle,
> And he's awake who thinks himself asleep.

Finally we arrive at a poem containing some beautiful lines that are recognisably 'Keatsian'. It is called *The Human Seasons* (March 1818) and talks about the autumn of a man's life. It is a good example of what Keats himself termed 'hieroglyphical language' and what Hazlitt described as turning thoughts into images. When a man has lived through his spring and summer, says Keats, his soul retires to 'quiet coves', reminiscent of the 'cavern's mouth' in *On the Sea* where the sea could simply be listened to:

> ...Quiet coves
> His soul has in its autumn, when his wings
> He furleth close, contented so to look
> On mists in idleness – to let fair things
> Pass by unheeded, as a threshold brook...

These lines are particularly poignant because, when he wrote this poem, the 22-year-old Keats had only three years left to live, so he could be said to have been in the autumn of his own life. He didn't know this, of course, but this image of someone nearing the end of his life, idly watching things pass him by, was to reappear in one of his greatest poems, the ode *To Autumn*:

> Who hath not seen thee oft amid thy store?
> Sometimes whoever seeks abroad may find
> Thee sitting careless on a granary floor,
> Thy hair soft-lifted by the winnowing wind;
> Or on a half-reaped furrow sound asleep,

Drowsed with the fume of poppies, while thy hook
Spares the next swath and all its twinèd flowers;
And sometimes like a gleaner thou dost keep
Steady thy laden head across a brook;
Or by a cyder-press, with patient look,
Thou watchest the last oozings hours by hours.

Keats: *To Autumn*, Stanza II (September 1819)

Keats was now maturing rapidly, both as a thinker and a poet, but for the time being he had to put his thoughts and his poetry aside and travel more than 200 miles by coach to the coastal resort of Teignmouth in Devon, to look after his sick brother.

***

Having alienated some of his closest friends and exhausted all his sources of financial support, Haydon now immersed himself in projects designed to procure invitations back into the dining rooms of the nobility. His meeting with the Grand Duke Nicholas at the British Museum in January 1817 finally paid off in January 1818, when he was invited to send casts of the Elgin Marbles to the Imperial Academy of St Petersburg in Russia, a singular honour that Haydon quickly brought to the attention of the Royal Academy. The contract to box up and ship the casts would be a profitable one, and Haydon decided to give it to Richard Westmacott, a sculptor and academician. Haydon invited him to tea at Lisson Grove and, when the sculptor arrived on a 'very wet, snowy night', Haydon welcomed him 'like a gentleman'. Haydon then cut in half his proposed shipping fee, and the sculptor was 'evidently annoyed'. Haydon recorded in his diary that Westmacott 'was a worthy little man, but I did it for fun.'[285]

In early February, Haydon learned that the government was intending to allocate huge sums of money for the building of new churches (£1,000,000 was allocated through the Church Building Act of 1818). He immediately set about writing a pamphlet urging the government to include money for commissioning religious paintings in the new churches. He wrote a letter to Charles Long, M.P., 1st Baron Farnborough, a known connoisseur of the arts who was married to Amelia Long, a skilful watercolourist and garden designer. Charles Long showed Haydon's letter to the Chancellor of the Exchequer, Nicholas Vansittart, but the response was muted. On Thursday 5 March, Haydon tried again; he wrote to George Canning M.P., a man with whom he had a tenuous connection:

> London, Lisson Grove North
> March 5th, 1818
>
> Sir,
>
> I had the honour of being introduced to you some years since by Lord Mulgrave. I am most anxious, with your leave, to impress you with the importance of the public encouragement of painting... Could one of your genius and fame be induced to take it under your protection in Parliament, depend upon it, it would be worthy of you...[286]

All of this activity and publicity brought the desired result because on 9 April Haydon was invited back to Lord Mulgrave's dinner table. Lady Mulgrave was present, as were Sir George and Lady Beaumont. Haydon, recalling that he had fallen out with these patrons nine years earlier because of his insistence on painting pictures that were too large for their drawing rooms, wrote in his diary, 'They all drank wine with me, which was symptomatic of concession to my views.'[287] Now that he had regained his entrée into high society, it became a priority for Haydon to be seen as a gentleman. He recalled that in earlier years, when he was painting *Dentatus*, he had behaved 'awkwardly, timidly and contemptibly' when in the company of 'ladies of high rank'. On 8 May 1818, he wrote that this was no longer the case:

> At the [British] Institution today a Lady of high rank was going to her carriage; another lady said, 'Mr Haydon will attend you.' I flew instantly, offered her my arm which she took and [in] the presence of all, I handed her out, & into her carriage perfectly at ease and retiring stood at the entrance till she drove off, bowing to her as [I] caught her eye... I felt highly pleased with myself.[288]

With his self esteem restored, secure in the knowledge that he had been rehabilitated in the eyes of Lord Mulgrave and his set, he arranged for his pamphlet on church paintings to be reviewed in the Tory periodical, the *Quarterly Review* and threw himself back into his work. Lord Mulgrave visited his studio to look at *Christ's Entry into Jerusalem* on Sunday 10 May and, around the same time, Keats came to dinner along with Bewick and an unknown guest that Haydon called 'a noodle'. Haydon appeared to be in good spirits:

> Keats, Bewick and I dined together. Keats brought some friend of his, a noodle. After dinner to his horror when he expected we should all be discussing Milton & Raphael &c., we burst into the most boisterous merriment. We had all been working dreadfully hard the whole week...

the Wise acre sat by without saying a word, blushing and sipping his wine...[289]

These high spirits were not to last. The first sign of a setback appears in Haydon's diary at the end of May when he began dictating his entries to Bewick. Clearly, despite the move from the cramped and fume-ridden studio in Great Marlborough Street to his large and airy studio in Lisson Grove, his eyes were once again failing him. On 14 August, Haydon himself wrote a single line: 'God protect me!'. His health then broke down completely and he left London to visit his sister, who now lived in the town of Bridgwater in Somerset. 'I left Town for the Country,' he said, 'in a state of wretched debility & nervousness.'[290]

***

Teignmouth is a coastal town about 200 miles to the south-west of London and 15 miles south of the old city of Exeter. It had a small port and a shipyard which built merchant vessels but, says a gazetteer of 1815, it 'is now become a fashionable watering place; the public rooms and theatre are situated in E[ast] Teignmouth. They are very commodious: and the surrounding country is very beautiful'.[291] On 8 March 1818, when Keats set off from London to visit his brother Tom, a fierce storm was raging across the south of England but the Exeter coach had a timetable to keep so it trundled along the miles of muddy, potholed roads despite the high winds and pouring rain. It was later reported in the Examiner that several people had been killed by falling masonry, that mail coaches had been delayed by flattened trees and that a man on board a Gravesend packet 'was blown overboard and drowned'. Almost a week after arriving at the lodgings where Tom was staying (George having already returned to London), Keats wrote a letter to Reynolds to say that it was still raining, and that Tom was still sick. He added that he was preparing the fourth book of Endymion for the press and writing a preface, but that he had lost all enthusiasm for the task and wished 'it was all done'.

On the day that Keats left London, Haydon wrote him a letter to say that a gold ring and seal had been found in a field at Stratford-upon-Avon; Haydon believed it to have belonged to Shakespeare. The letter was sent to Teignmouth and Keats responded nearly three weeks later by writing some witty doggerel and saying that it had been raining almost constantly since his arrival, and that at last his brother's health seemed to be improving. Haydon replied with a friendly, gossipy letter:

> ...it has rained in Town almost incessantly since you went away, the fact is, you dog, you carried the rain with you as Ulysses did the Winds, and then opening your rain bags you look round with a knowing wink and say, 'curse this Devonshire, how it rains!'[292]

Keats replied again on 10 April in a more serious and thoughtful tone:

> I shall be in town in about a fortnight and then we will have a day or so now and then... we will have no more abominable Rows – for they leave one in a fearful silence...[293]

There is an air of admonishment in the letter, a warning from Keats that he could no longer tolerate the squabbles and bad feeling among his friends.

**

The newspapers of the early nineteenth century were fiercely divided along party lines, and the insults and threats exchanged between them were often vitriolic. (The former editor of the *Champion*, John Scott, was killed in a duel after he had been insulted in a newspaper.) The most belligerent of the Tory newspapers was *Blackwood's Edinburgh Magazine* and this had long had Keats in its sights as a young, middle-class, liberal-minded writer, the protégé of the enemy of all Tory journalists, Leigh Hunt. Keats, they knew, was the son of a stableman and had given up his medical studies in order to become a poet – a pursuit which they considered to be the domain of a wealthy and cultured minority. Writing under the pseudonym 'Z', a Blackwood's writer called John Gibson Lockhart reviewed Keats' poetry (*Poems 1817* and the newly published *Endymion*) and chose to turn this into a personal attack on the poet. Knowing that Keats was only five feet tall and possibly aware that the poet was painfully self-conscious of his short stature, Lockhart wrote:

> Mr Hunt is a small poet but he is a clever man. Mr Keats is a still smaller poet, and he is only a boy of pretty abilities...[294]

Alluding to Keats' criticism of eighteenth-century poetry in his poem *Sleep and Poetry* (Keats had described the poet Alexander Pope and his contemporaries as 'a schism nurtured by foppery and barbarism'), Lockhart says:

> ...to deny [Pope's] genius, is just about as absurd as to dispute that of Wordsworth, or to believe in that of Hunt. Above all things, it is most

pitiably ridiculous to hear [Pope et al] reviled by uneducated and flimsy striplings... fanciful dreaming tea-drinkers who, without logic enough to analyse a single idea, or imagination enough to form one original image, or learning enough to distinguish between the written language of Englishmen and the spoken jargon of Cockneys presume to talk with contempt of some of the most exquisite spirits the world ever produced...[295]

Lockhart was a brilliant scholar who was only a year older than Keats. He had studied at Glasgow University and Balliol College, Oxford, and he was proficient in French, German, Italian and Spanish. He looked down his nose at Keats with genuine contempt, and dismissed his poetry outright:

> The phrenzy of the 'Poems' was bad enough in its way, but it did not alarm us half so seriously as the calm, settled, imperturbable drivelling idiocy of 'Endymion'.[296]

Keats would have been dismayed that in attacking his 'Great Spirits' poem, *Addressed to Haydon*, Lockhart wrote:

> [Haydon], that clever, but most affected artist who as little resembles Raphael in genius as he does in person, notwithstanding the foppery of having his hair curled over his shoulders in the old Italian fashion...[297]

By the time of this review (and others just as hurtful), Keats had much more important and painful things demanding his attention and his energy. His beloved brother Tom had been brought back to Hampstead in a serious condition and was getting worse; he died of tuberculosis on 1 December 1818. Keats was devastated because his second brother George had by then married and emigrated to America, and his sister Fanny was still under the guardianship of Richard Abbey. This meant that, effectively, Keats was left without any family at all. After the poet's own death in 1821, Haydon wrote:

> The death of his brother wounded him deeply, and it appeared to me from that hour he began seriously to droop.[298]

***

Keats and Haydon came close to an estrangement in January 1819, just weeks after Tom's death, when Haydon turned to Keats for a loan even though Keats was himself facing financial difficulties. He had left the lodgings he had shared with Tom and moved into the house of Charles Brown, the friend of Charles Dilke. Brown and Dilke had built a house together in Hampstead and called it Wentworth Place (a Dilke family name; it is now Keats House), and Brown lived in one half of it. He charged Keats £5 a month for the two back rooms, that is to say a parlour overlooking the garden and a bedroom on the first floor. Soon after Keats moved in, Haydon sent his servant Sammons – Keats called him 'Salmon' – to Wentworth Place with a letter asking Keats for a loan. In a carefully worded reply, Keats said he would try to help Haydon but only after Haydon had exhausted all other avenues:

> ...Believe me Haydon I have that sort of fire in my heart that would sacrifice everything I have to your service... I open my heart to you in a few words... let me be the last stay – ask the rich lovers of art first – I'll tell you why – I have a little money which may enable me to study

and to travel [for] three or four years.... Try the long purses. I am sorry I was not at home when Salmon called...[299]

Haydon immediately seized his opportunity:

> Keats! Upon my Soul I could have wept at your letter... you have behaved to me as I would have behaved to you, my dear fellow, and if I am constrained to come to you at last, your property shall only be a transfer for a limited time... Ah my dear Keats my illness has been a severe touch! – I declare to God I do not feel alone in the World now you have written me that letter... I believe you from my soul when you say you would sacrifice all for me...[300]

Keats wrote to his publisher John Taylor on Christmas Eve, 1818, the day after writing to Haydon: 'Can you lend me 30£ for a short time?' he asked, '– ten I want for myself – and twenty for a friend.' We do not know whether in this instance 'the friend' was Haydon, but it seems likely because on 7 January Haydon wrote to Keats to tell him he would accept his 'friendly offer' and that 'my only hope for the concluding difficulties of my picture lie in you.' He added that he would get a two-year bond ready as surety, which suggests he was expecting a much larger loan than £20 (it will be remembered that he had borrowed £300 from Mr Harman, ostensibly to finance his move to Lisson Grove, and then £400 from Thomas Coutts a few months later, just to cover his living expenses).

Keats wrote back to say that he would have 'a little trouble in procuring the Money' but that he would try to help. He also mentioned that he had been feeling unwell with a sore throat, adding that he felt discontented and melancholic. He said that he was once again planning to spend some time away from London, this time in Hampshire. The letters between Lisson Grove and Hampstead continued in this way until Keats wrote to explain that the money he was trying to obtain was part of his dead brother's share of the family inheritance, and that he was having difficulty obtaining it. Still not taking the hint, Haydon replied, 'Your letter was balm to my heart and soul', but Keats had by then left London. Despite feeling unwell, he had travelled with Charles Brown to Chichester and Bedhampton, about 70 miles south of London. It was during this visit that he would write *The Eve of St Agnes*, the first complete poem of 1819 and one of the poems that would earn him a place among the greatest of English poets.

Chapter 13

Thy end is truth's and beauty's doom and date...
Shakespeare, Sonnet XIV

At the end of January 1819, Keats went with Charles Brown to visit Charles Dilke's elderly parents in Chichester, and also Dilke's sister and brother-in-law at nearby Bedhampton. Chichester was a small city dominated by a cathedral whose tower could be seen for miles around, with a bishop's palace and several houses belonging to the dean and prebendaries. Also within the city walls stood five parish churches and a magnificent guildhall. According to a contemporary gazetteer, the four main streets, called North, South, East and West, met at a 'curious cross and market house' (the Chichester cross, an ornately carved Gothic edifice, still stands there). Every second Wednesday a sheep and cattle market would block the streets with livestock, and there was also a weekly fish market.[301] Gas lighting (whether in the streets or for houses) was still several years away even though it was beginning to appear in parts of London. All in all, Chichester was a genteel place with a predominantly medieval ambience. Drunks and miscreants could still find themselves punished by being put in the stocks.

On the 18 or 19 January Charles Brown met Keats off the coach and the two men then spent two or three days in a secluded part of the town called Eastgate Square. As the guests of the Dilkes and their friends, they joined in 'dowager card parties' and were popular with the old ladies. On 23 January they walked the twelve or so miles along the coast to the village of Bedhampton, to stay at the home of Charles Dilke's sister, Letitia, and her husband, John Snook. Keats regularly walked long distances, and about a month after walking to the Snooks' house he wrote in a letter, 'The nothing of the day is a thing called a velocipede. It is a wheel carriage to ride cock-horse upon, sitting astride and pushing along with the toes.'[302] The velocipede, the forerunner of the bicycle, clearly didn't appeal to him.

The Snooks were bakers and millers who lived in a house next to their flour-mill near the mouth of the Hermitage Stream at Bedhampton. It was a picturesque setting complete with a mill pond and weir. Keats and Brown settled in quickly and were soon writing a letter full of jokes and puns to Charles Dilke and his wife in London:

> [A lady] has persuaded Brown to shave his whiskers– he came down to Breakfast like the Sign of the Full Moon.[303]

On 23 January, they took John Snook's son to the dedication of a chapel in a splendid parkland called the Stansted Estate, some 20 miles away. Although they travelled in a chaise, it proved to be a miserable experience for Keats; it was raining and he had a sore throat. He later wrote to his sister, 'At Bedhampton I was unwell and did not go out of the Garden Gate but twice or thrice during the fortnight I was there'.[304] In fact, when Brown returned to London, Keats stayed behind and spent his time in the warmth and comfort of the mill house, nursing his sore throat and writing his new poem, *The Eve of St Agnes*. This is a romance set in a medieval Gothic castle and chapel (Keats may have had in mind Carisbrooke Castle on the Isle of Wight). The poem is based on a folk tale conceived around the legend of St Agnes, the patron saint of chastity whose feast day is 21 January. St Agnes was a Roman girl who was sentenced to execution on account of her Christianity but had to be ravished in a brothel before she could be killed since it was illegal to execute virgins. A miracle occurred, and her virginity remained intact. The legend went that on St Agnes' Eve, 20 January, a young woman who completed certain bedtime rituals would dream of her future husband, and Keats wove an elaborate romance around this notion. (As Keats was in 'medieval' Chichester on 20 January, perhaps the subject of the legend had come up in conversation with the old ladies in the Dilkes' circle of friends.)

The Eve of St Agnes is perhaps the first of Keats' completed poems that demonstrates his mature genius as a poet. He creates a scene so rich and colourful that the language is, again to use his own phrase, 'hieroglyphical', transforming his thoughts into visible images. At the start of the poem, Keats evokes the coldness of the weather on a January night when an old beadsman is at prayer in a chapel (a beadsman was a poor old man whose job it was to pray for the well-being of his lord or king). The beadsman is kneeling down in an aisle bordered by rows of tombs. These are adorned with the sculpted effigies of knights and ladies, and high above them are carved angels below a cornice. The old man's breath is beautifully described – it is rising in the cold air as if making its way to heaven along with his prayer:

> St Agnes' Eve – ah, bitter chill it was!
> The owl, for all his feathers, was a-cold,
> The hare limped trembling through the frozen grass,
> And silent was the flock in woolly fold.
> Numb were the Beadsman's fingers, while he told
> His rosary, and while his frosted breath,
> Like pious incense from a censor old,
> Seemed taking flight for heaven, without a death,
> Past the sweet virgin's picture, while his prayer he saith.
>
> His prayer he saith, this patient, holy man;
> Then takes his lamp, and riseth from his knees,
> And back returneth, meagre, barefoot, wan,
> Along the chapel aisle by slow degrees.
> The sculptured dead, on each side, seem to freeze,
> Imprisoned in black, purgatorial rails.
> Knights, ladies, praying in dumb orat'ries,
> He passeth by; and his weak spirit fails
> To think how they may ache in icy hoods and mails.

As he shuffles along the aisle, the beadsman is made aware that preparations for a pageant in the castle are complete. The carved angels overhead are beautifully rendered:

> The ancient beadsman heard the prelude soft,
> And so it chanced for many a door was wide
> From hurry to and fro. Soon, up aloft,
> The silver, snarling trumpets 'gan to chide;
> The level chambers, ready with their pride,
> Were glowing to receive a thousand guests;
> The carvèd angels, ever eager-eyed,
> Stared, where upon their heads the cornice rests,
> With hair blown back, and wings put cross-wise on their breasts.

At the centre of the poem are two young lovers, Porphyro and Madeline, loosely based on Shakespeare's *Romeo and Juliet*. Madeline lives in the castle, and Porphyro has managed to gain access to it, but there is a deadly enmity between Porphyro and Madeline's families, and Porphyro's life would be in danger if he were to be caught within its walls. An old nurse called Angela discovers him, 'with heart on fire for Madeline', hiding behind a pillar, and takes him to Madeline's bedchamber where he hides in a closet and sees her undress.

In Chapter 2 we saw how Keats was judicious in his use of colour almost from the very start of his writing career, that there had been heraldic overtones in the *Imitation of Spenser* in which the kingfisher's blues and greens had vied with the brilliant golds and rubies of the fish below:

> There the king-fisher saw his plumage bright
> Vying with fish of brilliant dye below,
> Whose silken fins and golden scales light
> Cast upwards through the waves a ruby glow...

The Pursuit of Beauty and Truth

That had been written five years earlier, when Keats was just 18. He was now 23, and he infused *The Eve of St Agnes* with a richness of colour never before seen in English poetry. Its 'depth of impression' was emulated by poets and captured by painters (particularly the Pre-Raphaelites) for decades after Keats' death and the following two stanzas are among the most famous in the whole of Keats' poetry. They describe a triple-arched window in Madeline's bedchamber surrounded by carvings of fruits and flowers. The window glass is full of 'splendid dyes' and the coloured light from it falls upon Madeline as she kneels down in prayer. There is rose-bloom, a symbol of beauty, amethyst, a symbol of sincerity, and *gules*, the colour of rubies and a symbol of passion. Keats openly acknowledges the heraldic nature of this imagery (*'mong thousand heraldries*) and the effect is both complex and beautiful, but note how brilliantly he spreads his alliteration (**c**asement, **c**arven; **g**arlanded, **g**rass; **d**iamonded, **d**evice, **d**yes) and assonance (the repetition of vowel sounds, e.g., g<u>ar</u>landed, c<u>ar</u>ven; p<u>a</u>nes, qu<u>ai</u>nt, st<u>ai</u>ns, s<u>ai</u>nts) across several lines of each stanza. As a display of technical virtuosity, it is perhaps unrivalled in English poetry:

> A casement high and triple-arched there was,
> All garlanded with carven imageries
> Of fruits, and flowers, and bunches of knot grass,
> And diamonded with panes of quaint device
> Innumerable of stains and splendid dyes,
> As are the tiger-moth's deep-damasked wings;
> And in the midst, 'mong thousand heraldries,

> And twilight saints, and dim emblazonings,
> A shielded scutcheon blushed with blood of queens and kings.
>
> Full on this casement shone the wintry moon,
> And threw warm gules on Madeline's fair breast
> As down she knelt for heaven's grace and boon;
> Rose-bloom fell on her hands, together pressed,
> And on her silver cross soft amethyst,
> And on her hair, a glory, like a saint.
> She seemed a splendid angel, newly dressed,
> Save wings, for Heaven. Porphyro grew faint;
> She knelt, so pure a thing, so free from mortal taint.

Her vespers done, Madeline frees her hair of its wreathed pearls; she

> Unclasps her warmèd jewels one by one;
> Loosens her fragrant bodice; by degrees
> Her rich attire creeps rustling to her knees...

Porphyro looks on 'entranced' as Madeline climbs into bed and then falls asleep. The muffled music in the rest of the castle provides a backdrop as he cautiously emerges to begin laying a table at her bedside. In the distance, a hall door is shut and silence finally descends on the castle. Porphyro quietly furnishes the table with succulent food: 'candied apple, quince and plum... and lucent syrops, tinct with cinnamon'. The next stanza, though not as rich in colour, is just as technically brilliant as the previous ones (Porphyro's 'glowing hand' is being illuminated by moonlight. This small touch alone shows the power of Keats' imagination and the distinctiveness of his poetical sensibility):

> These delicates he heaped with glowing hand
> On golden dishes and in baskets bright
> Of wreathèd silver; sumptuous they stand
> In the retired quiet of the night,
> Filling the chilly room with perfume light.
> 'And now my love, my seraph fair, awake!
> Thou art my heaven, and I thine eremite.
> Open thine eyes, for meek St. Agnes' sake
> Or I shall drowse beside thee, so my soul doth ache.

Madeline eventually awakes when Porphyro plays some music to her on a lute. But is she *really* awake, or is she dreaming? Keats leaves the question open, but eventually Madeline and Porphyro 'melt' together with 'solution sweet' as the wind howls outside and sleet patters against the stained glass window. Early the next morning, while the revellers in the rest of the castle are still asleep, Madeline and Porphyro glide down the corridors and escape like phantoms, disappearing over the moor:

> And they are gone – aye, ages long ago
> These lovers fled away into the storm...

Keats ends the poem by telling us that Angela the nurse died 'palsy-twitched' and the old beadsman 'slept among his ashes cold'.

When Keats packed his bags and left the Snooks' mill at Bedhampton, he had the draft of *The Eve of St Agnes* in his luggage. His sore throat hadn't fully cleared up even though he had not gone 'out of the Garden Gate but twice or thrice' during the fortnight that he was a guest at the mill house. We do not know whether he suspected that his illness was an early sign of a more serious problem, but as a trained medical practitioner, it is likely that he did. (Around this time he wrote to his sister that his sore throat had 'haunted' him 'at intervals nearly a twelve-month'.)[305] After the return journey to London, he moved back into Wentworth Place with Brown and on the morning of Sunday 14 February 1819, St Valentine's Day, he began a journal-letter to his brother and sister-in-law in America:

> ...I am still at Wentworth Place – indeed, I have kept indoors lately, resolved if possible to rid myself of my sore throat... I was nearly a fortnight at Mr John Snook's and a few days at old Mr Dilke's – Nothing worth speaking of happened at either place. I... wrote... a little Poem called 'St Agnes Eve'... I see very little now, and very few Persons, being almost tired of Men and things.[306]

***

Around the time that Haydon was preparing a two-year bond as surety for the loan he was expecting from Keats, he was also writing to other potential benefactors asking for help. One of them, the wealthy collector Thomas Hope, duly sent him £200 (he was the same Thomas Hope of Deepdene who had bought Haydon's first painting, *The Flight into Egypt*). With £200 in the bank and his eyes rested, Haydon continued with his efforts to regain a place in the hearts, homes and dining rooms of the aristocracy. Sending casts of the Elgin Marbles to the Imperial Academy of St Petersburg in Russia had resulted in a correspondence with the President of the Academy, the Russian historian and statesman, Aleksei Olenin, and also with his old friend the Italian sculptor Canova, who had taken an interest in the casts. From the very start of their correspondence, Olenin praised Haydon highly. After mentioning that he had read some of Haydon's writings, including the controversial *On the Judgement of Connoisseurs on Works of Art*, he said:

> I have resolved to begin my desired acquaintance with you by sending, for your own use, some casts from the best remains of antiquity that are in the possession of his Imperial Majesty at St. Petersburg, as the beautiful bust of Achilles, a statue of Venus, a true antique Grecian work which the connoisseurs of fine arts think to be equal to the Venus of [the] Medicis, and a small statue of Silenus, which articles I hope you will receive as a mark of the esteem I have for you...[307]

We can only imagine Haydon's pleasure at being praised by such an important man as Olenin, and being told that he was to receive a cast of a statue that would have been worthy of the Medicis themselves. The Achilles, Venus and Silenus duly arrived at Haydon's studio and were proudly put on display. Haydon wrote a letter of thanks to Olenin:

> The head of the Silenus **for beauty of execution and intense truth of expression** is one of the finest specimens I know of Greek sculpture. It is universally admired, and has made a great noise among those whose judgment I estimate.[308] [My emphasis]

As for the Venus, Haydon said it

> is indeed a most beautiful statue, and has all the air of a fresh and pure Virgin, young elastic, and lovely, uninjured by the passions of our nature, and without having suffered from the anxieties of life.[309]

This idea, that a piece of sculpted art can be seen as virginal, 'uninjured by the passions of our nature, and without having suffered from the anxieties of life' became the central theme in Keats' *Ode on a Grecian Urn*. He may or may not have seen the correspondence between Haydon and Olenin (although, knowing Haydon's pride in such matters, it is more than likely that Haydon did show it to him), but even if he did not, he would almost certainly have seen the idea restated in an article that Haydon published over two Sundays in the *Examiner* of early May 1819. Keats was still an avid reader of the *Examiner* and often mentioned it in his letters.

Back in 1816, Haydon had used his influence with his old friend William Seguier, a well-connected painter and art dealer, to have two of the famous and extremely valuable cartoons of Raphael sent from the royal palace at Hampton Court to the grand gallery of the British Institution in Pall Mall in order that Haydon's pupils could copy them. ('Cartoons', from Italian *cartone*, were large drawings designed to be transferred to walls for the making of frescoes, or to cloth for the making of tapestries.) The original ten cartoons of Raphael depicted scenes from the lives of St Peter and St Paul; only seven survive but they are considered masterpieces of the Renaissance. They were the designs for a set of tapestries to be hung on the lower walls of the Sistine Chapel in the Vatican and were commissioned by Pope Leo X in 1515. On 25 January, 1819, the *Examiner*'s Fine Arts section stated,

> We see that MR HAYDON intends shortly to exhibit the drawings of his pupils... The object of the exhibition, we understand, is to impress

the public mind with the nature and principles of preparatory study, on which the old masters proceeded.[310]

On 30 January, an exhibition of his pupils' drawings from the cartoons and the Elgin Marbles was held (under the auspices of the British Institution) at the Thatched House Tavern in St James's Street. Despite its rustic name, this was a large building which had a spacious exhibition room and was popular with various societies for their meetings. A drawing by a caricaturist called J.L. Marks places the building on the south west side of the street, within sight of St James's Palace. The drawing is called 'St James's Street in an Uproar, or the Quack Artist and his Assailants' and the nobility are shown alighting from their coaches and flocking into the building while Haydon stands opposite in a large brimmed hat and blue longcoat, surrounded by geese (presumably *quacking* at the artist). In fact, the exhibition was very well received and added greatly to Haydon's reputation as a commentator on the arts. The *Examiner*, much to Leigh Hunt's credit, made this clear in an article published on 7 February:

> The Drawings from the Cartoons are not only strong and very novel evidences of the beneficial effects resulting from the plan adopted by the Directors of the Institution, but are so many fresh leaves added to the laurel crown which decorates the brow of Mr HAYDON, inasmuch as they are performed by his Pupils... Two of the three excellent youths who have made these beautiful Chalk Copies, hitherto perhaps unequalled in England by any other hands besides Mr HAYDON'S, are of too intellectual a family, too conspicuously

brilliant in the cultivation of the Fine Arts, not to make us more than commonly sanguine... There are likewise some faithful Engravings... in imitation of Chalk Drawings, from charming heads, hands, &c., by Mr HAYDON... superior for **truth and beauty** to any... yet published in England.[311] [My emphasis]

As if this weren't enough, a subsequent notice appeared in the *Examiner*:

> Mr HAYDON'S EXHIBITION – The archduke MAXMILIAN [sic]... yesterday inspected the masterly drawings from the cartoons and Elgin Marbles by Mr HAYDON'S pupils, and expressed himself highly gratified at such productions at so early an age.[312]

And this was not the last of the *Examiner*'s panegyrics – others followed over the ensuing weeks. In the afterglow of such a public success, Haydon could respond in a calm and measured way when the following criticism appeared in print (it was written anonymously by someone calling themselves 'Castigator'):

> [Haydon's pupils]... had shown their abilities in the Royal Academy before [Haydon] cajoled them to call themselves his pupils. This, we are informed, has been his uniform plan: where he has seen a youth exhibit ability, he has tried every means which flattery could suggest to induce him to join his party... I advise young men to shake off the trammels of this imposter...[313]

This was unfair; indeed, it was blatantly untrue. Bewick's letters clearly show that he was refused admission to the Royal Academy and that Haydon subsequently gave generously of his time for free, and Cripps, though not involved in the exhibition, had never attended the Royal Academy. On Sunday 7 March, Haydon was given the space in the *Examiner* to refute the accusations and he did so calmly, point by point. We know that Keats read the 'imposter' piece and Haydon's measured response because he said in a letter to Haydon, postmarked 8 March, 1819, 'You got out gloriously in yesterday's *Examiner*'.[314]

Haydon was to write his scholarly article about one of Raphael's Cartoons in the coming weeks, but in the meantime he mused on the lessons he had learned from the popular success of his exhibition, particularly the praise heaped on the drawings of the Elgin Marbles. After writing in his diary that the private exhibition day was 'the proudest day of my life' he went on to quote from the *Epigrams* of the Roman poet, Martial. He quoted a comment in which Martial praises the sculptor, Phidias, the man who is understood to have created the Elgin Marbles:

> 'Adde aquam & natabunt', says Martial of Phidias. This explains more in four words of the principles of Phidias than pages of discussion. Put his fish in water & they will swim! Give his cows grass and they will eat! Shew his dogs a hare & they will run! Sound a trumpet to his horses & they will neigh! & point out a lovely girl to his men & their eyes will melt![315]

We can recall that Haydon had said of the statue of Venus sent to him by Aleksei Olenin that it was

> indeed a most beautiful statue, and has all the air of a fresh and pure Virgin, young elastic, and lovely, uninjured by the passions of our nature, and without having suffered from the anxieties of life.

What he meant, of course, was that the statue of Venus was wholly lifelike but had never actually *lived*, hence the goddess had retained both her beauty and her purity. Now, musing on the Elgin Marbles, he said that the fish, cows, dogs, horses and men are so lifelike that with a little encouragement they might spring to life and swim, or chase a hare, or 'melt' over a lovely woman. Haydon was saying that both the Venus and the Elgin Marbles are held in stasis; they are thoroughly *lifelike* but forever unable to become *alive*. This was the idea that Haydon wove into his forthcoming article about one of the Raphael Cartoons, and it was also the idea that was central to Keats' *Ode on a Grecian Urn*. Both were written in May 1819.

***

Keats stayed at Wentworth Place in Hampstead throughout the spring and early summer of 1819. In many ways he was 'furling his wings', spending a lot of time alone among his books. His reading included Robert Burton's *Anatomy of Melancholy*, a huge encyclopaedia of melancholia, as well as Dante's *The Divine Comedy* and William Robertson's *The History of America*. Keats was missing his brother George terribly, and thinking about life's joys and sorrows, or 'light and shade', moved his intellectual focus back from poetry to philosophy. In October 1818, he had written to Richard Woodhouse, a legal clerk at his publisher Taylor and Hessey's office:

> As to the Poetical character itself (I mean that sort of which, if I am any thing, I am a Member; that sort distinguished from the wordsworthian or egotistical sublime; which is a thing per se and stands alone) it is not itself – it has no self – It has no character – it

enjoys light and shade; it lives in gusto, be it foul or fair, high or low, rich or poor, mean or elevated – It has as much delight in conceiving an Iago as an Imogen. What shocks the virtuous philosopher delights the chameleon poet.[316]

Yet again his thinking had been heavily influenced by Hazlitt – not just in saying that the poetical character lives in gusto, but also in his echo of Hazlitt's *Round Table* piece, *Mr Booth's Iago* (we noticed in Chapter 8 that Hazlitt had praised the actor Junius Brutus Booth for playing Iago with 'the chameleon quality of reflecting… all objects that come in contact with him'). At the time he wrote to Woodhouse, Keats clearly saw himself as a poet *if he was anything*. But from 14 February to 3 May, roughly from the time he wrote *The Eve of St Agnes* to the appearance of Haydon's article about the Raphael Cartoons in the *Examiner*, he wrote the journal-letter to his brother in America that we noted above, and it is through this letter that we can see his thoughts moving towards a mature philosophical stance based on Hazlitt's description of the disinterested mind. He had made a friend called William Haslam (a friend of the family into which his brother George had married) and after hearing that Haslam's father was dying, he said:

> Circumstances are like Clouds, continually gathering and bursting – While we are laughing the seed of some trouble is put into the wide arable land of events… [it] grows and bears a poison fruit which we must pluck… From the manner in which I feel Haslam's misfortune I perceive how far I am from any humble standard of disinterestedness… I have no doubt that thousands of people never

heard of had hearts completely disinterested: I can remember but two – Socrates and Jesus – their Histories evince it...[317]

Mentioning Jesus makes Keats wonder if there is a 'superior being' who is aware of the 'instinctive attitude' his mind sometimes falls into. If there is such a being, he may actually be entertained by Keats' lack of disinterestedness, just as Keats himself may be entertained by watching the instinctive 'alertness of a stoat' or the 'anxiety of a deer'. I am young, says Keats, and I am 'writing at random – straining at particles of light in the midst of a great darkness':

> This is the very thing in which consists poetry, and if so it is not so fine a thing as philosophy – for the same reason that an eagle is not so fine a thing as a truth – Give me this credit – Do you not think I strive to know myself? Give me this credit and you will not think that on my own account I repeat Milton's lines –
>
> How charming is divine Philosophy
> Not harsh and crabbed, as dull fools suppose
> But musical, as is Apollo's lute...[318]

Know thyself is, of course, one of the most famous injunctions in the history of philosophy. It was said to have been inscribed in the forecourt of the Temple of Apollo at Delphi, and Plato made it central to the philosophy of Socrates. Keats remembered that Thomas Taylor had said Socrates was a 'great man' who left his 'mind and his sayings and his greatness' to posterity without actually leaving any writings of his own. It was this observation from Taylor that had led Keats to compare Socrates with Jesus.[319]

***

By the time Keats began writing this long journal-letter to his brother, Haydon was once again asking him for money. The exhibition of the drawings of the Raphael Cartoons had been costly for Haydon; it had earned him a good deal of public notice and approval but had returned little in financial terms. He had spent many hours writing long tracts in his diary, letters to foreign dignitaries and articles for the *Examiner* while his great painting had languished on its easel. When he finally turned his attention back to the painting he found that he needed to buy more brushes (from Paris) as well as linseed oils and expensive pigments, but he had insufficient money to pay for them. Having exhausted the purses of every other friend and patron he could think of, he finally asked Keats to fulfil his earlier promise of a loan, but in so doing he put Keats in a very awkward position.

Keats' financial affairs were muddled. The small family inheritance from the Jennings' business at the Swan and Hoop had for years been administered by the guardian of the Keats children, Richard Abbey. Some of it was being contested in the Court of Chancery, and Tom Keats' death in December 1818 had only made things worse. George Keats had more of a business mind than his older brother but he was out of reach in America, so Keats was left to deal with matters on his own (he was in fact almost completely ignorant when it came to the administration of his inheritance). When a letter containing the following comment arrived from Haydon, Keats was, perhaps for the first time, genuinely annoyed with the seemingly never-ending demands of his friend:

> ...My dear Keats – now I feel the want of your promised assistance – as soon as it is convenient it would indeed be a great, the greatest of blessings... Before the 20th if you could help me it would be nectar and manna...[320]

Keats seems to have ignored this letter because Haydon wrote to him again on Monday 12 April 1819:

> My dear Keats,
>
> Why did you hold out such delusive hopes [in] every letter on such slight foundations? You have led me on step by step, day by day; never telling [me] the exact circumstances; you paralysed my exertions in other quarters – and now when I find it is out of your power to do what your heart led you to offer I am plunged into all my old difficulties with scarcely any time to prepare for them... I declare to you I scarcely know which way to turn...[321]

The tone of this letter was wholly inappropriate – Haydon wrote as if he were scolding a wayward child. He effectively said that Keats was deluded when he led Haydon on, day by day, and that it was Keats' fault that Haydon was left with his 'old difficulties' – his growing mountain of debt and his seemingly endless need to borrow money. The reproachful tone of the letter was only slightly lessened by a postscript in which Haydon said he was 'sensible' of the trouble Keats had taken and that he was (still) attached to Keats 'as much & more than to any Man'. Keats' reply shows that he was irritated, but it was still measured:

> When I offered you assistance I thought I had it in my hand... The difficulties I met with arose from the alertness and suspicion of

> [Richard] Abbey: and especially from the affairs being still in a Lawyer's hand – who has been draining our property for the last six years of every charge he could make – I cannot do two things at once, and thus this affair has stopped my pursuits in every way... I assure you I have harassed myself ten times more than if I alone had been concerned in so much gain or loss... from my own imprudence and neglect all my accounts are entirely in my Guardian's Power. This has taught me a lesson. Hereafter I will be more correct...[322]

He went on to point out that he had been in the habit of lending small sums of money to his friends which he now realised had little chance of being repaid and that the total, around £200, could have bought him a library of books. He then answered Haydon's complaint directly:

> It has not been my fault. I am doubly hurt at the slightly reproachful tone of your note and at the occasion of it, – for it must be some other disappointment; you seemed so sure of some important help when I last saw you – now you have maimed me again; I was whole, I had began reading again – when your note came I was engaged in a Book...[323]

The letter breaks off when Keats says he will 'walk over the first fine day' to see where Haydon's affairs stand. If the painter was still desperate for money, Keats says, he would take the 'gloomy walk' into the City to confront Richard Abbey. It seems Keats was successful this time because he lent Haydon £30 and the next time Keats wrote to him, on 17 June 1819, it was to tell him he was in serious difficulty himself, and to ask for the loan to be repaid. It was probably through sheer necessity that Haydon ignored the request but Keats, in a letter to his brother in America, said that Haydon 'did not seem to care much about it, and let me go without my money with almost nonchalance'. After the tone of Haydon's recent letters and incessant demands, Keats considered this an unforgiveable discourtesy. 'He ought to have sold his drawings to supply me,' he continued. 'I shall perhaps still be acquainted with him, but [as] for friendship, that is at an end.'[324]

***

Six weeks before these events, on 2 May 1819, the first part of Haydon's 'Raphael Cartoons' article appeared in Leigh Hunt's *Examiner*. It was called *On The Cartoon of the Sacrifice at Lystra* and was about the picture that Raphael had based on the Biblical story in Acts Chapter 14, in which St Paul and St Barnabus cure a man from Lystra who was widely known to be lame. In the story, when St Paul ordered the man to get up and walk, he *leaped* and *walked*. The italics are Haydon's – he had talked of this miracle in his diary as having the ring of truth about it, adding that it was one of the reasons he believed in Christianity. Any lame man who had just been cured, thought Haydon, would not merely stand up, but would leap with joy and astonishment.

In the Biblical account, this event was witnessed by the Roman pagans of Lystra. They quickly brought a white bull with gilt horns and a garland to sacrifice to the 'gods' who had performed this miracle before their very eyes (St Paul and St Barnabus. It was entirely typical of Haydon that in discussing the ceremony of sacrifice he borrowed descriptions in Latin from the Roman writers, Juvenal, Ovid and Livy). As for St Paul himself, said Haydon, he had an expression of 'confused astonishment and horror' that the locals were going to sacrifice a bull to *him*. Haydon described the scene in great detail before telling his readers that his article would be completed in the following week's *Examiner*.[325]

The second part of the article appeared on 9 May. Haydon opened the piece by comparing Raphael with Phidias. Both artists, he contended, had produced figures (whether painted or sculpted) whose appearances were completely natural and lacking the 'style' that Michelangelo created in his unnatural figures. Haydon then lifted his thoughts straight out of his diary and transposed them into his article:

> No doubt the conception of a character may be so grand, the novelty of an idea may be so beautiful, the pathos of an idea may be so deep, that the errors or inadequacy of the means of representation may be forgiven...[326]

After saying that an art which imitates nature should have truth and purity in its language (again, taken from the diary), Haydon began a train of thought which developed and expanded his earlier comments about the statue of Venus and which would be echoed in Keats' *Ode on a Grecian Urn*:

> Michelangelo seemed to disdain to imitate creatures who are weak enough to yield to passion, and took refuge from this world's materials in the sublime and solitary feeling in imagining a higher order of beings and a world of his own. His Prophets and Sybils look as if they

were above the influence of time; **they seem as if they would never grow old, and had never been young**.[327] [My emphasis]

On March 25, 1820, after an exhaustive six year effort, Haydon finally exhibited his *Christ's Entry into Jerusalem*, but with reservations. He had been worrying about the head of Christ, for in attempting a 'supernatural' look with 'divine mildness' he had painted the face in pale colours. 'My great anxiety was the head of Christ,' he wrote many years later in his autobiography, 'which at last I believed I had succeeded in, but in swerving from the traditional type I had shocked some devout Christians, as if it were not like him!.. I endeavoured to combine in it power and humbleness, but power took the lead, and by overdoing the intellectual a little, I injured, I fear, the simplicity of that divine mildness which should always be the ruling expression in the Saviour's face.'[328]

Despite these misgivings, Haydon went ahead and hired the magnificently ornate Egyptian Hall in Piccadilly as the venue for his exhibition (the cost to be paid from the proceeds of the exhibition and sale). During the many years it had taken to paint, the picture had, said Haydon, 'been visited by fashion, beauty and rank, by genius and royalty' and the expectation was, he said, 'very high indeed'. The frame alone weighed 600lbs, and at the first attempt to hang it, snapped its iron ring. It was finally lifted by 'the strongest soldiers' and various contraptions of machinery. Sir George Beaumont sent £30 towards the cost of the exhibition but 'this soon went' and everything came to a halt. Fittings and hangings were still required. Haydon flew down to Coutts bank and saw a Mr Antrobus and a Mr Majoribanks:

> I said, 'I am going to exhibit a picture which has taken six years to paint.' They stared. 'Six years over a picture?'... 'Yes, sir.' 'Well, what do you want?' 'Why I am ashamed to say I have no money left, and am overdrawn.' 'How much do you want?' said Mr Majoribanks, putting on the banker look... 'Why,' said I, '£50 would do.' 'You shall have it,' said both... I went off to a wholesale house, bought all the fittings wanted of the right colour (purple brown), [and] galloped back to the Egyptian Hall, where whispers were already beginning to be heard.[329]

With the picture up, Haydon signed the invitations to the private viewing, 800 in all. It was to be the best show in London with all the ministers and their ladies attending, and 'all the foreign ambassadors, all the bishops, all the beauties in high life, the officers on guard at the palace, all the geniuses in town, and everybody of any note, all were invited and came'. With the time of admission approaching, Haydon's nerves got the better of him. He sat in the nearby Hatchett's Coffee Room, literally watching the clock. When he finally went back to the Egyptian Hall, a crowd of carriages was blocking Piccadilly. There were servants in the passageways and 'bustle and chat, and noise and [the] hallooing of coachmen'. The room was full, and everybody was straining to see the great painting. Keats and Hazlitt were 'up in the corner', said Haydon, and 'really rejoicing'.[330]

***

Some two months earlier, on 3 February 1820, Keats had returned from town in bitterly cold weather. He had gone out without a coat, and walked the short distance from the coach stop in Pond Street to his lodgings in Wentworth Place. 'He came into the house in a state that looked like fierce intoxication,' wrote his friend Charles Brown. 'I knew this was impossible.' Keats was fevered, and he explained to Brown that he had travelled on the outside of the coach until he had become severely chilled, 'but now I don't feel it'. Brown put him to bed and brought him a glass of spirits. At that moment Keats had coughed and produced a drop of blood. There were few people in England who could have seen more clearly what that drop of blood represented. Many years later, Brown could still remember what Keats had said:

> Bring me the candle, Brown and let me see this blood… I know the colour of that blood, it is arterial blood. I cannot be deceived in that colour. That drop of blood is my death warrant.[331]

Keats looked up at Brown's face 'with a calmness of countenance I can never forget'. The young poet knew that he had developed the dreadful disease that had claimed the lives of his mother and beloved younger brother, and his use of the phrase 'death warrant' was not chosen lightly. As a qualified medical practitioner, he knew that his chances of survival were very slim. In the last letter he wrote before his death on 23 February, 1821, he said, 'I have an habitual feeling of my real life having past, and that I am leading a posthumous existence.'[332] By the time of Haydon's exhibition, Keats had already produced the poetry that was to make him historically famous and his 'posthumous existence' had effectively begun. Despite his earlier comment that his friendship with Haydon was over, he made a huge effort to leave his sick bed and join Hazlitt at the Egyptian Hall in Piccadilly. Haydon, of course, did not know that Keats had been coughing up blood. As the crowd bustled and jostled to get a better look at the picture, the artist looked on. He was still worrying about the head of Christ. It 'startled people', he said. 'It was not the traditional head; not the type, not orthodox.' Then, almost miraculously, in walked the majestic Mrs Siddons, the actress and intellectual who was the city's arbiter of taste:

> The whole room remained dead silent and allowed her to think. After a few minutes Sir George Beaumont, who was extremely anxious, said in a very delicate manner: 'How do you like the Christ?' Everybody listened for her reply. After a moment, in a deep, loud, tragic tone she said: 'It is completely successful... The paleness of...Christ gives it a supernatural look.'[333]

Sir George Beaumont, a potential purchaser, may have been relieved, but Haydon himself was not deceived. He knew he had failed by his own standards. 'The Christ's head,' he later wrote, 'was certainly not successful.'[334] He was aware that the 'supernatural' face he had painted was, unlike, say, the face of Christ in Michelangelo's *Pieta* or the face of any person in a painting of Raphael, far from beautiful. Even more importantly, this face of a Jewish man who had spent a lifetime out of doors in the simmering heat of the Holy Land had the complexion of a man who had spent his life under cloudy northern skies.

The Pursuit of Beauty and Truth

Beauty of form; truth of conveyance. As Haydon took in the scene at the Egyptian Hall in Piccadilly, as he talked to Sir George Beaumont and glanced at Keats, even as he listened to the opinion of Mrs Siddons, he knew that he had failed on both counts.

***

Around the time Haydon's *On The Cartoon of the Sacrifice at Lystra* had appeared in the *Examiner*, Keats wrote four of the five 'Great Odes' that would help secure his historical fame (the *Ode to Autumn*, which we noted earlier, was written later in the year). He wrote an *Ode to Psyche*, an *Ode on Melancholy* and an *Ode on Indolence*, all three of which are among the treasures of English literature. He also wrote what is perhaps the most famous of the odes, the *Ode on a Grecian Urn*.

Keats once wrote to Benjamin Bailey at Oxford about the difference between things that are 'real' and things that are 'semi-real':

> ...Things real – such as existences of Sun, Moon and Stars and passages of Shakespeare – Things semi-real, such as Love, the Clouds, etc., which require a **greeting of the Spirit** to make them wholly exist...[335] [My emphasis]

All of the subjects of the Great Odes are things 'semi-real', that's to say they are fleeting objects or personifications which require the imagination, or a dream – a 'greeting of the spirit' – to make them *wholly* exist. Thus we have Psyche (*Surely I dreamt today, or did I see / The wingèd Psyche with awakened eyes?*), Autumn (*Who hath not seen thee oft amid thy store?*), Melancholy (*Aye, in the very temple of Delight / Veiled*

Melancholy has her sovran shrine), Indolence (*The blissful cloud of summer indolence / Benumbed my eyes...*), the Nightingale (*Was it a vision, or a waking dream?*) and then the Grecian Urn itself (*...a friend to man, to whom thou sayest...*).

Keats had seen several Greek and Roman vases at the British Museum and perhaps also in one of the many private collections in existence at this time. Thomas Hope, for example, Haydon's generous patron, had bought part of the vase collection of Sir William Hamilton, the Scottish diplomat, antiquarian and former Ambassador to Naples. There exists (at the Keats-Shelley museum in Rome) a picture which Keats drew of a decorated volute krater called the Sosibios Vase, an Attic shaped vessel used to mix wine and water. It is believed that Keats copied or traced it from a book of engravings by a man called Henry Moses.[336]

But Keats' 'Grecian urn' is entirely imaginary, an amalgam of various images he had seen in museums, in paintings and in books. We can recall his comment when comparing his own poetry with Lord Byron's: 'He describes what he sees – I describe what I imagine – Mine is the hardest task', and his comment to Benjamin Bailey in his important letter of November 1817:

> I am certain of nothing but the Holiness of the heart's affections and the truth of Imagination. What the Imagination seizes as Beauty must be Truth whether it existed before or not, for I have the same idea of all our passions as of Love: they are all, in their sublime, creative of essential Beauty.

In writing the *Ode on a Grecian Urn*, Keats imagined a marble urn decorated with a pastoral scene from the Vale of Tempe in Thessaly, or an idealised vale of Arcady. Technically, this transformation of a work of art – a vase, or a sculpture – into another, often more vivid and descriptive artistic medium – poetry, or painting – is a rhetorical device called ekphrasis. The structure of this poem is very complex with, as we have come to expect, an elaborate intermingling of alliteration (**s**till, **qu**ietness, **f**oster, **s**ilence, **s**low, **s**ylvan) and assonance (br**i**de, ch**i**ld, s**i**lence, t**i**me, rh**y**me; fl**ow**ery, **ou**r) along with a high degree of repetition (*what* men, *what* maidens, *what* mad pursuit) across the whole poem. Its ten line stanza with its complex rhyme scheme was invented by Keats himself in order to make the first four lines and the second three of each stanza consistent – a,b,a,b,c,d,e – but the last three variable. In the first stanza, the last three lines have a rhyme scheme of d,c,e and rely heavily on repetition for their effect of movement and noise from this *silent* urn. Note how, despite its vast age, the urn is described as virginal, unaffected, uninjured, *unravished* by time itself. This mirrors Haydon's comment to Aleksei Olenin that the statue of Venus had 'all the air of a fresh and pure Virgin… uninjured by the passions of our nature, and without having suffered from the anxieties of life':

> Thou still unravished bride of quietness,
> Thou foster-child of silence and slow time,
> Sylvan historian, who canst thus express
> A flowery tale more sweetly than our rhyme!
> What leaf-fringed legend haunts about thy shape

> Of deities or mortals or of both?
> In Tempe or the dales of Arcady?
> What men or gods are these? What maidens loth?
> What mad pursuit? What struggle to escape?
> What pipes and timbrels? What wild ecstasy?

Keats has personified the urn and asked it several questions. Who *are* these people? What are they doing? What are they playing on their pipes and timbrels? Are they gods, or men? He sees a youth singing to his lover under a tree, a tree like the one he saw by the brook at Burford Bridge, the 'too happy, happy tree', which was living in a 'drear-nighted December'. But unlike the tree at Burford Bridge which next year will 'bud at the prime', the tree on the urn will never change, will never be bare of leaves. Similarly, the youth will always be singing, always be on the verge of kissing his love. Keats offers some consolation:

> Fair youth beneath the trees, thou canst not leave
> Thy song, nor ever can those trees be bare;
> Bold lover, never, never canst thou kiss,
> Though winning near the goal – yet do not grieve:
> She cannot fade, though thou hast not thy bliss,
> Forever wilt thou love, and she be fair!

More questions arise. To what green altar is that 'mysterious priest' leading a heifer like the one famously depicted in the Elgin Marbles, 'lowing at the skies', a heifer garlanded like the one depicted in the *Sacrifice at Lystra*? And the people in the procession, from where have they come?

> Who are these coming to the sacrifice?
> To what green altar, O mysterious priest,
> Lead'st thou that heifer lowing at the skies,
> And all her silken flanks with garlands dressed?
> What little town by river or sea shore,
> Or mountain-built with peaceful citadel,
> Is emptied of this folk, this pious morn?
> And, little town, thy streets for evermore
> Will silent be; and not a soul to tell
> Why thou art desolate can e'er return.

The urn has no answer, and in the final stanza Keats accepts that it is a 'silent form', though full of contradictions – it is made of stone and it is cold, and yet it portrays a scene that is intense, dramatic and musical.

These contradictions are perplexing and difficult to apprehend (as thinking about the Elgin Marbles brought about a 'dizzy pain') until Keats remembers that he must cease speculation and acknowledge the fact that they do not exist outside of his own imagination (they tease him 'out of thought', as did eternity). This was by now the mature imagination of a poetic genius who had studied the Elgin Marbles with Haydon, the singular artist who had spent six years trying to produce a painting that was both beautiful and true. It was the imagination of a poet-philosopher who alluded to the flowers and bees of the *Ion*, Plato's treatise on poetic inspiration, after spending several weeks in Oxford with a scholar who had an assortment of Platonic dialogues on his bookshelves. These interactions had brought Keats to the understanding that what is imagined necessarily belongs to that celestial, heavenly realm where our minds are 'full alchemised', a realm where, according to Plato's philosophy, perfection exists as it does not exist anywhere on earth. What is imagined as beautiful *must* be beautiful, said Keats. 'What the Imagination seizes as Beauty must be Truth.'

The urn finally answers, but of course it is the poet himself who is addressing the urn and telling it that *he* finally understands. Before he so disastrously transferred it onto his canvas, Haydon had said of his head of Christ, 'I saw the Divine face for the first time – distinctly in my mind'. But Keats' Grecian urn will never leave the celestial realm of the imagination. As such, it will always be truly beautiful, and beautifully true:

> ...When old age shall this generation waste,
> Thou shalt remain, in midst of other woe
> Than ours, a friend to man, to whom thou sayest,
> 'Beauty is truth, truth beauty' – that is all
> Ye know on earth, and all ye need to know.

Epilogue

Keats' *Poems 1820* was published by Taylor & Hessey with moderate success. It contained *The Eve of St Agnes*, the Great Odes and many other poems that would eventually secure him a place among the greats of English literature. But by then Keats was too ill to take much notice, perhaps even to care. He had famously fallen in love with a young woman called Fanny Brawne and was devastated by the realisation that he would never be able to marry her. He wrote to her in February 1820 as follows:

> How illness stands as a barrier 'twixt me and you! Even if I was well – I must make myself as good a Philosopher as possible. Now I have had opportunities of passing nights anxious and awake, I have found other thoughts intrude upon me. 'If I should die,' said I to myself, 'I have left no immortal work behind me – nothing to make my friends proud of my memory – but I have lov'd the principle of beauty in all things, and if I had had time I would have made myself remembered.'[337]

Keats' doctors advised a trip to the warm climate of Italy, and after a terrible journey aboard a brig called the *Maria Crowther*, he arrived in Naples on Saturday 21 October 1820. Reports of a typhus epidemic in London meant that the port authorities held the ship in medical quarantine for 10 days.[338] The quarantine ended on October 31, Keats' 25th birthday, and from there he went to Rome and lodgings in the Piazza di Spagna. He died there of consumption on Friday 23 February 1821. Up until his dying day Keats considered that he had failed as a poet, and he would have been astonished to learn that future generations of scholars and historians would mention him in the same breath as Shakespeare and Milton.

By the time of his final illness, many of his friends had already begun to collect his letters and manuscripts. Taylor and Hessey's legal adviser, Richard Woodhouse, was the most assiduous collector among Keats' admirers and Charles Brown was the first to attempt a biography, but it was Reynolds to whom Keats had confided the most varied of his speculations and the most profound of his inner thoughts, and it was Reynolds whom posterity considered his greatest friend. As he grew older, Reynolds became tormented by the realisation that he had wasted his considerable literary talents in the pursuit of a profession that he had found dull and unprofitable. The handsome and witty young poet who, back in December 1817, had been proclaimed by Leigh Hunt as one of the new 'Young Poets' along with Keats and Shelley, had spent the next 30 years as an impoverished second-rate solicitor, an occasional contributor to (and sometimes editor of) various magazines, and a popular raconteur among the erudite literary men of the famous Garrick Club in London.

The Pursuit of Beauty and Truth

A friend at the club, Lord John Russell, had used his influence to have Reynolds appointed as the assistant clerk at the new county court in Newport on the Isle of Wight, and so it was that in April 1847 Reynolds and then his wife Eliza packed up their belongings and took the stagecoach and steamship to the island. They moved into lodgings about a mile from where Keats had stayed with Mrs Cook in April 1817, and from where Keats had sent the letter containing his beautiful sonnet, *On the Sea*. Reynolds still had that letter and he may have realised that exactly 30 years had passed since Keats had written it.

The new assistant clerk and his wife settled in at 36 Nodehill, and between their modest home and Reynolds' office in the guildhall was an area of slums containing a slaughterhouse, a malthouse and (Newport being a garrison town) several public houses with names like The Valiant Soldier, The Trooper and The Military Arms. These sold cheap ale and gin to impoverished people who sang bawdy songs, played darts and huddled over decks of cards. Reynolds fitted in well. He became widely known for his drunkenness and would have been a familiar sight in the public houses along the more fashionable High Street. Once a very handsome man, it is not difficult to imagine him standing at a bar, stiffened by brandy and water, recounting tales of his life as a young man in London, the popular friend of several famous artists and writers, a protégé of the famous London editor, Leigh Hunt.

Hunt continued to write poetry and in 1828 he published a popular book called *Lord Byron and Some of his Contemporaries* which included an account of Shelley and some years that Hunt had spent with Byron in Italy, but Hunt's tastes grew out of fashion and his life in London became a continual struggle against poverty and sickness. In later life he established several new journals and periodicals and lived for a long time in fashionable Kensington, but he was only kept from the debtors' prison by sympathetic friends who provided him with various annuities and pensions. Towards the end of his life, with his financial problems eased, he wrote his autobiography but Hunt is mostly remembered today for his discovery and early publication of Keats and Shelley.

Benjamin Haydon did not achieve the fame he craved as a painter and never recovered from the 1820 failure of his epic painting, *Christ's Entry into Jerusalem*. Despite Mrs Siddons' endorsement, nobody wanted to buy the painting so Haydon decided to exhibit it more widely in the hope of making a profit from the door receipts. He rolled the painting up and sent it with his servant, Sammons, to Edinburgh – they went on a 'Leith smack', a passenger and cargo vessel, while Haydon himself went by coach. After securing lodgings in Edinburgh, Haydon hired an exhibition hall and then went for a walk with a friend, William Allen, a Scottish painter who had entered the Royal Academy at Somerset House a year or two before Haydon. Allen was to Edinburgh what Haydon was to London, a famous historical painter who had many friends in the literary world. He was a friend of the novelist Walter Scott and the Tory *Blackwood's* journalists including John Gibson Lockhart, the man who had written the vindictive review of Keats' poetry and said that Haydon 'as little resembles Raphael in genius as he does in person'.

During their walk Haydon and Allen actually met Lockhart, and Allen made the introductions. Haydon later said that the journalist appeared 'nervous' but the two men got along with each other and even had dinner together.[339] Haydon met another of the Blackwood set, John Wilson, a professor, lawyer and poet as well as a journalist, of whom Haydon said, 'His light hair, deep sea-blue eye, tall athletic figure, and hearty hand grasp, his eagerness in debate, his violent passions, great genius and irregular habits, rendered him a formidable partisan, a furious enemy, and an ardent friend. His hatred of Keats, which could not be concealed, marked him as the author of all those violent assaults on my poor friend in *Blackwood*.'[340]

Whether it was because of his Tory politics or his desperate desire to enlist the help of the Edinburgh intellectuals in publicising his painting, Haydon was determined to set himself apart from Leigh Hunt, Keats, Hazlitt and the rest of the 'cockneys' while he was in Scotland. He did this by accepting invitations to dinners and going horse riding with the *Blackwood* journalists (*fine dogs*, Haydon called them). By the time he left Edinburgh, he and Lockhart were firm friends and Lockhart used his influence to raise a subscription for Haydon when the painter was facing jail for debt in 1827.[341]

Haydon learned of Keats' death five weeks after the event and, in March 1821, wrote a long, rambling and incoherent account of him in his diary:

> A genius more purely poetical never existed. In conversation he was nothing, and if anything, weak and inconsistent… He was the most unselfish of human creatures; he was not adapted for this world…his knowledge of the Classics was inconsiderable, but he could feel their beauties.[342]

He blamed Leigh Hunt for what he saw as Keats' weakness and irresolution and, bizarrely considering his adventure in Scotland, he blamed the Tory reviewers for Keats' later despondency. As we saw, Keats was yet another close friend that the painter had managed to disenchant, and their final parting was an unhappy one:

> The last time I saw [Keats] was at Hampstead, [where he was] lying in a white bed with a book, hectic, weak, & on his back, irritable at his feebleness… I told him to be calm, but he muttered if he did not soon recover he would cut his throat. I tried to reason on such violence, but it was no use; he grew angry, & I went away deeply affected.[343]

Haydon married a woman called Mary Hyman in October 1821. In 1823 he experienced the first of his many spells in the King's Bench Prison for debt; he said in his diary that he was kept awake during the night by the 'songs and roarings of the other prisoners'. In later years, between his spells in prison, he maintained a modest amount of fame as a writer and public lecturer but when the great art critic John Ruskin published his masterful, four-volume *Modern Painters* between 1843 and 1856 he wrote, '…nothing except disgrace and misguidance will ever be gathered from such work as that of Haydon…'[344]. It was a small mercy that the comment was published after Haydon's death – he had finally given up the struggle and committed suicide in the most horrible manner on 22 June 1846. Standing in front of his last painting, he had cut his throat, survived the ordeal, and then shot himself.

History would not remember Haydon for his paintings; few have survived, though his *Christ's Entry into Jerusalem* now hangs in a chapel at the Mount St Mary's Seminary in Cincinnati, United States. Haydon is instead remembered for his voluminous, gossipy, sometimes vindictive but often brilliant diary, a record of a life spent pursuing an art for which he lacked the technical skills required to secure a place in history, but which is a valuable record of his daily interactions with some of the greatest painters and writers of his day. The tragedy is that Haydon could almost certainly have secured the lasting fame he craved had he chosen to be a writer instead of a painter.

William Hazlitt's fame as a journalist and essayist turned to infamy when he fell in love with a young servant girl and was almost driven mad by her rejection. He wrote a book about his experience, *Liber Amoris*, which was widely mocked and disparaged. He married a rich widow and with his new found wealth he toured Europe and wrote a monumental biography of Napoleon. The marriage did not last and Hazlitt increasingly spent time at the coaching inn, the Hut, on the outskirts of his beloved Winterslow. He died in London on 18 September 1830, in poverty once again, despite his marriage. History remembers him as one of England's greatest prose writers and a major influence on Keats.

Percy Bysshe Shelley moved abroad in 1818 and never set foot in England again. Upon hearing that Keats was desperately ill, Shelley offered him sanctuary in the warm climate of Italy, at his home near Pisa. Keats was somewhat ambivalent in his reply, but Shelley was clearly expecting him as a letter to Leigh Hunt's wife, Marianne, shows. 'I am aware... that I am nourishing a rival who will far surpass me and this is an additional motive, and will be an added pleasure.'[345] When Shelley heard of Keats' death he wrote an elegy for him. It is called *Adonais* and it contains some of Shelley's most beautiful poetry. The following lines are typical, and would surely have been appreciated by Keats:

> The One remains, the many change and pass;
> Heavens light forever shines, Earth's shadows fly;
> Life, like a dome of many-coloured glass,
> Stains the white radiance of Eternity...

When Shelley himself was drowned while sailing in the Gulf of La Spezia on 8 July 1822, a copy of Keats' last book of poems was found in his pocket – it was recovered when his body was later washed ashore.

A wealthy aristocrat called Richard Monkton Milnes, 1st Baron Houghton, was a friend of some of the nineteenth century's greatest literary men. When it became known in the mid 1840s that Milnes was writing a biography of Keats (his *Life, Letters and Literary Remains of John Keats* came out in 1848), many of Keats' former friends contacted him and offered their memories, manuscripts and letters. There is a treasure trove of correspondence between Milnes (and his publisher Edward Moxon) and Charles Brown (who handed a 'biography' over to Milnes), George Felton Mathew, Leigh Hunt, Charles Cowden Clarke, Benjamin Bailey, Benjamin Haydon and others, all sharing their memories of Keats.

Reynolds initially had a dispute with Edward Moxon over the copyright of his valuable collection of letters from Keats, including the letter containing the sonnet *On the Sea*. Moxon wrote to Milnes on 19 December 1846:

> Dear Mr Milnes,
>
> I am glad to hear that you are at work on the Memoir of Keats. You will I hope when you come to Town bring the MS. with you ready for press. I enclose you Keats's 1st volume... I also enclose you two notes which I sometime ago received from John Hamilton Reynolds. I would suggest that you write to him. As he was Keats's most intimate friend he is perhaps offended that no application has been made to him...[346]

Reynolds wrote to Milnes on 22 December 1846 to try to clear up any misunderstanding. He was not interested in making money from his ownership of Keats' letters, he was considering writing his own *Recollections of Keats*, but was now happy to hand his material over to Milnes:

> [Keats] had the greatest power of poetry in him of any one since Shakespeare! He was the sincerest Friend, the most loveable associate, the deepest Listener to the griefs & disappointments of all around him 'that ever lived in the tide of times'. Your expressed intentions as to

the Life are so clear & good; that I seem to have the weight of an undone work taken from me...[347]

When he died, drunk, disappointed and impoverished in November 1852, Reynolds left behind his devoted wife of nearly 30 years, Eliza Drewe Reynolds, but his gravestone in St Thomas's Church in Newport does not even mention her. Nor does it state that he had been a father, and that his daughter, Lucy, had died tragically young. His work at the county court in Newport is not recorded, neither is the fact that he was once a popular member of the Garrick Club. There is no mention of his early achievements as a newspaper editor in London, nor of his once being a promising young poet. His parents are not mentioned, neither are his sisters. But decades after his death, an additional four words were added to the inscription in order to acknowledge the contribution he had made to English literature:

In

Memory of

John Hamilton Reynolds

Who died

November 15th, 1852

Aged 58 years

The Friend of Keats

Notes

Abbreviations

Autobiography: Malcolm (ed.), *The Autobiography and Journals of Benjamin Robert Haydon*, London, Macdonald, 1950

Correspondence and Table-Talk: Haydon, Frederic Wordsworth (ed.), *Benjamin Robert Haydon: Correspondence and Table-Talk*, 2 vols, Boston, Estes & Lauriat, 1877

Diary: Pope, Willard Bissell (ed.), *The Diary of Benjamin Robert Haydon*, vols 1&2, Cambridge, Mass., Harvard University Press, 1960

Letters of John Keats: Buxton Forman, H. (ed.), 2 vols, part of *The Complete Works of John Keats*, 5 vols, Glasgow, Gowars & Gray, 1901

Chapter 1

1 - *Autobiography* p.20

2 - ibid., p.10

3 - ibid., p.15

4 - *Correspondence and Table-Talk*, vol.1, p.16

5 - *Autobiography* p.15

6 - *Autobiography* p.47

7 - Von La Roche, Sophie, *Sophie in London 1786*, trans., Williams, C., London, Jonathan Cape, 1933 pp.141-142

8 - *Autobiography* p.21

9 - ibid., p.17

10 - *The Literary Works of Sir Joshua Reynolds*, 2 vols, London, T Cadell, 1835, vol.1, p313

11 - ibid., vol.1, p344-5

12 - *Autobiography* p.21

13 - The sculpture was unearthed in 1506, in a vineyard near Santa Maria Maggiore. Pope Julius II sent Michelangelo to report back on the find. Discussed in Nickerson, Angela K., *A Journey into Michelangelo's Rome*, California, Roaring Forties Press, 2008, p108.

14 - John Paul Richter (trans.), *The Notebooks of Leonardo da Vinci*, (2 vols) London 1883 vol.1., IX, 488

15 - Bondanella, Julia Conaway & Peter (trans.), *Giorgio Vasari, The Lives Of The Artists*, Oxford University Press, 1991, P471

16 - *Autobiography* p.16

17 - Among Prince Hoare's many publications was a treatise on the progress of painting and sculpture in Great Britain called *Epoch Of The Arts*, London, John Murray, 1813

18 - Gwynn, Stephen, *Memorials Of An Eighteenth Century Painter*, London, T. Fisher Unwin, 1898, p12

19 - Opie was elected professor of painting at the Royal Academy in 1805 and delivered his first lectures in February 1807. It was said that the hard work involved in their preparation hastened his death, which occurred in April 1807.

20 - Fuseli's friend, the theologian Johann Casper Lavater, in a letter to the philospher Johann Gotfried von Herder dated November 4, 1773.

21 - *Autobiography* p.25

Chapter 2

22 - Haynes, J., *A Coroner's Inquest, 1804*, The Keats Shelley Memorial Bulletin, 1963, vol 14, p.46

23 - Gittings, *John Keats*, p.20

24 - Rollins, Hyder E. (ed.), *The Keats Circle: Letters and Papers 1816-1878*, 2 vols, Cambridge, Mass., Harvard University Press, 1948, vol.1, p.303

25 - The Keats family finances are discussed in Gittings, *John Keats*, pp.20-22

26 - Cowden Clarke, Charles & Mary, *Recollections of Writers*, New York, Charles Scribner's Sons, 1878 p.122

27 - Collected together in, for example, Parson's *Portraits of Keats*, 1954

28 - Clarke, *Recollections of Writers*, p.123

29 - ibid., p.146

30 - Adams, Francis (ed.), *The Extant Works of Aretaeus the Cappadocian*, London, The Sydenham Society, 1856, p.311

31 - Clarke, *Recollections of Writers*, p.125

32 - ibid., p.126

Chapter 3

33 - *The Literary Works of Sir Joshua Reynolds*, vol.1, p.360

34 - ibid., p.309

35 - *Diary*, vol.1, p.7

36 - *Autobiography*, p.26

37 - Cunningham, Allan, *The Life of David Wilkie*, 3 vols, London, John Murray, 1843, vol.1 p.45

38 - *Autobiography*, p.33

39 - *Correspondence and Table-Talk*, vol.1, p.250

40 - *Autobiography*, p.37

41 - Bell, Charles, *Essays on the Anatomy of Expression in Painting*, London, Longman, 1806, p.vi

42 - ibid., p.121

43 - ibid., p.150

44 - ibid., p.viii

45 - *Correspondence and Table-Talk*, vol.1, p.251

46 - Hooke, Nathaniel, *The Roman History, From The Building of Rome to the Ruin of the Commonwealth*, 5th edition, 4 vols, Hawkins, G. (etc.), London 1770, vol.1, p355

47 - *Autobiography*, p.51

48 - ibid., p.50

49 - ibid., p.77

50 - ibid., p.80

51 - *Diary*, vol.1, pp.15-16

52 - ibid., p.18-19

53 - ibid., p.19

54 - ibid., p.34

55 - ibid., p.313

56 - ibid., p.479

57 - *Autobiography*, p.114

58 - Diary, vol.1, pp.72-73

59 - ibid., p.119

60 - ibid., p.126

61 - *Autobiography*, p.159

62 - ibid., p.142

63 - Haydon's article, *To the critic on Barry's works in the Edinburgh Review, Aug 1810*, first appeared in the *Examiner* in three parts beginning on January 26th, 1812. With Haydon's permission, it was reprinted in two parts in the *Annals of Fine Arts*, London, Sherwood, Neely and Jones, etc., 1817, p.156 & 269

64 - *Examiner*, No.213, Sunday 26th January, 1812, p.61

65 - ibid.

66 - *Autobiography*, p.148

67 - ibid., p.152

68 - *Diary*, vol.2, pp.145-6

69 - *Diary*, vol.1, p.315

70 - ibid., the quote being from *The Faerie Queene*, I.v.1

71 - *Autobiography*, p.197

Chapter 4

72 - Dr Hammond's house was pulled down in 1931 according to the online version of *A History of the County of Middlesex*, Baker, T.F.T.

(etc., eds.), University of London & History of Parliament Trust, 2012, vol.5, pp.137-142

73 - *Letters of John Keats*, vol.1, p50

74 - Rollins, *The Keats Circle*, vol.2, p.277

75 - Beattie, James, *The Minstrel, or, The Progress of Genius*, London, C. Dilly, 1797, p.iii

76 - A quote widely attributed to Cooper, e.g., in *The British Medical Journal*, Wynter, Andrew M.D. (ed.) 1858, p.664.

77 - Cooper, Astley, *Principles and Practices of Surgery*, Philadelphia, Baswell, Harrington & Baswell, 1839, p.21

78 - The 'Old Operating Theatre' is now a museum in the roof space of St Thomas' church in Southwark, London. In Keats' day, the wards of the south wing of St Thomas' hospital were built around the church.

79 - Rollins, *The Keats Circle*, vol.2, p.209

80 - ibid., pp.208-209

81 - ibid., p.212

82 - Gill, Stephen, *William Wordsworth, The Major Works*, Oxford University Press, 1984, p.640

83 - ibid.

84 - ibid., p.641

Chapter 5

85 - Aldcroft, Derek, & Freeman, Michael (eds.), *Transport in the Industrial Revolution*, Manchester University Press, 1983, p.162

86 - Pilkington, Mrs, *Margate*, London, J. Harris, 1813, p.3

87 - Carey, George Saville, *The Balnea, or an Impartial Description of all The Popular Watering Places in England*, 2nd ed., London, W. West & C. Chapple, 1799, p.13

88 - Smith, John Thomas, *Nollekens And His Times*, 2 vols, London, Henry Colburn, 1829, vol.1, p.88

89 - Hunt, Leigh, *The Indicator*, London, Joseph Appleyard, 1820, p.278

90 - ibid., pp.270-271

91 - *Autobiography*, p.296

92 - *Letters of John Keats*, vol.1, p.3

93 - *Diary*, vol.2, p.62

94 - Taylor, Tom (ed.), *The Autobiography and Memoirs of Benjamin Robert Haydon 1808-1846*, with an introduction by Aldous Huxley, London, Peter Davies, 1926, p.856

95 - *Autobiography*, p.562

96 - ibid., p.297

97 - Clarke, *Recollections of Writers*, p.139

98 - *Correspondence and Table-Talk*, vol.1, p.96

99 - *Letters of John Keats*, vol.1, p.5

100 - Moore, Thomas, The *Life of Lord Byron*, London, John Murray, 1844, p.228

101 - Clarke, *Recollections of Writers*, p.139

102 - ibid.

103 - *The Examiner*, No.466, Sunday, December 1, 1816, p.761

104 - ibid.

Chapter 6

105 - White, Gilbert, *The Natural History of Selborne*, London, J. & A. Arch, etc., 2 vols, 1822, vol.1, p.23

106 - Hazlitt, William Carew (ed.), *Lamb and Hazlitt, Further Letters & Records Hitherto Unpublished*, London, Elkin Mathews, 1900, p.76

107 - ibid., pp.68-69

108 - Hazlitt, William, *Criticisms on Art with Catalogues of the Principal Picture Galleries of England*, 2nd series, edited by his son, London, C. Templeman, 1844, pp.1-2

109 - ibid., p.6

110 - ibid., p.14

111 - Sadler, Thomas (ed.), *Diary, Reminiscences and Correspondence of Henry Crabb Robinson*, 2 vols, Boston, Fields, Osgood & Co., 1869, vol.1, p.41

112 - *Correspondence and Table-Talk*, vol.1, p.96

113 - *Diary*, vol.1, p.303

114 - ibid., vol.2, pp.64-65

115 - Smith, Horace, *A Graybeard's Gossip about his Literary Acquaintance*, New Monthly Magazine 81, 1847, pp.238-240

116 - ibid.

117 - Dix, John, *Pen and Ink Sketches of Poets, Preachers and Politicians*, London, David Bogue, 1846, p.144

118 - Hogg, Thomas Jefferson, *The Life of Percy Bysshe Shelley*, 4 vols, London, Edward Moxon, 1858, vol.1, pp.69-70

119 - *The Monthly Review or Literary Journal*, London, J. Porter, 1816, p.433

120 - *Autobiography*, p.298

121 - ibid.

122 - *Correspondence and Table-Talk*, vol.1, p.313

123 - ibid., p.317

124 - Hazlitt, William, *Table Talk, or Original Essays*, London, John Warren, 1821, pp.354-357

125 - *Autobiography*, p.300

126 - Rollins, *The Keats Circle*, vol.2, p.154

127 - ibid., vol.1, p.140

128 - Moran, James, *Printing Presses, History and Development, etc.*, Berkeley and Los Angeles, University of California Press, 1973, pp.107-108

129 - Harper, Henry (ed.), *The Letters of Mary Shelley*, Norwood, Plimpton Press, 1918, pp.41-42

Chapter 7

130 - *Diary*, vol.2, p.88

131 - *Autobiography*, pp.303-304

132 - *Diary*, vol.2, p.88

133 - *Autobiography*, p.304

134 - ibid., p.305

135 - Hunt, Leigh, *Autobiography*, 2 vols, New York, Harper & Brothers, 1850, vol.2, p.31

136 - Barnard, John, in *Romanticism*, Edinburgh University Press, vol.12, no.2, 2006, p.90

137 - *Diary*, vol.1, p.89

138 - ibid., p.87

139 - *Autobiography*, p.78

140 - *Diary*, vol.1, p.29

141 - ibid., pp.50-51

142 - ibid., p.113

143 - *Autobiography*, p.78

144 - *Diary*, vol.1, p.280

145 - *Correspondence and Table-Talk*, vol.2, p.3

146 - *Autobiography*, p.303

147 - *Autobiography*, p.284

148 - ibid., p.286

149 - *Diary*, vol.2, p.101

150 - Reynolds, John, *The Champion*, 9th March, 1817, pp.78-81

151 - *Letters of John Keats*, vol.1, p.5

152 - ibid., p.8

153 - Quoted in Buxton Forman, H. (ed.), *The Complete Works of John Keats*, (5 vols), London, Gowars & Gray, 1901, vol.1, p.4

154 - Rollins, *The Keats Circle*, vol.1, p.69

Chapter 8

155 - *Autobiography*, p.185

156 - *Diary*, vol.1, p.296

157 - Hazlitt, William, *The Champion*, November 13th, 1814, reprinted in *A View of The English Stage*, London, Robert Stodart, 1818, pp.27-33

158 - *Letters of John Keats*, vol.1, p.9

159 - *Diary*, vol.2, p.107

160 - ibid., p.101

161 - *Letters of John Keats*, vol.1, p.147

162 - Birket Foster, Myles, *History of the Philharmonic Society of London*, 1813-1912, London, John Lane, 1912, p.7

163 - *Letters of John Keats*, vol.1, pp.7-8

164 - *Correspondence and Table-Talk*, vol.2, pp.31-32

165 - ibid., pp.32-33

166 - *Diary*, vol.2, p.110

Chapter 9

167 - *Letters of John Keats*, vol.1, p.11

168 - ibid.

169 - Jones, Leonidas M., *The Letters of John Hamilton Reynolds*, University of Nebraska Press, 1973, p.3

170 - *Letters of John Keats*, vol.1, p.13]

171 - ibid.

172 - ibid.

173 - *Letters of John Keats*, vol.1, p.16

174 - *Diary*, vol.2, p.122

175 - ibid., p.124

176 - *Correspondence and Table-Talk*, vol.2, p.3

177 - *Letters of John Keats*, vol.1, p.17

178 - ibid.

179 - ibid., p.19

180 - ibid., p.18

181 - *Crosby's Complete Pocket Gazetteer of England and Wales*, London, Baldwin, Cradock & Joy, 1815, p.328

182 - Shelley, Mary (ed.), *Shelley Memorials from Authentic Sources*, Boston, Ticknor and Fields, 1859, p.99

183 - Kent, Elizabeth, *Flora Domestica*, London, Taylor & Hessey, 1823, p.xix

184 - Hunt, Leigh, *Foliage*, London, C&J. Ollier, 1818, p.13

185 - ibid., p.16

186 - ibid., p.18

187 - *Diary*, vol.2, p.81

188 - Hunt, Leigh, *Autobiography*, vol.2, pp.13-14

189 - *Letters of John Keats*, vol.1, p.20

Chapter 10

190 - *Diary*, vol.2, p.125

191 - Fordyce Mavor, William, *A New Description of Blenheim*, 11th edition, Oxford, H. Slatter, 1820, p.21

192 - Diary, vol.2, p.125

193 - ibid., p.126

194 - ibid.

195 - ibid.

196 - ibid.

197 - Turner, Dawson, *Synopsis of The British Fuci*, 2 vols, Yarmouth, F.Bush, 1802, vol.1, p.iii

198 - A *Catalogue of the Manuscript Library of the Late Dawson Turner, Esq* was prepared for the auctioneers Messrs Puttick and Simpson of Leicester Square, London, in June 1859

199 - Carey, George Saville, *The Balnea, or an Impartial Description of all The Popular Watering Places in England*, 2nd ed., London, W. West & C. Chapple, 1799, pp.262-263

200 - *Crosby's Complete Pocket Gazetteer of England and Wales*, p.535

201 - *Diary*, vol.2, p.127

202 - Rollins, *The Keats Circle*, vol.2, p.259

203 - ibid., p.260

204 - ibid., p.261

205 - ibid., p.267

206 - ibid., pp.157-158

207 - ibid., p.268

208 - ibid., p.270

209 - *Letters of John Keats*, vol.1, p.24

210 - ibid., p.27

211 - ibid., pp.28-30

212 - ibid., p.31

213 - Rollins, *The Keats Circle*, vol.2, p.270

214 - *Letters of John Keats*, vol.1, p.34

215 - Rollins, *The Keats Circle*, vol.2, pp.277-278

216 - *Correspondence and Table-Talk*, vol.2, pp.3-4

217 - *Letters of John Keats*, vol.1, p.36

218 - ibid., pp.36-37

219 - *Diary*, vol.2, p.132

220 - ibid.

221 - ibid., p.134

222 - ibid.

223 - Carter Hughson, Shirley (ed.), *The Best Letters of Percy Bysshe Shelley*, Chicago, A.C. McClurg & Co., 1892, pp.89-90

224 - *Letters of John Keats*, vol.1, p.31

225 - *Diary*, vol.2, pp.135-136

226 - *Letters of John Keats*, vol.1, pp.37-38

Chapter 11

227 - Bell, John, *Observations on Italy*, William Blackwood, Edinburgh, 1825, pp.333-335

228 - *Diary*, vol.2, pp.138-142

229 - *Letters of John Keats*, vol.1, p.46

230 - ibid.

231 - ibid., pp.41-42

232 - ibid., p.46

233 - ibid., vol.2, p.111

234 - ibid., vol.1, p.47

235 - *Diary*, vol.1, p.483

236 - Cornwell, Baron Wilson (Mrs), *Memoirs of Harriet, Duchess of St Albans*, 2 vols, London, Henry Colburn, 1839, vol.1, p.157

237 - ibid., p.338

238 - *Autobiography*, p.315

239 - *Diary*, vol.2, pp.168-169

240 - *Autobiography*, pp.315-316

241 - Jones, Leonidas M., *The Life of John Hamilton Reynolds*, University Press of New England, 1984, p.131

242 - *Letters of John Keats*, vol.1, p.58

243 - *Autobiography*, pp.317-319

244 - Dilke, Charles Wentworth, *The Papers of a Critic*, 2 vols, London, John Murray, 1875, vol.1, p.8

245 - ibid., p.21

246 - Dilke, Charles Wentworth, *Old English Plays*, 6 vols, London, John Martin, 1814, vol.1, p.v

247 - Part quoted in Colvin, Sydney, *Keats*, London, Macmillan & Co., 1942, p.81. The whole article was reproduced in the *Harvard Library Bulletin*, Cambridge, Mass., 1972, Vol, xx, No.4, pp.368-371

248 - Hazlitt, William, *The Round Table, A Collection of Essays on Literature, Men and Manners*, 2 vols, Edinburgh, Archibald Constable & Co., 1817, vol.2, pp.22-23

249 - ibid., p.26

250 - *Letters of John Keats*, vol.1, pp.49-50

251 - ibid., p.50

252 - *Correspondence and Table-Talk*, vol.1, p.309

253 - Hazlitt, *The Round Table*, vol.1, p.76

254 - *Letters of John Keats*, vol.1, p.48

255 - ibid., p.71

Chapter 12

256 - *Letters of John Keats*, vol.1, p.58

257 - Leigh Hunt Letters, Special Collections, University of Iowa Libraries, Iowa City, Iowa, *Haydon Letter to Leigh Hunt*, 31 December, 1817

258 - ibid., *Haydon Letter to Leigh Hunt*, 6 January, 1818

259 - *Letters of John Keats*, vol.1, p.56

260 - ibid.

261 - ibid.

262 - ibid.

263 - ibid., pp.57-58

264 - *Diary*, vol.2, p.183

265 - ibid., p.185

266 - ibid., p.187

267 - Landseer, Thomas (ed.), *Life and Letters of William Bewick*, 2 vols, London, Hurst & Blackett, 1871, vol.1, p.41

268 - ibid., p.118

269 - ibid., p.108

270 - *Letters of John Hamilton Reynolds*, p.9

271 - Hazlitt, William, *Lectures on the English Poets*, London, Taylor & Hessey, 1818, p.92

272 - ibid., p.95

273 - ibid., p.107

274 - Landseer, *Life and Letters of William Bewick*, pp.41-42

275 - ibid., pp.159-162

276 - *Letters of John Keats*, vol.1, p.65

277 - Rollins, *The Keats Circle*, vol.1, p.10

278 - ibid.

279 - *Five Dialogues of Plato Bearing On Poetic Inspiration*, with an introduction by A.D. Lindsay, London, J.M. Dent, 1910, pp.6-7

280 - *Letters of John Keats*, vol.1, p.47

281 - ibid., p.59

282 - ibid., p.67

283 - ibid., p.78

284 - ibid., p.85

285 - *Diary*, vol.2, p.181

286 - *Autobiography*, p.322

287 - *Diary*, vol.2, p.197

288 - ibid.

289 - ibid., p.198

290 - ibid., p.204

291 - *Crosby's Complete Pocket Gazetteer of England and Wales*, 1815, p.466

292 - *Correspondence and Table-Talk*, vol.2, p.9

293 - *Letters of John Keats*, vol.1, pp.98-99

294 - *Blackwood's Edinburgh Magazine*, Edinburgh, William Blackwood, 1818, vol.3, p.522

295 - ibid., pp.520-521

296 - ibid, p.519

297 - ibid., p.520

298 - *Diary*, vol.2, pp.317-318

299 - *Letters of John Keats*, vol.2, p.5

300 - ibid., pp.4-5

Chapter 13

301 - *Crosby's Complete Pocket Gazetteer of England and Wales*, 1815, pp.109-110

302 - *Letters of John Keats*, vol.2, p.35

303 - ibid., p.11

304 - ibid., p.12

305 - ibid.

306 - ibid., p.22. The date of Sunday 24th February in this edition is incorrect – the 24th February 1819 was a Wednesday. Most other sources have the date as Sunday 14th February, e.g., *John Keats, Selected Letters*, Oxford, 2002, p.196

307 - *Correspondence and Table-Talk*, vol.1, p.324

308 - ibid., p.330

309 - ibid.

310 - *The Examiner*, No.578, Sunday, 24 January, 1819, p.58

311 - ibid., No.580, Sunday 7 February, 1819, pp.93-94

312 - ibid., No.581, Sunday 14 February, 1819, p.102

313 - ibid., No.584, Sunday 7 March, 1819, p.157

314 - *Letters of John Keats*, vol.2, p.14

315 - *Diary*, vol.2, pp.216-217

316 - *Letters of John Keats*, vol.1, p.173

317 - ibid., vol.2, pp.36-37

318 - ibid., p.38

319 - ibid., p.37

320 - ibid., p.9

321 - ibid., p.19

322 - ibid., pp.19-20

323 - ibid., p.20

324 - ibid., p.116

325 - *The Examiner*, No.592, Sunday, 2 May, 1819, pp.285-287

326 - ibid., No.593, Sunday, 9 May, 1819, pp.300-301

327 - ibid., p.301

328 - *Autobiography*, p.329

329 - ibid., p.331

330 - ibid., p.331-332

331 - Rollins, *The Keats Circle*, vol.2, pp.73-74

332 - *Letters of John Keats*, vol.2. p.202

333 - *Autobiography*, p.333

334 - ibid., p.332

335 - *Letters of John Keats*, vol.1, p.84

336 - Moses, Henry, *A Collection of Antique Vases, Altars, Paterae, etc.*, London, I. Williams, 1814, plate 38

Epilogue

337 - *Letters of John Keats*, vol.2, p.156

338 - Walsh, John Evangelist, *Darkling I Listen*, New York, St Martin's Press, 1999, p.12

339 - *Autobiography*, p.341

340 - ibid., p.342

341 - ibid., p.428

342 - *Diary*, vol.2, p.316

343 - ibid., p.318

344 - Ruskin, John, *Modern Painters* (David Barrie, ed.), London, Andre Deutsch, 1987, p.506

345 - Holmes, Richard, *Shelley: The Pursuit*, London, Penguin Books, 1974, p.614

346 - Rollins, *The Keats Circle*, vol.2, p.167

347 - ibid., p.173

Select Bibliography

The following books and pamphlets are the sources to which I have chiefly turned. I have also consulted a number of other nineteenth-century books, newspapers, maps and periodicals at the British Library in London:

Allot, Miriam (ed.), *Keats, The Complete Poems*, London, Longman, 1970

Bailey, James Blake, *The Diary of a Resurrectionist* 1811-1812, London, Swan Sonnenschein & Co., 1896

Bate, Walter Jackson, *John Keats*, London, Hogarth Press, 1992

Buxton Forman, H. (ed.), *The Complete Works of John Keats*, (5 vols), Glasgow, Gowars & Gray, 1901

Carey, George Saville, *The Balnea, or an Impartial Description of all The Popular Watering Places in England*, 2nd ed., London, W. West & C. Chapple, 1799

Chilcott, Tim, *A Publisher And His Circle, The Life and Work of John Taylor, Keats's Publisher*, London, Routledge & Kegan Paul Ltd, 1972

Colvin, Sydney, *Keats*, London, Macmillan & Co., 1942

Cooper, Bransby Blake, *The Life of Sir Astley Cooper*, 2 vols, London, John W. Parker, 1843

Coote, Stephen, *John Keats, A Life*, London, Hodder & Stoughton, 1995

Cornwell, Baron Wilson (Mrs), *Memoirs of Harriet, Duchess of St Albans*, 2 vols, London, Henry Colburn, 1839

Cowden Clarke, Charles & Mary, *Recollections of Writers*, New York, Charles Scribner's Sons, 1878

Crosby's Complete Pocket Gazetteer of England and Wales, London, Baldwin, Cradock & Joy, 1815

Cunningham, Allan, *The Life of David Wilkie*, 3 vols, London, John Murray, 1843

Davenport Adams, W.H., *The History, Topography and Antiquities of The Isle of Wight*, London, Smith, Elder & Co., 1856

Everest, Kelvin (ed.), *Shelley Revalued, Essays from the Gregynog Conference*, Leicester University Press, 1983

Gill, Stephen, *William Wordsworth, A Life*, Oxford: Clarendon Press, 1989

Gill, Stephen, *William Wordsworth, The Major Works*, Oxford University Press, 1984

Gittings, Robert, *John Keats*, London, Heinemann, 1968

Gray, Charles Harold (ed.), *Essays by William Hazlitt*, New York, The Macmillan Company, 1926

Grayling, A.C., *The Quarrel Of The Age, The Life and Times of William Hazlitt*, London, Phoenix Press, 2001

Harper, Charles G., *The Exeter Road, The Story of the West of England Highway*, London, Chapman & Hall, 1899

Haydon, B.R., *Lectures on Painting And Design*, London, Longman, Brown, Green, And Longmans, 1844

Haydon, B.R., and Hazlitt, William, *Painting and the Fine Arts*, Edinburgh, Adam and Charles Black, 1838

Haydon, Frederic Wordsworth (ed.), *Benjamin Robert Haydon: Correspondence and Table-Talk*, 2 vols, Boston, Estes & Lauriat, 1877

Hazlitt, William, *A View Of The English Stage; or, A Series of Dramatic Criticisms*, London, Robert Stodart, 1818

Hazlitt, William, *An Essay on the Principles of Human Action*, London, J Johnson, 1805

Hazlitt, William, *Criticisms on Art with Catalogues of the Principal Picture Galleries of England*, 2nd series, edited by his son, London, C. Templeman, 1844

Hazlitt, William, *Lectures on the English Poets*, London, Taylor & Hessey, 1818

Hazlitt, William, *The Round Table, A Collection of Essays on Literature, Men and Manners*, 2 vols, Edinburgh, Archibald Constable & Co., 1817

Holmes, Richard, *Shelley: The Pursuit*, London, Penguin Books, 1974

Howe, Will D., *Charles Lamb and His Friends*, Indianapolis, The Bobbs Merrill Company, 1944

Hughes-Hallett, Penelope, *The Immortal Dinner*, London, Viking-Penguin Books Ltd, 2000.

Hunt, Leigh, *Autobiography*, 2 vols, New York, Harper & Brothers, 1850

Hunt, Leigh, *Correspondence*, 2 vols, London, Smith, Elder & Co., 1862

Jack, Ian, *Keats And The Mirror Of Art*, Oxford University Press, 1967

Jones, Leonidas M., *The Letters of John Hamilton Reynolds*, University of Nebraska Press, 1973

Jones, Leonidas M., *The Life of John Hamilton Reynolds*, University Press of New England, 1984

Jones, Stanley, *Hazlitt: A Life, from Winterslow to Frith Street*, Oxford University Press, 1991

Landseer, Thomas (ed.), *Life and Letters of William Bewick*, 2 vols, London, Hurst & Blackett, 1871

Lowell, Amy, *John Keats*, 2 vols, Boston, Houghton Mifflin Company, 1925

Malcolm (ed.), *The Autobiography and Journals of Benjamin Robert Haydon*, London, Macdonald, 1950

Motion, Andrew, *Keats*, London, Faber, 1997

Olney, Clarke, *Benjamin Robert Haydon, Historical Painter*, Athens, The University of Georgia Press, 1952

Parson, Donald, *Portraits of Keats*, Cleveland, The World Publishing Company, 1954

Pilkington, Mrs, *Margate*, London, J. Harris, 1813

Pope, Willard Bissell (ed.), *The Diary of Benjamin Robert Haydon*, vols 1&2, Cambridge, Mass., Harvard University Press, 1960

Reynolds, Joshua, *The Literary Works of Sir Joshua Reynolds, with a Memoir of the Author by Henry William Beechey*, 2 vols, London, T Cadell, 1835

Ridley, M.R., *Keats' Craftsmanship*, London, Methuen & Co. Ltd, 1964

Roe, Nicholas, *Fiery Heart, The First Life Of Leigh Hunt*, Pimlico, 2005

Rollins, Hyder E. (ed.), *The Keats Circle: Letters and Papers 1816-1878*, 2 vols, Cambridge, Mass., Harvard University Press, 1948

Sadler, Thomas (ed.), *Diary, Reminiscences and Correspondence of Henry Crabb Robinson*, 2 vols, Boston, Fields, Osgood & Co., 1869

Scudder, Horace E., *The Complete Poetical Works and Letters of John Keats*, Boston & New York, Houghton Mifflin Company, 1899

Shelley, Mary (ed.), *Shelley Memorials from Authentic Sources*, Boston, Ticknor and Fields, 1859

Sikes, Herschel Moreland, et al. (eds.), *The Letters of William Hazlitt*, New York University Press, 1978

Spenser, Edmund, *The Faerie Queene, with an Introduction by Helen Moore*, Ware, Wordsworth Editions Limited, 1999

Spurgeon, Caroline F.E., *Keats's Shakespeare*, Oxford University Press, 1928

Taylor, Tom (ed.), *The Autobiography and Memoirs of Benjamin Robert Haydon 1808-1846*, with an introduction by Aldous Huxley, London, Peter Davies, 1926

The Oxford University Calendar. 1817. Oxford, J. Parker et al. 1817

The Oxford University and City Guide, Oxford, Henry Slatter, 1839

The Theatrical Inquisitor and Monthly Mirror, Vol XI, 1817, London, C. Chapple, 1818

Printed in Great Britain
by Amazon